The Limits of a Text

Journal of Theological Interpretation Supplements

University of Otago, New Zealand
Editor-in-Chief

The Limits of a Text

Luke 23:34a as a Case Study in
Theological Interpretation

JOSHUA MARSHALL STRAHAN

Winona Lake, Indiana
EISENBRAUNS
2012

Printed in the United States of America

www.eisenbrauns.com

Library of Congress Cataloging-in-Publication Data

Strahan, Joshua M.
    The limits of a text : Luke 23:34a as a case study in theological
        interpretation / Joshua M. Strahan.
            p. cm. — (Journal of theological interpretation supplements ; 5)
    The author's thesis.
    Includes bibliographical references (p.   ) and index.
    ISBN 978-1-57506-704-9 (pbk. : alk. paper)
    1. Bible. N.T. Luke XXIII, 34a—Criticism, interpretation, etc.
    2. Bible—Hermeneutics.   I. Title.
    BS2595.52.S77   2012
    226.4′06—dc23

                                                          2012036362

For Lauren

I love you now and always

Table of Contents

Acknowledgments

The writing of this book would not have been possible without the support of numerous people. It is impossible to express the fullness of my gratitude for my wife, Lauren, for believing in me more than I believed in myself, for moving across the country and working (sometimes at grueling jobs) to support me, for being my best friend whose company I could look forward to on long days, for living on a tight budget, for raising our daughter into the special girl she is, and for so many more things. I love you now and always. And little Sophi, thank you for all the smiles and giggles, the hugs and kisses, which reminded your daddy not to lose perspective by taking his work too seriously.

I owe my deepest gratitude to my supervisor, Joel Green, for giving me a chance when others did not, for investing in me beyond what was required, for pushing me to a standard that I didn't know I could reach, for sharing insight that I would never have acquired on my own, and for teaching by example that my research and writing should serve the church. I have always felt lucky to be your student. Special thanks are also due David Downs, Murray Rae, and Jim Eisenbraun for their perceptive feedback and encouragment.

I must thank my Mom, for instilling in me the belief that I could do anything, and for the safety net of knowing she would love me even if I failed at everything; and my Dad, for his quiet sacrifice that allowed me to get a good education, and for showing me day in and day out that hard work is a virtue. You are better parents than any kid deserves. Thanks are certainly due to David and Debbie Scobey for loving me like one of their own children and supporting me in countless ways, even when that meant moving their daughter across the country. I could not have done this without you.

Finally, I am grateful for the financial support I received from The Christian Scholarship Foundation, the Harrison Award, the CATS Scholarship, the Scholer Fellowship, and also Jason Baxter, who gave me the computer on which I wrote much of this book. I am honored by these gifts that lifted a heavy financial burden.

ABBREVIATIONS

Ancient Texts

Agr.	Philo, *De agricultura*
Ant.	Josephus, *Antiquitates judaicae*
DDC	Augustine, *De Doctrina Christiana*
Ebr.	Philo, *De ebrietate*
Fug.	Philo, *De fuga et inventione*
Haer.	Irenaeus, *Adversus Haereses*
Hist. eccl.	Eusebius, *Historia Ecclesiastica*
Imm.	Philo, *Quod deus sit immutibalis*
Mig.	Philo, *De migratione Abrahami*
Pos.	Philo, *De posteritate Caini*
Sac.	Philo, *De sacrificiis Abelis et Caini*
Spec.	Philo, *De specialibus legibus*

Modern Texts

AB	Anchor Bible
ABRL	Anchor Bible Reference Library
ACW	Ancient Christian Writers. 1946-
ANF	*Ante-Nicene Fathers*
AUSS	*Andrews University Seminary Studies*
BECNT	Baker Exegetical Commentary on the New Testament
BibInt	*Biblical Interpretation*
CBQ	*Catholic Biblical Quarterly*
ChristAnt	Christianisme antique
DSS	Dead Sea Scrolls
EKKNT	Evangelisch-katholischer Kommentar zum Neuen Testament
ExpTim	*Expository Times*
FC	Fathers of the Church. Washington, D.C., 1947-
FN	*Filologia Neotestamentaria*
GOTR	*Greek Orthodox Theological Review*
HNT	Handbuch zum Neuen Testament
HTKNT	Herders theologischer Kommentar zum Neuen Testament
HTR	*Harvard Theological Review*
HTS	Harvard Theological Studies
ICC	International Critical Commentary
IDB	*The Interpreter's Dictionary of the Bible.* Edited by G.A. Buttrick. 4 vols. Nashville, 1962.
IJST	*International Journal of Systematic Theology*
Int	*Interpretation*
JBL	*Journal of Biblical Literature*

JSNT	*Journal for the Study of the New Testament*
JSNTSS	Journal for the Study of the New Testament: Supplement Series
JTI	*Journal of Theological Interpretation*
JTS	*Journal of Theological Studies*
KJV	King James Version
LCL	Loeb Classical Library
NA^{27}	*Novum Testamentum Graece*, Nestle-Aland 27th ed.
Neot	*Neotestamentica*
NETS	*A New English Translation of the Septuagint and the Other Greek Translations Traditionally Included under That Title*
N.F.	Neue Folge
NICNT	New International Commentary on the New Testament
NICOT	New International Commentary on the Old Testament
NIGTC	New International Greek Testament Commentary
NIV	New International Version
NPNF[1]	*Nicene and Post-Nicene Fathers*, Series 1
NRSV	New Revised Standard Version
NTAbh	Neutestamentliche Abhandlungen
NTS	*New Testament Studies*
NTTSD	New Testament Tools, Studies and Documents
OECT	Oxford Early Christian Texts. Edited by H. Chadwick. Oxford, 1970-
ÖTK	Ökumenischer Taschenbuch-Kommentar
PatByzRev	*Patristic and Byzantine Review*
PEGLMWBS	*Proceedings: Eastern Great Lakes and Midwest Biblical Societies*
RNT	Regensburger Neues Testament
RP	*The New Testament in the Original Greek: Byzantine Textform 2005*, compiled and arranged by Maurice A. Robinson and William G. Pierpont (Southborough, MA: Chilton, 2005)
SBLSP	*Society of Biblical Literature Seminar Papers*
SNT	Studien zum Neuen Testament
SJP	*Southern Journal of Philosophy*
SJT	*Scottish Journal of Theology*
SP	Sacra pagina
StPatr	Studia patristica
THKNT	Theologischer Handkommentar zum Neuen Testament
THNTC	Two Horizons New Testament Commentary
TPINTC	TPI New Testament Commentaries
Treg	Samuel Prideaux Tregelles, *The Greek New Testament, Edited Ancient Authorities, with Their Various Readings in Full, and the Latin Version of Jerome* (London: Bagster; Stewart, 1857-1879)

TUGAL	Texte und Untersuchungen zur Geschichte der altchristlichen Literatur
UBS[4]	*The Greek New Testament*, United Bible Societies, 4th ed.
VetChr	*Vetera Christianorum*
WBC	Word Biblical Commentary
WH	Westcott-Hort
WSA	The Works of Saint Augustine: A Translation for the 21st Century
WUNT	Wissenschaftliche Untersuchungen zum Neuen Testament
ZBK	Zürcher Bibelkommentar

1

Reading an Ambiguous Text

Introduction

In brief, this book offers an attempt to deal with the enigmatic text of Luke 23:34a: "Then Jesus said, 'Father, forgive them, for they know not what they do'" (ὁ δὲ Ἰησοῦς ἔλεγεν· πάτερ, ἄφες αὐτοῖς, οὐ γὰρ οἴδασιν τί ποιοῦσιν).[1] Despite its brevity, this text is debated on several grounds, including its originality, its (socio-cultural and/or intertextual) interpretive background(s), the identity of the prayer's referents, the nature of their misunderstanding, and the text's consequent communicative intent. Each of these disputed issues will be examined in more detail below. Accordingly, the primary goal of this study is to examine critically the evidence on these interrelated issues and to make a case for my own solutions to these matters. More specifically, after arguing for the originality of Luke 23:34a, I will demonstrate 1) that both historiographical theory and theological insight allow for multiple readings of this text, although 2) these readings should be constrained according to certain interpretive parameters for which I will contend.

An Enigmatic Text

Beginning with the text-critical ambiguity of Luke 23:34a, the NA[27] places the prayer in double brackets as does the UBS[4], the latter of which also attributes the highest degree of certainty (the letter A) to this decision. At first glance, the external evidence would seem to favor its unoriginality, as the text is absent from two of the earliest and best mss. (p[75], B) and is also missing in the earliest Western and Caesarean codices (respectively, D*, Θ). Further, it may seem hard to explain why a scribe would deliberately omit Jesus' merciful prayer. For reasons such as these, some scholars join the UBS[4] and NA[27] in regarding the text as unoriginal.[2] Nevertheless, many have challenged this verdict, arguing that 1) the external evidence is balanced by the early and familially diverse presence of this text in the Fathers (e.g., Origen, Diatessaron), 2) valid reasons exist for why a

---

1. For the sake of familiarity, I have retained the KJV translation of Luke 23:34a. Unless otherwise noted, English translations in what follows are from the NRSV.

2. See, e.g., Jacobus H. Petzer, "Anti-Judaism and the Textual Problem of Luke 23:34," *FN* 5 (1992): 199-203; Jason A. Whitlark and Mikeal C. Parsons, "The 'Seven' Last Words: A Numerical Motivation for the Insertion of Luke 23:34a," *NTS* 52 (2006): 188-204; Bruce M. Metzger, *Textual Commentary on the Greek New Testament: A Companion Volume to the United Bible Societies' Greek New Testament (Fourth Revised Edition)* (2d ed; Stuttgart: United Bible Societies, 1994), 154.

scribe would omit this prayer (e.g., antiJudaic tendencies), and 3) the internal evidence—such as Lukan wording (e.g., πατέρ [Luke 22:42; 23:46]) and themes (e.g., the ignorance motif [Acts 3:17; 17:30])—strongly suggests this is a Lukan text.[3]

Concerning the possible (socio-cultural and/or intertextual) interpretive background(s) of Luke 23:34a, several options have been put forward. For example, George Carras avers that Luke 23:34a should be read in view of the Pentateuchal laws on unintentional sin (e.g., Num 15:22-31), given the "thematic" links between these texts.[4] In contrast, I. Howard Marshall sees the primary intertextual link to be Isa 53:12, wherein the prayer of Jesus "exemplifies the statement of Isa 53:12 that the Servant makes intercession for the transgressors."[5] Shelly Matthew argues that Jesus' prayer must be understood in light of Roman clemency, particularly the clemency of emperors.[6] Recent research in circa-first-century documents on the matter of unintentional sin may also shed new light on the background of Luke 23:34a. For instance, Gary Anderson shows that, in the *Community Rule* and the *Damascus Document*, intentional sin is defined as any violation of the revealed law whereas unintentional sin is violation of the hidden law.[7] Perhaps, then, Jesus' prayer should be understood as forgiving those sinning against a hidden law, a reading that I will later suggest finds some overlap in Luke-Acts. My own research into Philo will also reveal a

---

3. See, e.g., Matthais Blum, *"... denn sie wissen nicht, was sie tun": Zur Rezeption der Fürbitte Jesu am Kreuz (Lk 23, 34a) in der antiken jüdisch-christlichen Kontroverse* (NTAbh N.F. 46; Münster: Aschendorff, 2004), 17-27; Thomas Bolin, "A Reassessment of the Textual Problem of Luke 23:34a," *PEGLMWBS* 12 (1992): 131-44; Raymond E. Brown, *The Death of the Messiah—From Gethsemane to the Grave: A Commentary on the Passion Narratives in the Four Gospels* (vol 2; ABRL; New York: Doubleday, 1994), 975-81; François Bovon, *Das Evangelium nach Lukas* (EKKNT 3/4 ; Zürich: Benziger Verlag, 2010), 461-62. The most recent work on this text-critical question argues that the history of interpretation reveals how Luke 23:34a was a troubling text to early Christians, thereby furthering the claim that early readers had motives for omitting the text (Nathan Eubank, "A Disconcerting Prayer: On the Originality of Luke 23:34a," *JBL* 129 [2010]: 521-36).

4. George Carras, "A Pentateuchal Echo in Jesus' Prayer on the Cross: Intertextuality between Numbers 15:22-31 and Luke 23:34a," in *The Scriptures in the Gospels* (ed. C.M. Tucket; Leuven: Leuven University Press, 1997), 605-16.

5. I. Howard Marshall, *Luke: Historian and Theologian* (Downers Grove, IL: InterVarsity, 1998), 172; see also Darrell L. Bock, *Luke 9:51-24:53* (BECNT 2; Grand Rapids: Baker Academic, 1994), 1849; contra John Nolland, *Luke 18:35-24:53* (WBC 35c; Dallas: Word, 1993), 1146.

6. Shelly Matthews, "Clemency as Cruelty: Forgiveness and Force in the Dying Prayers of Jesus and Stephen," *BibInt* 17 (2009): 118-46.

7. Gary A. Anderson, "Intentional and Unintentional Sin in the Dead Sea Scrolls," in *Pomegranates and Golden Bells: Studies in Biblical, Jewish, and Near Eastern Ritual, Law, and Literature in Honor of Jacob Milgrom* (ed. David P. Wright, David Noel Freedman, and Avi Hurvitz; Winona Lake, IN: Eisenbrauns, 1995), 49-64.

rather complex understanding of unintentional sin wherein, for example, ignorant offenders can even be seen as instruments of God—an idea picked up in
other texts bearing witness to the Lukan ignorance motif (e.g., in Acts 3:17-18,
God fulfills prophecy through the actions of the ignorant). Clearly, these various
interpretive schemas could influence various readings of a single text.

As for the nature of the misunderstanding, the debate is whether "not know
(οἶδα)" refers to lack of information or miscomprehension. As Daube writes,
"In the former case, a man is reprieved because he is not in possession of the
relevant facts or doctrine.... In the latter case, a man is reprieved because,
though fully instructed, he fails to appreciate the implications of the facts or to
rise to the doctrine offered."[8] Blum contends for the former and Carras
the latter.[9]

With regard to the prayer's referents (i.e., the "them" who do not know
what they "do"), the confusion arises from the ambiguous terms, αὐτοῖς and
ποιοῦσιν (v. 34a). Does "them" refer to the soldiers (e.g., v. 36) and/or the Jewish leaders (e.g., v. 35) and/or the people (e.g., v. 35)? Does "do" refer to the
crucifixion (e.g., v. 33) and/or the mockery (e.g., vv. 35-38) and/or the division
of clothes (v. 34b)? On the one hand, Blum and Flusser maintain that Jesus'
prayer is directed only to the Roman soldiers on the basis of both the immediate
cotext (i.e., "they crucified Jesus" in v. 33, and the division of clothes in v. 34b)
and the historical situation of which the original audience would presumably
have been aware (i.e., the Roman soldiers, not the Jews, performed crucifixions).[10] On the other hand, Carras claims that the prayer is on behalf of "the Jerusalem religious establishment" because it is clear throughout Luke-Acts that
they are responsible for Jesus' crucifixion (e.g., "...our chief priests and leaders
handed him over to be condemned to death and crucified him" [Luke 24:20]).[11]
Between these two extremes is Raymond Brown who, in light of evidence similar to what is presented above, allows for "both the Romans and the Jews" to be
the prayer's referents.[12] And Schneider understands the prayer as including the
mockers, given the present tense of ποιοῦσιν.[13]

---

8. David Daube, "'For They Know Not What They Do': Luke 23:34," StPatr 4
(1961): 60.

9. Blum, *Denn Sie Wissen Nicht*, 36; Carras, "Numbers 15:22-31 and Luke 23:34,"
613

10. David Flusser, "'Sie Wissen Nicht, Was Sie Tun: Geschichte eines Herrnwortes," in *Kontinuität und Einheit: Für Franz Mussner* (ed. Paul-Gerhard Müller and
Werner Stenger; Freiburg: Herder, 1981), 394-95; Blum, *Denn Sie Wissen Nicht*, 28.

11. Carras, "Numbers 15:22-31 and Luke 23:34," 609; see also Joseph A. Fitzmyer,
The Gospel According to Luke (vol. 2; AB 28a; New York: Doubleday, 1985), 1503-4.

12. Brown, *Death*, 973. For a similar reading, see Nolland, *Luke*, 1146; Gerhard
Schneider *Das Evangelium nach Lukas: Kapitel 11-24* [ÖTK 3; Gütersloh: Gütersloher
Verlagshaus Mohn, 1977], 483]). David Crump reads the prayer as even more far-
reaching, referring to "the entire scene and all its actors" (*Jesus the Intercessor: Prayer
and Christology in Luke-Acts* [WUNT 2/49; Tübingen: Mohr Seibeck, 1992], 86).

13. Schneider, *Lukas*, 483.

Not surprisingly, there are numerous opinions about the text's meaning and function in its pericope and in Luke-Acts as a whole. For example, Nolland notes that this text displays Jesus carrying out his own teachings (e.g., Luke 6:27-28).[14] Shelly Matthews claims the prayer serves to highlight Jesus' character, but has "no effect on the prayer's objects" when understood against the background of Roman clemency.[15] Carras claims that Luke 23:34a, which he avers depicts Jesus forgiving the Jewish religious leaders, shows that Luke is not antiJudaic.[16] Flusser and Blum, contra Carras, claim that reading the prayer as forgiving the Jews is antiJudaic, as it assigns blame to the Jews.[17] Consequently, much of their research into the history of interpretation of Luke 23:34a focuses on whether the prayer is read as forgiving the Jews. For Blum, such interpretations are disallowed by appeal to both historical criticism and authorial intent.

Blum's appeal to interpretive delimiters brings us to a significant question in our study—namely, is a text's meaning confined to what can be determined by historical criticism and/or to authorial intent;[18] or are there theological and historiographical reasons that allow a text to be heard differently by different readers? Furthermore, if biblical texts are polysemic, are valid readings constrained by congruency with authorial intent,[19] theology,[20] one's community,[21] or some other guideline(s)? In the case of an ambiguous text such as Luke 23:34a, how might one evaluate the various proposed interpretations of Jesus' prayer? Is there only one right interpretation? If so, how is it discovered? If not, are all readings equally valid? What are the proper criteria for evaluating a reading of a biblical text?

Proposal and Preview

In short, my solution for dealing with the ambiguities of Luke 23:34a is fivefold. First, I will argue for the text's originality, showing how a thorough investigation of the external and internal evidence attests to the originality of Luke 23:34a (ch. 2). Second, I will call into question attempts to delimit interpretation that appeal *exclusively* to historical-critical research, authorial intent, and/or the interpretations of early readers (ch. 3). Third, with help from Augustine's *De*

---

14. Nolland, *Luke*, 1144.

15. Matthews, "Clemency as Cruelty," 118.

16. Carras, "Numbers 15:22-31 and Luke 23:34," 615.

17. See ch. 3 for an extended discussion of Blum and Flusser.

18. See, e.g., Krister Stendahl, "Biblical Theology, Contemporary," in *IDB* 1:418-32.

19. See, e.g., Murray Rae, "Texts in Context: Scripture and the Divine Economy," *JTI* 1 (2007): 23-45.

20. See, e.g., Stephen E. Fowl, "The Role of Authorial Intention in the Theological Interpretation of Scripture," in *Between Two Horizons: Spanning New Testament Studies and Systematic Theology* (ed. Joel B. Green and Max Turner; Grand Rapids: Eerdmans, 2000): 71-87.

21. See, e.g., A. K. M. Adam, *Faithful Interpretation: Reading the Bible in a Post-modern World* (Minneapolis: Fortress, 2006).

Doctrina Christiana, I will offer a renewed, ecclesially located strategy for handling polysemy in biblical texts (ch. 4). Fourth, given the importance of authorial communicative intent that will be noted in *De Doctrina Christiana*, I will make a case for the most textually coherent reading of the aforementioned interpretive ambiguities in Luke 23:34a (ch. 5). Fifth, I will survey patristic readings of Luke 23:34a in order to further deal with attending to and delimiting polysemic readings within an ecclesially located exegetical paradigm (ch. 6). This study ends with a summary of the previous chapters and an example of what an ecclesially located reading of Luke 23:34a might look like in a more contemporary context (ch. 7).

In more detail, ch. 2 will address the text-critical question of Luke 23:34a more thoroughly than any extant work, particularly by examining the reliability (or not) of the text's appearance in the Fathers. I will argue that the external evidence is too ambiguous to warrant a claim of unoriginality, and that the internal evidence, clearly conforming to Lukan style and theology, indicates the text's originality. When examining the external evidence, I will compare the witnesses' dates, familial diversity, and reliability. I will also look at whether the shorter or longer reading better accounts for scribal error. As for the internal evidence, I will demonstrate that the evidence is not balanced; rather, the vocabulary, structure, and theology of the longer reading clearly conform to Lukan style, thereby indicating the prayer's originality.

The various interpretations and interpretive schemas put forward for Luke 23:34a raise the issue of how to properly read a text, especially an ambiguous text. Accordingly, ch. 3 opens by reviewing Matthias Blum's recent monograph on Luke 23:34a, where he argues that proper readings of Luke 23:34a must be constrained by congruency with historical-critical research and authorial intent.[22] Although I think that Blum wrongly conflates historical criticism and authorial intent, his argument nevertheless represents an appeal that is common in biblical studies—namely, that a text's meaning is ultimately determined by historical-critical research and/or what the author intended. By bringing representatives of such appeals (specifically, Heikki Räisänen and Krister Stendahl[23]) into conversation with contemporary hermeneutical and historiographical theory, I will argue three points. First, no universal norms privilege any reading strategy. Consequently, if there are no certain rules that dictate proper reading, then the interpreter must appeal to some unverifiable starting point that will guide and delimit readings. Second, an appeal to authors is incapable of determining *the* meaning of a text, because of the inescapable distance between the author's mind and the reader's mind, a distance that is further complicated by the equivocality of language. Third, for those who might claim that the distance between the author and *early* readers would not have been sufficient to allow for much ambiguity, I demonstrate that an appeal to the interpretive schemas of early readers of Luke

---

22. Blum, *Denn Sie Wissen Nicht*.

23. Heikki Räisänen, *Beyond NT Theology: A Story and a Programme* (2d ed.; London: SCM, 2000); Stendahl, "Biblical Theology," 418-32.

23:34a is likewise unable to establish *the* meaning of our text. Not only is our information about the Lukan audience limited, but socio-cultural research suggests that even in the first century there would have been multiple ways for early readers to interpret Jesus' prayer of forgiveness.

Having argued that no interpretive paradigms are neutral, I open ch. 4 with an example of what a *Christian* interpretive paradigm might look like. For help with this, I turn to Augustine's *De Doctrina Christiana* (*DDC*), which will be shown to have a hermeneutic with *a priori* theological convictions. Augustine's ecclesially located hermeneutical framework results in an exegesis that 1) calls for humble, submissive, and virtuous readers; 2) highly values authorial communicative intent; 3) is nonetheless open to polysemy; and 4) delimits interpretations by appealing to the rule of faith, the double love commandment, and clearer canonical texts. Insights from *DDC* will then be brought into conversation with the hermeneutical paradigms surveyed in ch. 3, particularly those of Räisänen and Stendahl. In brief, Augustine's hermeneutic clashes with Räisänen's, because Augustine reads Scripture from the standpoint of Christian faith whereas Räisänen attempts to read from a so-called neutral standpoint. Regarding Stendahl's exclusive privileging of authorial intent, an ecclesially located theology would seem to challenge Stendahl because of 1) how NT writers often seem to read OT texts beyond the intent of the OT author, and 2) the inability of *sola scriptura* to determine crucial theological doctrines. The last section of ch. 4 notes how Augustine's approach to delimiting interpretation holds together many of the strengths offered by contemporary theological interpreters, including Max Turner, Richard Hays, Joel Green, Stephen Fowl, A.K.M. Adam, Richard Briggs, and others.[24] My hope is that, by bringing *DDC* into the conversation, I can contribute to the elusive task of making room for, while simultaneously bounding, polysemy in biblical interpretation.

Because this ecclesially located exegesis values authorial communicative intent, ch. 5 is devoted to studying whether the Lukan text guides its readers to interpret Jesus' prayer in certain ways. In other words, I will be noting how the text itself offer clues for answering questions about the referent(s), the intertextual background, and the nature of the misunderstanding. My research is guided by Umberto Eco's advice: "the only way [to prove a conjecture about the *inten-*

---

24. Max Turner, "Historical Criticism and Theological Hermeneutics of the New Testament," in *Between Two Horizons: Spanning New Testament Studies and Systematic Theology* (ed. Joel B. Green and Max Turner; Grand Rapids: Eerdmans, 2000), 44-70; Richard B. Hays, "Reading the Bible with Eyes of Faith: The Practice of Theological Exegesis," *JTI* 1 (2007): 5-21; Joel B. Green, "Scripture and Theology: Uniting the Two So Long Divided," in *Between Two Horizons: Spanning New Testament Studies and Systematic Theology* (ed. Joel B. Green and Max Turner; Grand Rapids: Eerdmans, 2000), 23-43; Fowl, "Authorial Intention," 71-87; Adam, *Faithful Interpretation*; Richard S. Briggs, *The Virtuous Reader: Old Testament Narrative and Interpretive Virtue* (Grand Rapids: Baker Academic, 2010).

tio operas] is to check it against the text as a coherent whole."[25] Thus, I ask, *What interpretation of Luke 23:34a makes the most sense of the text?* Seeking the textual coherence of a circa-first-century historiographical narrative such as Luke-Acts will require my paying attention to 1) the language, repetition, and order of events in the surrounding pericope; 2) other Lukan texts whose subject matter closely overlaps that of Luke 23:34a; and 3) other circa-first-century documents to show that my interpretation would have made sense in Luke's socio-cultural milieu. My thesis from this investigation is as follows: first, the "not know[ing]" of Luke 23:34a is essentially a *misperception* of Jesus' paradoxical identity and ministry—exemplified by the cross; second, such misperception in Luke-Acts is linked not only with untransformed minds and untransformed exegesis but also with the fulfillment of God's purposes; third, the most likely intertextual echo is to the Pentateuchal laws on unintentional sin (e.g., Lev 5:18); and fourth, the primary referents of Jesus' prayer are the Jewish leaders and the Jerusalem inhabitants, with the Roman actors being less emphasized.

Since my ecclesially located exegetical paradigm does not make authorial communicative intent the gatekeeper of valid biblical readings, ch. 6 presents a case study of patristic readings of Luke 23:34a in order to illustrate what it might look like to hear and delimit multiple readings of a text. What things might one be illumined by or be compelled to regulate when attending to those influential Christians who read biblical texts in ways that often differ so much from contemporary scholarly readings? How might one put into practice the matter of delimiting readings by appeal to the rule of faith, the twofold love commandment, and clearer canonical texts?

Finally, ch. 7 concludes our study by summarizing the findings of the previous chapters, then noting how Martin Luther King Jr.'s sermon on Luke 23:34a ("Love in Action") functions as a helpful example of a contemporary ecclesially located reading.[26]

---

25. Umberto Eco, *The Limits of Interpretation* (Indianapolis: Indiana University Press, 1990), 59.

26. This sermon is in Martin Luther King Jr., *Strength to Love* (Philadelphia: Fortress, 1963), 39-48.

2

A Text-Critical Analysis of Luke 23:34a

Introduction

In light of the ecclesially located framework that informs this book, one might wonder whether the text-critical approach that follows should have been different. As Childs writes, "The discipline of text criticism is not a strictly objective or non-theological activity, but is an integral part of the same interpretive enterprise which comprises the church's life with its scriptures."[1] An ecclesially located reader is ultimately concerned with the canonical text(s), which raises the question of how text-criticism is related to canon.[2] Epp lays out the issue well: "If one can establish a text or reading to be 'as close as possible' to an autographic text-form…, does that text-critical decision in fact create an authoritative text or reading?"[3] In light of how "our multiplicities of texts may all have been canonical (that is, authoritative) at some time and place,"[4] it is possible that I could have bypassed the text-critical discussion altogether by simply noting that Luke 23:34a has been held as canonical in countless churches for centuries, and therefore deserves to be treated by ecclesial readers regardless of its origin. Nonetheless, a text-critical methodology is important in this study for two reasons. First, even if one acknowledges varying canonical witnesses, establishing that a particular witness was likely to be Lukan, for example, might help one interpret the authorial communicative intent by locating a text in its socio-cultural milieu. In the case of Luke 23:34a, the argument that this text was originally Lukan results in my investigation of first-century concepts of unintentional sin, rather than second- or third-century concepts. Second, it would seem that even those who accept multiple canonical forms must apply text-critical restraints at some point. A text-critical strategy that seeks to clarify the original author's words would seem to fit well in the ecclesially located interpretive framework I will put forward later that values authorial communicative intent. Thus, I contend that my text-critical approach is a legitimate one but not the *only* valid approach.

---

1. Brevard S. Childs, *The New Testament as Canon: An Introduction* (Philadelphia: Fortress, 1984), 529.
2. Ibid., 522.
3. Eldon J. Epp, "The Multivalence of the Term 'Original Text' in New Testament Textual Criticism," *HTR* 92 (1999): 278.
4. Ibid.

The Text-Critical Dilemma

According to Luke 23:34a, while mocked and crucified between two criminals, Jesus prays, "Father, forgive them, for they know not what they do" (Luke 23:34a). But is this verse original to Luke's Gospel? The NA[27] places the prayer in double brackets to "indicate that the enclosed words...are *known* not to be a part of the original text."[5] Similarly, the UBS[4] not only places v. 34a in double brackets, but also attributes the highest degree of certainty (the letter A) to this decision.[6] Lukan theologians such as Creed and Parsons agree that the verse is unoriginal.[7] A significant number of Lukan scholars, however, challenge this verdict.[8] The present question about the verse's originality illuminates the need for further text-critical analysis.

The difference of opinion between text critics and most Lukan scholars likely stems from the dissimilar weight allotted to internal and external evidence. Thus, Lukan specialists attach more significance to the internal evidence of v. 34a, whereas text critics assign greater authority to the external evidence. For this reason, a more detailed investigation is necessary, one that attempts to take seriously the external evidence while also allotting the appropriate influence to the internal evidence. Therefore, this chapter will investigate both the external and internal evidence regarding the text.

This chapter is organized in the following way.[9] First, I will evaluate the external evidence, comparing the a) date, b) familial diversity, and c) reliability of the conflicting witnesses, then assess which reading best accounts for the possibility of d) scribal error. Second, I will consider the internal evidence by investigating the verse's relationship to the a) vocabulary, b) structure, and c) theology of Luke. By means of this investigation, I will argue that the external evidence is

---

5. Introduction to *Novum Testamentum Graece*, 27th ed., 50* (italics mine).

6. The SBL Greek NT does not bracket the prayer, although the only evidence cited is the prayer's presence in the editions of Treg, NIV, and RP, contrasted with the double brackets of WH. In a separate essay, the editor of the SBLGNT, Michael W. Holmes, reveals his preference for reasoned eclecticism. Interestingly, however, his example of practicing textual criticism focuses solely on external evidence ("Reconstructing the Text of the New Testament," in *The Blackwell Companion to the New Testament* [ed. David Aune; Oxford: Wiley-Blackwell, 2010], 85-87).

7. E.g., John Martin Creed, *The Gospel According to St. Luke: The Greek Text with Introduction, Notes, and Indice* (London: Macmillan, 1950), 286-87; Whitlark and Parsons, "Seven Last Words," 188-204. Cf. Metzger, *Textual Commentary*, 154.

8. E.g., Bovon, *Lukas*, 461-62. Luke Timothy Johnson, *The Gospel of Luke* (SP 3; Collegeville, MN: Liturgical, 1991), 376; Nolland, *Luke*, 1141; I. Howard Marshall, *The Gospel of Luke: A Commentary on the Greek Text* (NIGTC 3; Grand Rapids: Eerdmans, 1978), 867-68; Josef Ernst, *Das Evangelium nach Lukas* (RNT 3; Regensburg: Friedrich Pustet, 1977), 485; Walter Schmithals, *Das Evangelium nach Lukas* (ZBK 3; Zurich: Theologischer, 1980), 226; Schneider, *Lukas*, 483; Flusser, "Sie Wissen Nicht ," 399-400; Blum, *Denn Sie Wissen Nicht*, 17-27.

9. For a similar, though less developed approach, see Bolin, "Reassessment," 131-44.

too ambiguous to warrant a claim of unoriginality, and that the internal evidence, clearly conforming to Lukan style and theology, indicates the text's originality.

External Evidence

The following chart offers a summary of the witnesses and their assumed dates, families, and categories.[10]

Witnesses with v. 34a absent:

SOURCE	FAMILY	CENTURY	CATEGORY
p^{75}	Alex	III	1
$\aleph^1$	Alex	IV-VI	
B	Alex	IV	1
D*	Western	V-VI	4
W	Byz	V	3
Θ	Caes	IX	2
070		VI	3
579	Alex	XIII	2
1241	Alex	XII	3
pc			
a	Western	IV	
sy^s	Western	IV-V	
sa	Alex	IV-V	
bo^{pt}	Alex	IV-V	
Cyril of Alex	Alex	V	

---

10. Dates and categories compiled from Kurt Aland and Barbara Aland, *The Text of the New Testament: An Introduction to the Critical Editions and to the Theory and Practice of Modern Textual Criticism* (rev. ed.; Grand Rapids: Eerdmans, 1989).

Witnesses with v. 34a present:

SOURCE	FAMILY	CENTURY	CATEGORY
א*	Alex	IV	1
א²	Alex	VII	
A	Byz	V	3
C	Alex	V	2
D²	Western	IX	
L	Alex	VIII	2
Ψ	Alex	VIII-IX	3
0250		VIII	3
ƒ¹·⁽¹³⁾	Caes	XII-XIII	3
33	Alex	IX	2
𝔐	(mostly) Byz		
lat	Western		
sy^c.p.h	Caes/West	V,V, VIII	
(bo^pt)	Alex	IV-V	
(Ir ^lat)	Western	III-IV; 200-396	
Diatesseron	Western		
Ephraim		IV	
Hegessipus		II	
Origen^lat	Caes/Alex	II-III	
Hippolytus	Western	II-III	

Dating of the Witnesses

p⁷⁵, the earliest Greek ms. of Luke 23, does not contain v. 34a. Thus, the text is absent as early as the turn of the third century.[11] In contrast, the earliest Greek ms. containing the text is א from the fourth century. The presence of this reading emerges, however, as early as the second century among the Fathers, including Hegesippus and Irenaeus. Moreover, the Diatessaron includes Jesus' prayer, as does Ephraim's commentary (310-373)—a strong witness in favor of the verse's presence in the Diatessaron in the second century.[12] Whitlark, Parsons, and Petzer, who regard the text as unoriginal, acknowledge its early presence.[13] Oddly, Whitlark and Parsons claim "that the absence of this logion is attested by the

---

11. For a survey of the proposed dates for p⁷⁵, see James R. Royce, who opts for a date around 200 (*Scribal Habits in Early Greek New Testament Papyri* [NTTSD 36; Leiden: Brill, 2008], 615 n.1).

12. "[Other Diatessaronic] versions with their variants cannot compare in textual value with the witness of Ephraem's commentary" (Aland, *Text*, 193); cf. also Joël Delobel, "Luke 23:34a: A Perpetual Text-Critical Crux?" in *Sayings of Jesus: Canonical and Non-canonical: Essays in Honour of Tjitze Baarda* [ed. William L. Peterson, et al.; Brill, 1997), 29.

13. "[It] must be admitted to be impressive from the point of view of its age" (Petzer, "Textual Problem," 200); cf. Whitlark and Parsons, "Seven Last Words," 190.

three major streams from the second century."[14] Though they twice claim se-cond-century absence, they not only fail to offer any evidence, but they earlier claim that the absence "runs from the beginning of the third century to the thir-teenth century."[15] Thus, they seem to be confusing their data.

Despite the earlier documents that witness to the text's inclusion, two fac-tors must be noted. First, according to Aland and Aland's rules of text criticism, "the primary authority for a critical textual decision lies with the Greek manu-script tradition, with the versions and Fathers serving no more than a supple-mentary and corroborative function."[16] Hence, one might claim that a third-century Greek ms. trumps second-century Fathers and versions. Although this rule has undeniable merit, one must question its limits. Should a single ms. out-weigh the testimony of older witnesses?[17] I will argue below that it should not. Furthermore, without p^{75}, the evidence of dating is similar, with both readings supported by fourth-century codices (i.e., absent in B; present in ℵ).

Second, and related, the survey thus far has taken into account neither the familial diversity nor the reliability of these documents, both of which are vital elements in a demanding text-critical investigation such as this. Even if agree-ment could be reached about the documents' dates, an earlier date assures nei-ther accuracy nor closer proximity to the autograph (e.g., a sixth-century ms. may have an earlier exemplar than a fourth-century ms.).

Despite the inherent limitations of this survey, we have already begun to no-tice the ambiguity of the external evidence. In particular, the earliest Greek ms. does not contain the text, but the Diatessaron and two Fathers from the second century do. Moreover, outside of p^{75}, the Fathers, and versions, the dates are similar between the readings with each containing codices dating from the fourth and fifth centuries.

Familial Diversity
The shorter reading appears among the Alexandrian family in the third century (p^{75}, cop^{sa}), among the Western family in the fourth (a, sy^s) and fifth/sixth centu-ries (D), among the Byzantine family in the fifth century (W), and among the Caesarean family in the ninth (Θ). On the other hand, the longer reading is found among the Alexandrian family in the third and fourth centuries (Origen, ℵ), among the Western family in the second century (Hegesippus and Irenaeus), among the Byzantine family in the fifth century (A), and among the Caesarean family in the fourth (Basil), fifth (Armenian) and twelfth/thirteenth centuries ($f^{1.(13)}$).

---

14. Whitlark and Parsons, "Seven Last Words," 189.
15. Ibid., 189, 191.
16. Aland and Aland, *Text*, 280.
17. Cf. A. von Harnack, "Probleme im Texte der Leidensgeschichte Jesu," in *Kleine Schriften zur älten Kirche: Berliner Akademieschriften, 1890-1920* (ed. A. von Harnack and Jürgen Dummer; 2 vols.; Leipzig: Zentralantiquariat der Deutschen Demokratischen Republik, 1980), 1:476.

When comparing the spread of the documents, Whitlark and Parsons comment that the shorter reading "is widely attested among text-types and geographically," whereas the longer reading "is restricted to the Western prior to the fourth century."[18] Similarly, Petzer remarks, "the short reading has in fact a wide basis of diverse evidence in its favor," whereas "the long reading has a distinctive Western flavour around it especially early in the history."[19] These articles, however, seem inconsistent in their treatments of the evidence. First, contra Whitlark and Parsons, the longer reading appears outside the Western family before the fourth century in Origen's writings, as even Petzer acknowledges.[20] Second, the measuring stick of diversity changes as they apply it to the two readings. Thus, the shorter reading is not attested in three families until the fifth century, whereas the longer reading appears in three by the fourth century, and all four by the fifth century. In other words, the longer reading is criticized for its lack of diversity before the fourth century, even though the shorter reading is also lacking diversity prior to the fourth century.[21] It appears that the longer reading is stigmatized as Western and local merely because it is found earlier in the Fathers—as though it could be supported by non-existent, second and third-century papyri and codices.

In order to argue that the shorter reading is supported by diverse witnesses earlier, one would have to exclude the versions and Fathers from the evidence. In this case, both readings have Alexandrian and Byzantine support by the fifth century. The shorter reading appears in the Western family by the fifth/sixth century (D) and in the Caesarean family by the ninth (Θ), whereas the longer reading only occurs in these regions in the ninth and twelfth/thirteenth centuries (respectively, D^2 and $f^{1.(13)}$). Nevertheless, even this distance is mitigated by noting that D^2 and $f^{1.(13)}$, though centuries later, are the oldest mss. in their respective families after D and Θ.

Once again, as with the evidence for dating, the ambiguity of the familial diversity is apparent. Both readings have early and familial diverse support. The advantage of the shorter reading is its earlier occurrence in the Greek mss.. The advantage of the longer reading is both that it achieves diversity by the early third century and that it is witnessed in all four families by the fifth century. In order to draw a more definitive conclusion in support of either reading, one would have to ignore the compelling weight of either the Greek mss. or numerous versions and Fathers.

---

18. Whitlark and Parsons, "Seven Last Words," 191.

19. Petzer, "Textual Problem," 200.

20. Ibid.; Eubank, "A Disconcerting Prayer," 522.

21. For instance, Petzer notes the diversity of the witnesses attesting the shorter reading outside of Alexandria in D W sy^s a d, none of which are prior to the fourth century ("Textual Problem," 200).

Reliability

Based on Aland and Aland's system of ranking the reliability of mss. by catego-ry,[22] one notices a comparable spread of category 1-4 documents favoring both readings. On the one hand, the shorter reading is supported by two documents from category 1 (p^{75}, B), two from category 2 (Θ, 579), three from category 3 (W, 070, 1241), and one from category 4 (D). On the other hand, the longer reading has one from category 1 ($\aleph$), three from category 2 (C, L, 33), and four from category 3 (A, Ψ, 0250, $f^{1.(13)}$).

Regarding the shorter reading, two possible advantages stand out. First, it has an extra category 1 witness. Yet, one could question whether p^{75} and B should carry the combined weight of one witness or two, since p^{75} is likely "ei-ther an ancestor of B or a precursor of B."[23] Second, the shorter reading is sup-ported by Θ, a category 2 from outside the Alexandrian family. In contrast, the longer reading has only category 3 evidence outside the Alexandrian family ($f^{1.(13)}$).[24] Therefore, with regard to category, the weight of evidence tilts in favor of the shorter reading, but only slightly. After all, the scale is virtually balanced with the exception of one document, Θ, which is neither category 1, nor Alex-andrian, nor dated prior to the ninth century.

Beyond the categorical system, other factors warrant investigation, such as the reliability of the Diatessaron and certain Fathers.[25] Beginning with the for-mer, the Diatessaron has received scrutiny because, in the Arabic version, v. 34a appears out of Lukan order, whereas the other sayings of Jesus from the cross occur in order of their respective appearances in John and Luke. Thus, in the Arabic Diatessaron, Jesus' words in John 19:26-27 precede his words in John 19:28, which precede his words in John 19:30a; in contrast, Jesus' words in Luke 23:34a do not precede, but fall between, his words in Luke 23:43 and 23:46a.[26] Whitlark and Parsons cite this as evidence that v. 34a is a "floating tradition."[27] This, however, begs the question of the organizing principle of Tatian and/or of the Arabic Diatessaron. For example, other Diatessaronic wit-

---

22. For more details, see Aland and Aland, *Text*, 106-7.

23. Philip Wesley Comfort, *Early Manuscripts and Modern Translations of the New Testament* (Grand Rapids: Baker, 1990), 63; cf. Crump, *Intercessor*, 81. For a detailed account that notes the consistent agreement of variations and anomalies of p^{75} B, see Calvin L. Porter, "Papyrus Bodmer XV (P75) and the Text of Codex Vaticanus," *JBL* 81 (1962): 363-76.

24. Note that the shorter and longer readings have equal category support from Byz-antine (W A, respectively).

25. Given the witness to the shorter reading in D, one might also inquire about the matter of Western non-interpolation. This theory, however, carries little weight in the argument, since D has numerous shorter Lukan readings that are not considered original (e.g., 4:16; 11:42; 22:19b-20; 24:36, 40).

26. According to the Arabic version, Jesus' seven words from the cross are in the following order: Luke 23:43; John 19:26-27; Mark 15:34/Matt 27:46; John 19:28; John 19:30a; Luke 23:34a; Luke 23:46a.

27. Whitlark and Parsons, "Seven Last Words," 202.

nesses have arranged the order of sayings in ways different from the Arabic witness, presumably to achieve some aesthetic or theological end,[28] thereby making it reasonable to imagine that such intentions—rather than the text's unoriginality—may also be behind the Arabic arrangement of sayings.[29] Elsewhere in the Arabic Diatessaron's passion narrative, there is not only reversal of Johannine order (e.g., singular Johannine material from John 19:23-24 [details concerning the division of Jesus' clothes] precedes singular material from 19:20-22 [details concerning the inscription above Jesus]) but also reversal of Markan/Matthean order (e.g., the statement of the crucifixion [Mark 15:24; Matt 27:35] precedes the offer and refusal of wine [Mark 15:23; Matt 27:34]) (Diatessaron 51). It would appear, then, that the arrangement of Jesus' sayings in Diatessaronic witnesses is an unreliable indicator of a text's originality.

Beyond the Diatessaron itself, Whitlark and Parsons also suggest that Ephraim was uncertain about the verse's status, because Ephraim's commentary alludes to v. 34a only in passing and out of order.[30] Yet, by applying this logic, one must assume that all three Johannine sayings of Jesus on the cross were untrustworthy as well, since Ephraim does not mention any of them in his passion narrative, and when he alludes to them, it is out of Johannine order (e.g., when discussing John 2:5).[31] Consequently, the arguments of Whitlark and Parsons against the presence of our text in Ephraim and the Diatessaron are unconvincing.

In fact, regarding v. 34a, there may be reason to attach more significance to the Diatessaron and Fathers than is normally given. The difficulty, particularly with regard to the Fathers, is determining whether a Father is citing Luke or a logion from another source such as the oral tradition. Andrew Gregory and François Bovon have each suggested methods for resolving this dilemma. Bovon seems to assume a Father's dependence on Luke when his citation is found in no extant sources except Luke's Gospel. He does offer "caution"—but little else—when recognizing that the patristic author might actually be citing a Lukan source and not Luke himself.[32] In contrast, Gregory, who follows the lead of Koester, adopts a self-proclaimed "minimalist" approach whereby the patris-

---

28. E.g., unlike the Arabic version, the Middle-English Pepysian places Luke 23:43 after John 19:26-27; unlike the Arabic, the Persian witness not only groups all three Johannine sayings together, but also places them before Luke 23:43.

29. In fact, the Arabic Diatessaron's placement of Jesus' prayer of forgiveness at the end, rather than beginning, of the crucifixion scene (as in Luke) does not seem to lack theological intention—namely, clarifying that forgiveness extends to the crucifixion in its entirety.

30. Whitlark and Parsons, "Seven Last Words," 202.

31. Ephraim, *Commentary on Tatian's Diatessaron*, 5.5.

32. François Bovon, "Issues in Reception History and Reception Theory: The Reception and Use of the Gospel of Luke in the Second Century" in *Reading Luke: Interpretation, Reflection, Formation* (ed. Craig G. Bartholomew et al.; Grand Rapids: Zondervan, 2005), 382-83.

tic author must betray Lukan redactional elements in order to be certain that the citation is from Luke and not a shared source.[33] Whereas Bovon's approach offers no methodology for distinguishing Lukan material from the lost traditions,[34] Gregory's approach is overly rigorous and often inapplicable to single-tradition material where redactional elements are hidden, such as Luke 23:34a.[35] Therefore, I will adopt a strategy in-between that of Bovon and Gregory, wherein patristic dependence on Luke is assumed in citations that include elements that are both 1) consistent with the cotext of Luke 23:34a and 2) distinctive to Lukan style. Such a strategy acknowledges the possibility of lost traditions while simultaneously offering accessible criteria for discerning (what Gregory refers to as) Luke's "fingerprints" in single tradition material.[36]

Before examining whether such Lukan elements are present in some of the Fathers and the Diatessaron, the most compelling evidence that a Father is quoting Luke must first be mentioned. Andrew Gregory avers, "A direct quotation, containing verbatim parallels to material in *Luke*…and referring explicitly to [Luke] as its source would of course constitute the strongest possible evidence."[37] In *Homilies on Leviticus* (ca. 240 AD), Origen offers a verbatim parallel of Luke 23:34a (*Pater, remitte illis, non enim sciunt, quid faciunt*) while also claiming that this quotation is said by Jesus "in the Gospels" (2.1.5). Given that no manuscript places this quotation anywhere in the canonical Gospels other than in Luke 23:34a, and given Origen's intimate familiarity with Luke's Gospel,[38] as well as his allusion to this prayer in the setting of the crucifixion,[39] it is highly unlikely that he is referring to anything other than Luke's Gospel at 23:34a.

---

33. Andrew Gregory, *The Reception of Luke and Acts in the Period before Irenaeus: Looking for Luke in the Second Century* (WUNT 2/169; Tübingen: Mohr Siebeck, 2003), 8-13.

34. Gregory, *Reception of Luke*, 16-20.

35. "[I]t is precisely in single tradition that it is most difficult to identify what is tradition and what is redaction" (Andrew Gregory, "Looking for Luke in the Second Century: A Dialogue with François Bovon," in *Reading Luke: Interpretation, Reflection, Formation* [ed. Craig G. Bartholomew et al.; Grand Rapids: Zondervan, 2005], 404).

36. Ibid., 403.

37. Gregory, *Reception of Luke*, 6.

38. He wrote not only at least thirty-nine homilies on Luke, but also five books of Lukan commentary that are no longer extant (Joseph T. Lienhard, forward to *Origen: Homilies on Luke, Fragments on Luke* [FC 94; Washington, D.C.: Catholic University of America Press, 1996], xxxvi).

39. In περὶ πάσχα Origen writes, "The sacrificing of this lamb [Jesus] was carried out by them in ignorance *because they do not know what they are doing and that is why it is forgiven them*" (διὰ τὸ μὴ αὐτοὺς γινώσκειν ὃ ποιοῦσιν ἔθνεν καὶ ἀφίεται αὐτοῖς [43-44]). The differences in vocabulary and syntax result from this being an allusion, whereas in *Homilies on Leviticus* Origen expressly identifies the citation as a quotation. Cf. Kim Haines-Eitzen, *Guardians of Letters: Literacy, Power, and the Transmitters of Early Christian Literature* (New York: Oxford University Press, 2000), 120.

In the short phrase, Πάτερ, ἄφες αὐτοῖς, οὐ γὰρ οἴδασιν τί ποιοῦσιν, Lukan fingerprints are recognizable. I argue in more detail below that the anarthrous and adjective-free vocative Πάτερ is distinctively Lukan, appearing eleven times and being the only form of address to the Father in Luke (contra Matt 6:9; 11:26; 26:39, 42; Mark 14:36; John 17:11, 25). Also unique to Luke is the formula ἄφες...γάρ, which occurs in the Lord's prayer at Luke 11:4 in contrast to ἄφες...ὡς, which occurs in the parallel at Matt 6:12. These two Lukan elements are present in the Greek writings of Hippolytus[40] and Hegesippus.[41] In the Latin, the adjective-free vocative address to the Father (*Pater*) is present in the writings of Origen (*Lev.* 2.1.5), Irenaeus (*Against Her.* 3.18.5), and *Acta Pilati* (10).[42] To these Lukan stylistic elements can be added the consistent relation of this prayer to the context of the crucifixion. Thus, Irenaeus writes that Jesus exclaims this prayer "upon the cross...for those putting him to death"—a setting that fits the immediate cotext of v. 34a wherein Jesus is being crucified in v. 33. Similarly, Ephraim, who is perhaps the most valuable witness to Tatian's Diatessaron, connects the prayer with the crucifixion three times (10.14; 21.3, 18).

Therefore, the evidence that several Fathers and the Diatessaron are referencing Luke and not an otherwise unknown tradition is indicated by 1) Origen's verbatim parallel quotation wherein he cites the Gospel as his source, 2) the consistent connection of this prayer with the crucifixion, and 3) the presence of Lukan stylistic traits. Consequently, the likelihood that these second and third century witnesses are citing Luke should—at the very least—balance the shorter reading's lone third century witness, p[75].

To summarize, a survey of the documents' reliability reveals a fairly balanced picture that moderately favors the shorter reading. The categorical weight was similar, though Θ gave a slight advantage to the shorter reading. Allegations about the manuscripts' tendencies and reliability amounted to very little when the evidence was evaluated. Therefore, as with the familial diversity and dating, ambiguity remains. For this reason, it is necessary to explore the puzzling issue of why a scribe might omit or insert this text.

Scribal Error
Three theories are commonly offered as explanations for an intentional error: the scribes have antiJudaic tendencies, the scribes are crafting a high Christology, or the scribes are harmonizing Luke's account with Stephen's, James', or Mark's. An exploration of each will reveal that no theory can adequately explain why a scribe might omit *or* insert this text.

---

40. Πάτερ ἄφες αὐτοῖς οὐ γὰρ οἴδασι ὃ ποιοῦσι (*Blessing of Jacob*, 9 [132]).

41. κύριε θέε Πάτερ ἄφες αὐτοῖς οὐ γὰρ οἴδασι τί ποιοῦσιν (Eusebius, *Hist. eccl.* 2.23.16).

42. For the possibility of early sources behind *Acta Pilati*, a text that clearly is working with Luke's passion narrative, see Blum, *Denn sie wissen nicht*, 55-63.

AntiJudaic tendencies. Jewish and Christian relationships were undoubtedly hostile in the first century as is indicated by NT texts (e.g., Acts 13:50; 14:2, 19, 17:5; 1 Thes 2:14-16) and other writings (e.g., Josephus, *Ant.* 200).[43] The ongoing nature of this hostility is seen in the words of Justin Martyr: "[Although] you have slain Christ, you do not repent; on the contrary, you hate and, whenever you have the power, kill us...[and] you cease not to curse him and those who belong to him" (*Dialogues* 133.6). Thus, it has been suggested that v. 34a is omitted for antiJudaic reasons—i.e., removing Jesus' forgiveness of the Jews.

Epp describes the following as antiJudaic alterations in D, a ms. that lacks v. 34a: addition of πονηρός to emphasize the Jews' wicked actions (Acts 3:17); an excuse of ignorance added in relation to the Gentiles to draw a contrast with the Jews (Acts 16:39); and the addition of γραφή in Acts 13:27 to suggest that the Jews are ignorant regarding *Scripture*, which Epp regards as "an excuse hardly complimentary or acceptable to the Jews."[44] To these, George Rice adds the following: addition of πονηρός to the scribes' actions in Luke 5:22 and πονηρία to their actions in Luke 20:23; addition of ὑποκριτής to modify the Pharisees (Luke 11:39); omission of Jesus' commendation of Jewish practices (11:42); omission of the claim that Jesus "was brought up" in Nazareth, and omission of the claim that it was "his" [Jesus'] custom to go to synagogue (Luke 4:16).[45]

Though antiJudaic bias is possibly seen in these variants, five counterpoints are in order. First, as Rice acknowledges, many of his examples are explicable on other grounds as synoptic harmonizations. Second, some of these variants that are labeled as antiJudaic are not clearly antiJudaic.[46] Third, D elsewhere adds narrative details to increase the drama, leading Barrett to suggest that D is merely increasing the drama rather than following an antiJudaic bias.[47] More importantly, fourth, Barrett notes proJudaic variants in D, such as changing "you/your" to "us/our" when Peter refers to the Jews (e.g., Acts 2:39; 3:22).[48] Fifth, there is no certainty that a scribe would attribute Jesus' prayer of for-

---

43. For a concise summary of these and other citations, see Brown, *Death,* 2:979.

44. E.J. Epp, "The 'Ignorance Motif' in Acts and the Antijudaic Tendencies in Codex Bezae," *HTR* 55 (1962): 51-62. He offers other examples, but these are his strongest.

45. George F. Rice, "The Anti-Judaic Bias of the Western Text in the Gospel of Luke," *AUSS* 18 (1980): 51-57; idem, "Some Further Examples of the Anti-Judaic Bias in the Western Text of the Gospel of Luke," *AUSS* 18 (1980): 149-56.

46. E.g., the addition of γραφή in Acts 13:27 may simply be an attempt to clarify the verse's convoluted Greek: οἱ γὰρ κατοικοῦντες ἐν Ἰερουσαλὴμ καὶ οἱ ἄρχοντες αὐτῶν τοῦτον ἀγνοήσαντες καὶ τὰς φωνὰς τῶν προφητῶν τὰς κατὰ πᾶν σάββατον ἀναγινωσκομένας κρίναντες ἐπλήρωσαν (see pages 77-78 below).

47. E.g., the addition of εὐθέως παραχρῆμα to the healing of the lame man (Acts 14:10); addition of δραμόντες εἰς τὸ ἄμφοδον to the Ephesians' actions (C.K. Barrett, "Is There a Theological Tendency in Codex Bezae?" in *Text and Interpretation: Studies in the New Testament Presented to Matthew Black* [ed. Ernest Best and R. McL. Wilson; Cambridge: Cambridge University Press, 1979], 22-23).

48. Ibid., 25-26.

giveness to the Jews and not the soldiers or criminals.[49] Thus, Petzer turns the
tables by arguing that the *longer reading* is antiJudaic because Jesus forgives the
Romans, thus placing full blame upon the Jews.[50] Although his case appears as
speculative as many of the examples of Epp and Rice, he is helpful in noting that
a discovery of an antiJudaic tendency in D cannot adequately explain the text's
absence from the older Alexandrian mss.[51] Therefore, on the one hand, the evidence of an antiJudaic bias accounting for the shorter reading is far from deci-
sive. On the other hand, the aforementioned conflict and attitude toward the
Jews make the idea of an addition by the fourth century similarly unlikely.[52]

High Christology. A high Christology might lead to an omission for several
reasons. First, a scribe may believe that killing Christ was too heinous to be ex-
cusable.[53] Second, the text may seem to contradict Jesus' words that the ignorant
sinner will still receive punishment (Luke 12:48; 19:44). Third, a scribe might
also see an inconsistency with 23:29-31 ("For the days are surely coming when
they will say, 'Blessed are the barren...'") if he were to interpret these verses as
Jesus' prediction of punishment for the crucifixion. Fourth, since Jerusalem was
destroyed, Jesus' prayer for forgiveness might appear ineffectual or
unanswered.[54]

Unlike the antiJudaic theory, a high Christology may better account for the
omission in the earlier Alexandrian witnesses. For instance, a high Christology
is noticeable among early Alexandrians, such as the well-known example of St.
Alexander who argues that Jesus was *homoousios* with the Father in contrast to
the rival Alexandrian doctrine of Arianism.[55] More importantly, Parsons—who
considers Luke 23:34a unoriginal—elsewhere argues that the following variants
of p[75] may reflect a high christological tendency: in Luke 16:30-31 ἐγέρθη re-
places πορευθῇ, which could highlight Jesus' resurrection and the religious
leaders' guilt; the omission of αὐτούς in Luke 9:34 may envision only Jesus in
the cloud at the Transfiguration; in John 6:19, the scribe corrects the preposi-

---

49. Most important for the discussion is not Luke's intention, but early Christian interpretation, since the latter would influence textual editing. Nevertheless, Eubank makes
a strong argument that early commentators of Luke 23:34a never applied this prayer to
the soldiers ("A Disconcerting Prayer," 526-32); contra Daube who reads the Didascalia
(ii.16; iv.14) as referring it to the soldiers ("For They Know Not What They Do," 59).

50. Petzer, "Textual Problem," 201-3.

51. Ibid., 201.

52. Bolin, "Reassessment," 139; Michael Wolter, *Das Lukasevangelium* (HNT 5;
Tübingen: Mohr Siebeck, 2008), 757.

53. Note John Chrysostom's comment, "You did slay Christ...This is why you have
no chance for atonement, excuse, or defense.... Is it not clear that you dared a deed much
worse and much greater than any sacrifice of children or transgression of the Law when
you slew Christ?" (*Adversus Judaeos Oratio* 6.2.10).

54. Note Jerome's attempt to explain Jesus' prayer as bringing about the delay of the
temple's destruction (*Epistle* 120.8.2); Brown, *Death*, 2:979; Wolter, *Lukasevangelium*,
757; Bovon, *Lukas*, 462.

55. Cf. also Cyril of Alexandria's emphasis on Jesus' divinity (ca. 378-444 CE).

tional agreement of θάλασσα so that Jesus clearly walks *on* the sea, not *beside* it; and in Luke 24:27, τὰ περὶ ἑαυτοῦ precedes ἐν πάσαις ταῖς γραφαῖς, which may suggest that Jesus is above the Scriptures, or it may emphasize the extent to which he fulfills them.[56]

Nevertheless, p[75] is well-recognized as a reliable document. Moreover, one might argue that a high Christology accounts for the *longer* reading. For instance, Jesus would be practicing his own teachings (Luke 6:35); his grace would contrast with the cursing of other Jewish martyrs (e.g., 2 Macc 7:9, 11, 14, 16-17, 18-19, 21-23); and, without the prayer, he may appear less gracious than Stephen (Acts 7:60). For these reasons, a high christological tendency cannot prove the text's originality. Nevertheless, the four reasons listed above, as well as the possible christological tendency in p[75], challenge the assumption that a scribe would more likely add than omit v. 34a. Once again, the external evidence proves to be ambiguous.

Harmonization. The text could be explained as a harmonization with Stephen's martyrdom, James' martyrdom, or Mark's passion narrative. The last option is the least likely and warrants little consideration. In light of what Harnack identifies as the "Gewicht der Worte," it is doubtful that a scribe would omit v. 34a simply to harmonize Luke's account with Mark's.[57]

The evidence regarding the harmonization of the martyr accounts is more disputable. For instance, when James dies, his words follow Jesus' verbatim: πάτερ ἄφες αὐτοῖς οὐ γὰρ οἴδασιν τί ποιοῦσιν (Eusebius, *Hist. eccl.* 2.23.16).[58] When writing of James' martyrdom, Eusebius cites Hegesippus, one of the early witnesses of the originality of v. 34a. This might suggest that he and other Fathers attributed (wittingly or unwittingly) James' words to Jesus. Regarding Stephen's martyrdom, the UBS[4] suggests a possible harmonization of Luke 23:34a with Stephen's dying words: κύριε μὴ στήσῃς αὐτοῖς ταύτην τὴν ἁμαρτίαν (Acts 7:60). Consequently, the important question emerges, which account(s) most likely influenced the other(s)?

The most helpful solution to this question arises by first comparing Jesus' martyrdom with Stephen's. Even if one assumes v. 34a is not original, it is still obvious that Luke has shaped Stephen's death so that it parallels Jesus'. For instance, both accounts include false witnesses (Luke 23:2; Acts 6:13-14), a Sanhedrin trial (Luke 22:66; Acts 6:12), a cry with a great voice (φωνῇ μεγάλῃ [Luke 23:46; Acts 7:60]), seeing Jesus/Son of Man at the right hand of God/power (Luke 22:69; Acts 7:55), and the prayer of committing one's spirit (εἰς χεῖράς σου παρατίθεμαι τὸ πνεῦμά [Luke 23:46]; δέξαι τὸ πνεῦμά μου

---

56. For these and other potential high christological variants in p[75], see Mikeal C. Parsons, "A Christological Tendency in P[75]," *JBL* 105 (1986): 463-79. For an argument against Parsons on this point, see Royce, *Scribal Habits*, 698-703.

57. Harnack, "Probleme," 1:478.

58. The only difference are titles preceding the prayer's addressee: πάτερ (v. 34a); κύριε θεὲ πάτερ (Eusebius, *Hist. eccl.* 2.23.16)

[Acts 7:59]).[59] Since Luke describes Stephen's death with such unmistakable parallels with Jesus' death, it seems likely that Stephen's prayer for his enemies is another deliberate Jesus-Stephen parallel. In other words, given the Jesus motif in Acts 6-7, Stephen's prayer for his enemies in Acts 7:60 works best if Luke 23:34a is original rather than a later addition. Moreover, a comparison of the Jesus-Stephen parallels in Luke-Acts reveals that Luke's tendency was to alter the vocabulary and order of events between the accounts.[60] In contrast, when scribes harmonize accounts they often retain similar vocabulary and word order.[61] Therefore, given the dissimilarity of word choice between the two prayers, and given the aforementioned paralleling of Stephen's and Jesus' deaths, it seems more likely that Luke wrote v. 34a and crafted Stephen's martyrdom in light of it, than that a scribe added v. 34a so as to harmonize it with Acts 7:60.[62]

In contrast, it appears likely that a deliberate harmonization, and not merely paralleling, occurs between Jesus' prayer and James', since the two prayers are verbatim with the exception of the addressees.[63] In favor of the priority of the prayer in Hegessipus, the *Second Apocalypse of James* (ca. 2nd century CE [?]) also records James making a similarly graceful remark, "He will not judge you for those things that you did, but will have mercy on you" (59). In favor of Lukan priority are two related factors. First, James' martyrdom appears to be influenced by Stephen's martyrdom. For instance, both see "the Son of Man...at the right hand" in heaven (Acts 7:56; Eusebius, *Hist. eccl.* 2.23.13); both make public pleas (7:2-53; 2.23.11);[64] and both are stoned by religious leaders (7:57-58; 2.23.16). These elements suggest that Hegessipus is already borrowing from NT texts to relate James' story. Second, Hegessipus also adapts Jesus-motifs to James' account. For example, James sees the Son of Man sitting at the right hand of "power" (Luke 22:69; *Hist. eccl.* 2.23.13; cf. "God" in Acts 7:56). Hence, Hegessipus not only borrows NT texts, but blends accounts in retelling.

---

59. Assuming Lukan familiarity with Mark's Gospel, one could also note parallels such as an accusation of blasphemy (Mark 14:64; Acts 6:11), the presence of the high priest (Mark 14:63; Acts 7:1), and accusations about Jesus destroying the temple/holy place (Mark 14:58; Acts 6:13-14); see Brown, *Death*, 2:978.

60. E.g., compare the prayers for committing one's spirit (εἰς χεῖράς σου παρα—τίθεμαι τὸ πνεῦμά μου [Luke 23:46]; δέξαι τὸ πνεῦμά μου [Acts 7:59]). The variation of order and vocabulary among parallels is also seen in the two post-resurrection accounts (Luke 24:36-49; Acts 1:2-12), the three Pauline conversion accounts (Acts 9:1-19; 22:1-21; 26:9-18), and the two accounts of Peter and Gentile converts (Acts 10:9-48; 11:4-17) (Henry J. Cadbury, "Four Features of Lucan Style" in *Studies in Luke-Acts* [ed. Leander E. Keck and J. Louis Martyn; Nashville: Abingdon, 1966], 88-96); see also Haines-Eitzen, *Guardians*, 120. Similarly, Bovon claims, "Lukas vermeidet mechanische Wiederholungen" (*Lukas*, 461).

61. Eubank, "A Disconcerting Prayer," 526.

62. Bolin, "Reassessment," 137.

63. Delobel, "Crux," 34 n.30.

64. "[Stand] on the battlement ...that your words may be audible to all the people" (2.23.11).

With evidence of Hegessipus' tendency to 1) borrow and 2) blend *undisputed* NT texts, it seems most likely that Hegessipus borrows by adapting James' martyrdom to Stephen's, and blends by inserting Jesus' prayer into James' mouth. The best solution, then, is that Hegessipus harmonizes James' death with Jesus' (and Stephens') and not that a later scribe harmonizes Jesus' death with James' or Stephen's.[65]

On the possibility of intentional error, no easy answers exist. A text that at first glance appears too "sublime"[66] to be purposefully omitted may seem the opposite to early Christian scribes. Thus, antiJudaic sentiment may not fully explain an omission, but it does question the likelihood of a proJudaic addition. Similarly, though christological tendencies cannot prove the originality of the longer reading, they do question the likelihood of a scribe adding a prayer that could either minimize the crime against Jesus or appear ineffective. Moreover, an exploration of potential harmonizations suggests the priority of v. 34a vis-à-vis both Stephen's and James' martyrdoms. Consequently, the external evidence is again inconclusive, though this survey of harmonizational tendencies favors the longer reading.

Summary of External Evidence
Both readings have strengths and weaknesses with regard to external evidence. The longer reading has the earliest witnesses, but the shorter reading has the earliest Greek manuscript. The longer reading achieves broader familial diversity earlier, but the shorter reading has earlier diversity among the Greek manuscripts. The longer reading has early and reliable witnesses, but the shorter reading has more early Greek manuscripts. Finally, although intentional errors cannot adequately account for either reading, harmonizational tendencies favor the priority of v. 34a vis-à-vis accounts of Stephen's and James' martyrdoms.

Internal Evidence
Whereas the external evidence is ambiguous, I will argue that internal evidence of structure, vocabulary, and theology favor the longer reading.

Structure
The claim that v. 34a is unoriginal because it interrupts the narrative[67] fails to notice the possible intentionality of the verse's placement. For instance, if original, v. 34a could highlight the contrast between Jesus and his mockers, particularly since it occurs between the soldiers' acts of crucifixion and division of his clothes.[68] Perhaps the prayer also explains the responses of the onlookers, the penitent criminal, and the centurion;[69] or perhaps Luke records two prayers to

---

65. For a similar argument, see Brown, *Death*, 2:977-78.
66. Creed, *Luke*, 286-87.
67. C.F. Evans, *Saint Luke* (TPINTC; London: SCM, 1990), 867.
68. Brown, *Death*, 2:976.
69. Crump, *Intercessor*, 87-89.

correspond to the two references to Jesus' crying out in Mark 15:34, 37. Whatever the case, v. 34a could serve Luke's purpose at its location in the pericope.
Therefore, any suggestion that v. 34a interrupts Luke's narrative and is therefore
unoriginal fails to recognize that Luke might "interrupt" his narrative for
a reason.

In fact, familiarity with Lukan tendencies would suggest that v. 34a belongs
in the pericope. Certainly, some attempts to argue the text's originality from
structure place unnecessary strain on the text. For instance, Marshall may be
correct to argue that v. 34a is necessary since Jesus' sayings "are found in each
[other] main section of the Lukan crucifixion narrative (23:28-31, 43, 46)."[70]
Yet, it is questionable whether, as he suggests, vv. 32-38 constitute a distinctive
"main section" or are part of a larger "main section" (vv. 32-43) that already
contains a saying (v. 43).[71] Similarly, Schweizer argues that Luke's tendency
toward triads would lead him to offer three sayings from the cross.[72] Once again,
though a possible structuring principle, it requires one to group narrative details
according to debatable categories (e.g., why is Jesus' cry a "sign"?).

The simplest solution to determining Luke's structural tendency is to observe another account of Lukan martyrdom. As mentioned above, Luke apparently parallels Stephen's martyrdom with Jesus' (e.g., false witnesses, a Sanhedrin trial, a cry with a great voice, seeing Jesus/Son of Man at the right hand of
God/power, and the prayer of committing one's spirit). Therefore, it is reasonable to assume that, just as Luke records Stephen's dying prayer for his enemies,
so he would have previously recorded Jesus doing the same. Though the differences in the two accounts prevent any certainty in this regard,[73] the overwhelming similarities suggest the originality of v. 34a. As John Nolland concludes,
"[Given] Luke's conscious paralleling of the deaths of Jesus and Stephen, it is
hard to see how Luke could have produced Acts 7:60 without being aware of a
tradition like 34a."[74]

In brief, the placement of v. 34a may evidence intention rather than interruption. Moreover, though Luke's precise structural principle is debatable, the
parallels between Jesus' and Stephen's martyrdoms indicate that, just as the
prayers in Luke 23:46 and Acts 7:59 correspond, so also would Stephen's prayer
in Acts 7:60 correspond to a parallel prayer of Jesus', such as v. 34a.

---

70. Marshall, *Luke*, 868.

71. Evans, *Luke*, 867.

72. E.g., three mockers taunting Jesus to save himself (soldiers, rulers, criminal);
"three signs: darkness, curtain, Jesus' cry"; and three responses to the crucifixion (centurion's, onlookers', acquaintances') (Eduard Schweizer, *The Good News According to
Luke* [Atlanta: John Knox, 1984], 359).

73. E.g., Stephen is stoned, not crucified; and he gives a lengthy speech, not a
brief one.

74. Nolland, *Luke*, 1141.

Vocabulary

The word choice is common to Luke as evidenced by the absence of any Lukan *hapax legomena* and by the following statistics: πάτερ (over 50x in Luke, 35x in Acts); ἀφίημι (31x in Luke, 3x in Acts); οὐ γάρ (7x in Luke, 6x in Acts); οἶδα (24x in Luke, 19x in Acts); and ποιέω (over 80x in Luke, over 60x in Acts). Whitlark and Parsons' claim that this is "simply stock NT vocabulary" has merit, since none of these terms is uniquely Lukan.[75] Nevertheless, the application of this "stock vocabulary" is consistent with, and often distinctive of, Luke:

- δέ – "The most obvious fact about Luke's use of co-ordinate conjunctions discovered by comparison with Mark is his preference for δέ over καί."[76]
- ἔλεγεν – As with the imperative ἄφες in v. 34a, the imperfect of λέγω elsewhere introduces imperatives (3:7-8, 11; 9:23; 10:2; 23:42).[77] Although the exact phrase ὁ δὲ Ἰησοῦς εἶπεν occurs in the aorist (5:34; 8:46), a similar phrase occurs with the imperfect: ὁ Ἰησοῦς ἔλεγεν (13:14). Moreover, despite Luke's preference for the aorist,[78] it is not uncommon to find the imperfect introducing a distinct statement (e.g., 5:36; 6:20; 12:54; 13:6; 14:7, 12; 16:5). Although Luke introduces Jesus' prayer in v. 46 with εἶπεν, a statement in v. 42 that utilizes ἔλεγεν offers closer parallels to v. 34a: "Then he said (ἔλεγεν), Jesus, remember (μνήσθητί) me when you come into your kingdom." Hence, as is the case v. 34a, in v. 42, ἔλεγεν introduces 1) a *distinct* saying, 2) in the form of a *request*, 3) to an *authoritative* (if not heavenly) *figure*, 4) in the *imperative*.
- πάτερ – In every recorded prayer in Luke, Jesus addresses God as "Father" (10:21; 11:2; 22:42; 23:46). Only in 10:21 does he address God by any other title (κύριε), and it immediately follows πάτερ. In contrast to the other synoptic Gospels, Jesus' address in Luke is always in the vocative (cf. Mark 14:36; Matt 11:26). Also unlike other Gospel writers, Luke never adds articles, adjectives, or possessives to πάτερ (cf. Matt 6:9; 26:39, 42; John 17:11, 25). Moreover, Jesus prays to the "Father" two other times in Luke's passion narrative (22:42; 23:46).[79]

75. "πάτερ (415x) ἀφίημι (142x) οἶδα (321x) ποιέω (565x)" (Whitlark and Parsons, "Seven Last Words," 191 n.13).

76. For over twenty possibilities of Luke substituting δέ for καί, see Henry J. Cadbury, *The Style and Literary Method of Luke* (HTS 6; Cambridge: Harvard University Press, 1920; repr., New York: Kraus, 1969), 142-43.

77. Brown, *Death*, 2:976.

78. See Cadbury, *Style*, 160, 169.

79. For more specific details regarding synoptic comparisons, see Haines-Eitzen, *Guardians*, 122.

- ἀφίημι – Luke frequently employs this verb or its related noun (ἄφεσις) in contexts that suggest forgiveness of sins (e.g., Luke 1:77; 3:3: 5:20-24; 9:5; 12:31; 24:47; Acts 2:38; 5:31; 10:43; 13:38). Moreover, the formula ἄφες...γάρ ("forgive...*for* [we forgive]") occurs in the Lord's Prayer in Luke 11:4, in contrast to ἄφες...ὡς ("forgive...*as* [we forgive]") in Matt 6:12.

- οἶδα – I will argue in greater detail in ch. 5 that the context of v. 34a suggests that οἶδα denotes "understanding," which corresponds to other occurrences of οἶδα in the Lukan narrative (e.g., Luke 2:49; 9:33).

- τί + ποιέω – These terms are frequently combined in Luke-Acts (e.g., Luke 3:12, 14; 6:11; 10:25; 12:17; 16:3, 4; 18:18; Acts 2:37; 4:16; 22:10). If original, the words would supplement the contrast between Jesus' innocence and his executioners' guilt.[80] Earlier in the narrative, τί...ποιέω represents the harm that the religious leaders desire to inflict upon Jesus (19:48; cf. also 6:11), which could correspond to the sin for which Jesus asks them to be forgiven.[81]

This survey indicates that v. 34a corresponds not only generally to Lukan vocabulary, but also specifically to Lukan usage, particularly in the cases of πατέρ and ἄφες...γάρ. The text's originality better explains this similarity than does a later scribal addition, so that Whitlark and Parsons would seem to overstate their case by claiming that the "skillful theological transformation" of "Western text representatives [such] as D" can equally account for the similarities between v. 34a and Luke.[82]

Theology

Verse 34a coincides with 1) the Lukan emphasis on prayer, 2) the Lukan portrayal of Jesus, and 3) the Lukan ignorance motif. Beginning with the first, Luke recounts Jesus praying numerous times (e.g., 3:21; 5:15-16; 6:12; 9:18-22; 9:29; 10:17-21; 11:1; 22:39-49; 23:46). Moreover, he tells parables about prayer (11:5; 18:1-8, 9-14) and instructs his disciples to pray (22:40). He withdraws to pray, and he prays at significant events (e.g., baptism, choosing of the disciples, Transfiguration, Mount of Olives, and the cross). Luke includes prayer when other Synoptics do not (e.g., Luke 5:16; 9:18; cf. Mark 1:45; 8:27 respectively; cf. also Luke 3:21; 6:12; 9:28-29).[83] Given this Lukan propensity toward prayer, particularly during important events, Jesus' prayer on the cross in v. 34a would certainly fit Luke's theological interests. Moreover, as mentioned above, this prayer's structure matches Jesus' prayer for forgiveness in 11:4.

Second, v. 34a corresponds with Luke's characterization of Jesus as Savior and as righteous through the use of irony and character contrasts. Regarding the

---

80. Cf. Luke 23:22, "What [τί] evil has he done [ποιέω]?"
81. Brown, *Death*, 2:976.
82. Whitlark and Parsons, "Seven Last Words," 192-93.
83. Cadbury, *Style*, 113.

former, this pericope highlights the theme of salvation through the repeated mockery of Jesus as the leaders, the soldiers, and a criminal each ridicule Jesus with a title (Messiah, King of the Jews, the Chosen One) and a jeer to "save himself" (23:35, 37, 39).[84] Just as the nature of Jesus' salvation is misunderstood throughout the Gospel, it is also misunderstood at the cross. Whereas the mockers understand salvation to be a release from crucifixion, they fail to see that, ironically, Jesus is saving them, in part by extending forgiveness to them.[85]

Jesus' righteousness is also a prevalent theme in the Lukan passion narrative.[86] For instance, Pilate repeats three times that Jesus is without "guilt" (αἴτιος [23:4, 14, 22]); Herod apparently finds him guiltless as well (23:15); and the centurion concludes the crucifixion scene by declaring that Jesus was "righteous" (δίκαιος; cf. "God's Son" [Mark 15:39]). Moreover, Luke contrasts Jesus' innocence by repeatedly characterizing Barabbas as a murderer and insurrectionist (23:19, 25). Luke explicitly highlights this contrast with Barabbas elsewhere: "You rejected the Holy and *Righteous* One and asked to have a murderer given to you" (Acts 3:14). In addition, the penitent criminal declares, "We indeed have been condemned justly, for we are getting what we deserve for our deeds, *but this man has done nothing wrong*" (23:41). Given these examples, v. 34a corresponds with Luke's habit of contrasting Jesus' righteousness with others' unrighteousness, for Jesus' gracious prayer of forgiveness would be a sharp contrast to the scornful jeer of the mockers.

Lastly, v. 34a is consistent with Luke's ignorance motif (e.g., Acts 3:17; 13:27; 17:30; cf. also Luke 24:45; Acts 26:9). Of the numerous examples, Acts 3:17 suffices to display the consistency of v. 34a with regard to Luke's ignorance motif. In Acts 3:17, Peter declares that the people and their rulers "acted in ignorance." Undoubtedly, "acted" refers to Acts 3:13-15, which describes their treatment of Jesus whom they "handed over," "rejected," replaced with a murderer, and "killed." Therefore, even though the Jews and their leaders might act willingly (e.g., 13:34), Luke believes they could still act unknowingly, *especially regarding the crucifixion*. An undisputed text such as Acts 3:17 reveals that Luke saw no contradiction between this ignorance motif and other passages that suggest impending punishment despite/because of ignorance (e.g., Luke 12:48; 19:44; 23:29-31).

Moreover, the act of forgiving the ignorant corresponds with the mercy of Jesus and his disciples elsewhere in Luke. For example, whereas forgiveness often follows an act of repentance or faith (e.g., Luke 7:47; 24:7; Acts 2:38; 5:31), Stephen's prayer reveals that forgiveness may be extended to those with neither faith nor repentance (7:60). Jesus calls his followers to love one's enemies and to "pray for those who abuse you" (6:27-28), which is exactly what

---

84. Johnson, *Luke*, 380.

85. Ibid.

86. For the characterization of Jesus that follows, see John T. Carroll, "Luke's Crucifixion Scene," in *Reimagining the Death of the Lucan Jesus* (ed. Dennis D. Sylva; Frankfurt-am-Main: Hain, 1990), 116-17.

occurs in v. 34a. Therefore, v. 34a fits well within Lukan concepts of ignorance and forgiveness as well as his portrayal of Jesus.

Summary of Internal Evidence
The closest structural parallel to Jesus' martyrdom, Acts 6:8–7:60, suggests that v. 34a belongs among Jesus' words from the cross. Regarding vocabulary, every word in v. 34a is not only familiar to Luke, but is also used in a way congruent with, if not distinctive of, Lukan style. Concerning theology, the longer reading corresponds with Luke's emphasis on prayer, Luke's use of irony and character contrast to portray Jesus as Savior and as righteous, and Luke's ignorance motif. Consequently, the structure, vocabulary, and theology of v. 34a support the text's originality. Even Whitlark and Parsons, who support the shorter reading, remark, "[I]f we were able to base our textual judgments concerning Luke 23:34a on internal evidence alone, we would likely conclude that the reading was original."[87]

Conclusion
By means of this investigation, I have argued that the external evidence is too ambiguous to warrant a claim of unoriginality, and that the internal evidence, clearly conforming to Lukan style and theology, indicates the text's originality. Given this evidence, it appears that the editors of the NA[27] and the UBS[4] have gone too far–the former by placing v. 34a in double-brackets and the latter by giving their evaluation an "A" rating. Even those who maintain support of the shorter reading must acknowledge in light of the evidence that this text cannot be "known" to be unoriginal. Though it is difficult to prove the text's originality, it would appear more difficult to prove its unoriginality. Why, then, should the burden of proof lie with the supporters of the longer reading and not vice versa? Instead, one should follow the weight of the evidence and not insist *a priori* that this text is unoriginal—or that the case for originality must be made with certainty. To deny the originality of the longer reading because it cannot be thoroughly proven is to place a standard upon the longer reading that the shorter reading could itself never meet. According to my sifting of the data, since the evidence tips the scale in the advantage of the longer reading, v. 34a should be regarded as original.

---

87. Whitlark and Parsons, "Seven Last Words," 194.

3

Historiography, Hermeneutics, and Luke 23:34a

The classical debate [is] aimed at finding in a text either (a) what its author intended to say or (b) what the text says independently of the intentions of its author. Only after accepting the second horn of the dilemma can one ask whether what is found is (i) what the text says by virtue of its textual coherence and of an original underlying signification system or (ii) what the addressees found in it by virtue of their own system of expectations.[1]

Introduction

The multiple proposed interpretations of Luke 23:34a—seen, for example, in ch. 1 where we surveyed various proposed readings of the referents, intertextual echo, and nature of the misunderstanding—raise the question of strategies for evaluating readings. In his essay, "'Sie Wissen Nicht, Was Sie Tun': Geschichte eines Herrnwortes," David Flusser argues that Jesus' prayer is on behalf of the Roman soldiers, not the Jews or their superiors. Though he is aware that Luke later applies the ignorance motif to the Jews (esp. Acts 3:13-17), he maintains that the referents of Jesus' prayer in Luke 23:34a are determined by the immediate textual context (i.e., the division of clothes in v. 34b) and the historical situation of which the original audience would presumably have been aware (i.e., the Roman soldiers, not the Jews, performed crucifixions).[2] According to Flusser, since the context and historical situation determine (for him) that this prayer refers to the Roman soldiers, any subsequent interpretation that refers this prayer to the Jews is anti-Semitic, or at least influenced by an anti-Semitic bias, insofar as it identifies the Jews as those guilty, that is, those needing forgiveness for the death of Jesus. For instance, when the Syrian Didascalia restates this prayer of Jesus in a direct reference to the Jews, Flusser regards this as anti-Semitic.[3]

Matthias Blum's monograph on Luke 23:34a is essentially an expanded version of Flusser's article. Blum writes, "Flusser's reference to the agraphon in the Syrian Didascalia as evidence that one understood Luke 23:34 at that time as a prayer for the guilty Jews has raised the question concerning which contexts the prayer of forgiveness is still stated and which referents are mentioned or

---

1. Eco, *Limits of Interpretation*, 50-51.
2. Flusser, "Sie Wissen Nicht," 394-95.
3. Ibid., 403.

assumed."[4] Blum follows Flusser by offering the same reasons for referring the prayer exclusively to the soldiers—i.e., the immediate context and the historical situation: "The fact that the prayer aims at the forgiveness of the Roman soldiers arises from the immediate context and the binding of the pronoun αὐτοῖς to the subjects of v. 33.... It is the assumed practice that there is exclusive jurisdiction of the Roman governor in Judea, according to which the soldiers are the executive agents of the crucifixion."[5] Similarly, Blum also considers those readings that refer the prayer to the Jews as anti-Semitic or as influenced by previous anti-Semitic portrayals that assign to the Jews guilt for the crucifixion of Jesus.[6] Blum hopes that an appeal to the yield of historical criticism is a sufficient delimiter of allegedly anti-Semitic interpretations of Luke 23:34a because he is convinced that such work undoubtedly shows that the soldiers are the sole addressees of the prayer:

> Because it can now be unambiguously shown with the help of historical-critical exegesis that the prayer of forgiveness refers in Luke to the Romans, historical-critical exegesis exercises here a correcting function. Therefore, the reception of a single word of the Lord, such as the forgiveness request, must always follow the original context-restraint...in order not to risk suggesting a meaning in the reception that contradicts the meaning within the context of the biblical text.[7]

Blum, however, is overly optimistic in supposing that attention to textual context and historical criticism is by itself sufficient to prevent anti-Semitic interpretations. For example, J.T. Sanders and Frank Matera, though both appealing to grammatico-historical evidence, reach conflicting conclusions regarding Luke's opinion of Jews—the former sees Luke as anti-Semitic, the latter does not.[8] Regarding our specific Lukan text, as we saw in ch. 1, historical critics themselves have not come to a consensus on the specific matter of the referent of Jesus' prayer in Luke 23:34a. Moreover, even if the historical situation and the textual context were sufficient to determine a referent of the prayer, the question remains whether such research can stand as the nonnegotiable arbiter of valid readings.

This brings us to a significant question in interpretive theory, and to the topic of the present chapter: Is a text's meaning determined via appeal to historical criticism, and/or to authors and texts, and/or to readers; or are there historio-

---

4. Blum, *Denn Sie Wissen Nicht,* 197; translations of Blum are my own.

5. Ibid., 28-29.

6. Rather than offering a *Wirkungsgeschichte*, Blum opts for an *Auslegungsgeschichte* because "the anti-Semitic reading of NT texts reflects not the history of [the text's] effect, but rather the history of its reception" (ibid., 9).

7. Ibid., 207.

8. J.T. Sanders, *The Jews in Luke-Acts* (Philadelphia: Fortress, 1987); Frank Matera, "Responsibility for the Death of Jesus according to the Acts of the Apostles," *JSNT* 39 (1990): 77-93.

graphical and hermeneutical reasons that allow a historiographical text to have multiple, valid readings? I will argue that 1) there are no indisputably verifiable norms that privilege any reading strategy, 2) that an appeal to texts/authors is incapable of determining *the* meaning of a text, and 3) that an appeal to the interpretive schemas of early readers of Luke 23:34a is likewise unable to establish *the* meaning of our text. The matter of delimiting multiple readings—i.e., Blum's main concern—must wait until ch. 4.

Historiographical and Hermeneutical Theory

Blum and Flusser appeal to two textual delimiters: the historical situation and the textual context. Blum apparently conflates these two elements with historical-critical exegesis.[9] In contrast, I might consider historical criticism more traditionally concerned with "what really happened" (see below), instead of, for example, what the text's immediate context indicates. Regardless of Blum's precise definition of historical criticism, the prevalence of the historical-critical paradigm in biblical research requires that a chapter devoted to "meaning" must deal with traditional historical-critical questions as well. Consequently, in what follows, our focus will be on the attempt to delimit meaning by appealing to 1) historical criticism, 2) texts/authors, and 3) the socio-cultural situation.

Historical Criticism

In light of advances in historiographical and hermeneutical theories, Blum's (and many others') historical-critical assumptions about the proper interpretation of historiographical texts must be rethought, particularly those assumptions dealing with the norms of reading. Beginning with the norms of historical criticism, a well-written apologetic for a proper historical-critical reading is found in Heikki Räisänen's *Beyond New Testament Theology*.[10] Räisänen composed this treatise from his conviction that nearly every extant NT theology has failed to take seriously the need to distinguish between the historical and theological tasks. In other words, most NT theologians have failed to practice historical criticism fully, but have only practiced in part. Thus, Räisänen lays out a fairly accurate survey of how these theologians do not fully comply with the norms of historical criticism (whether they intended to or not). His particular concern is the unacknowledged (or unrecognized) modernizing tendencies of biblical scholars. Räisänen stigmatizes any work as "modernized" if he thinks it fails to take seriously the historical situation on its own terms. For instance, he regards canonical boundaries or any notion of a unified canonical theology as symptomatic of modernization since canonization occurred subsequent to a text's origin. For Räisänen, then, a proper NT theology eschews all ecclesial and faith convictions in favor of a historical approach characterized by eight principles:

---

9. For example, note the three references to the delimiting work of historical criticism wherein he is apparently referencing his grammatico-historical research (Blum, *Denn Sie Wissen Nicht*, 206-8).

10. Räisänen, *Beyond NT Theology*.

1. Awareness of the problems involved in relating historical study to theology.
2. Recognition of theological diversity within the New Testament.
3. Awareness of the cultural gap between modernization and antiquity and, consequently, of the peril of modernization.
4. As a particularly important aspect of the former, recognition of the centrality of futuristic eschatology in large parts of the New Testament...
5. Recognition of the necessity to study the New Testament in a broad context of political, social, and religious history.
6. Appreciation of the role of human experience reflected in the religious and theological contents of the New Testament.
7. Willingness to admit the existence of problematic claims, arguments, and standpoints in New Testament texts.
8. Some concern for a fair presentation of competing traditions, notably Judaism.[11]

The end result of such an approach, according to Räisänen, is a surplus of neutral historical data, about which the entire global community could be in agreement.

Räisänen's proposed programme for NT theology, however, is not a self-evident method for proper historical work. Rather, it is founded on unverifiable assumptions about how the world is arranged. As Wright notes, "The crucial thing to realize is that what the positivist tradition would see as 'facts' already come with theories attached."[12] For example, when discussing theories of history, Terrence Tilley argues that modern historical presumptions—particularly Troeltsch's principles of analogy and correlation—are too frequently mistaken for universal truths, rather than understood as *unverifiable, ideological starting points* that have their own limitations and problems. One simply lacks the meta-empirical perspective necessary for determining whether, for example, the principles of analogy and correlation are sufficient means for discerning truth.[13] Such assumptions about the way the world is (and was) are based on "philosophical claims not necessitated either by religious conviction or by the practic-

---

11. Ibid., 4

12. N.T. Wright, *The New Testament and the People of God* (Minneapolis: Fortress, 1992), 43.

13. Wright helpfully notes, "the observer is looking from one point of view, and one only; and there is no such thing as a god's-eye view (by which would be meant a *Deist* god's-eye view) available to human beings, a point of view which is no human's point of view" (*New Testament*, 36). I am, however, wary of Wright's historical Jesus work, because of historiographical and theological reasons that Luke Timothy Johnson addresses well ("A Historiographical Response to Wright's Jesus," in *Jesus and the Restoration of Israel: A Critical Assessment of N.T. Wright's Jesus and the Victory of God* [ed. Carey C. Newman; Downers Grove, IL: InterVarsity, 1999], 206-24).

es of historical investigation."[14] Unfortunately, the presumptions of the histori-cal-critical paradigm are too frequently mistaken for universal truths, rather than being understood as unverifiable, ideological starting points.[15] This is perhaps best exemplified in a follow-up essay to *Beyond New Testament Theology,* wherein Räisänen denies the role of "metaemperical entities...as explanatory factors" in history, *while not recognizing that this denial is in itself a metaem-perical claim*: "I do not see how recent insights into historiography...could un-dermine my basic concern—which is simply that a 'historical' account of early Christianity is not to appeal to supernatural or 'metaemperical' entities (gods, revelation, inspiration) as explanatory factors."[16]

One sees similar problematic assumptions elsewhere in *Beyond New Testa-ment Theology.* For instance, while recognizing that "it depends on scholars what sort of questions they put to their sources,"[17] he overlooks the logical con-clusion that all historical analysis is thereby modernized by the historian's own worldview. Räisänen also never adequately addresses N.T. Wright's apt critique of the book's first edition that his eight criteria are by no means objective, but are Räisänen's own subjective creation.[18] Perhaps Räisänen's greatest moderniz-ing move is his neglecting to read NT texts on their own terms, thus never truly hearing "what kind of readings can do justice to the text in its historical con-text."[19] Most NT texts were presumably written to a believing audience under the assumption that their contents would be interpreted by those who had faith in

---

14. Terrence W. Tilley, *History, Theology and Faith: Dissolving the Modern Prob-lematic* (Maryknoll, NY: Orbis, 2004), 7, 37-66.

15. Todd Penner, noting the diversity of historical-critical approaches, is wary of cri-tiques directed against historical criticism "as a whole;" and he even claims that Räisänen's *Beyond NT Theology* is "working from the margins of historical-critical tradi-tion and discourse" ("The Challenge from Within: Reading Räisänen against Dominant Methodological Discourse," in *Moving Beyond New Testament Theology: Essays in Con-versation with Heikki Räisänen* [ed. Todd Penner and Caroline Vander Stichele; Göttin-gen: Vandenhoeck & Ruprecht, 2005], 26). Although I believe Räisänen is actually call-ing historical critics to follow their discipline more *consistently*, the diverse historical-critical approaches that Penner notes are still founded on unverifiable grounds, and could thereby fall under a critique similar to that which is here applied to Räisänen.

16. "What I Meant and What It Might Mean...An Attempt at Responding," in *Mov-ing Beyond New Testament Theology: Essays in Conversation with Heikki Räisänen* (ed. Todd Penner and Caroline Vander Stichele; Göttingen: Vandenhoeck & Ruprecht, 2005), 425. In this essay, Räisänen further nuances his programme in response to criticism of his *Beyond NT Theology.* Further, he clarifies that his goal is a NT theology for a "non-confessional academic context" (404), which would seem to call into question his aspira-tions for global communicability, given the narrowness of his audience. Nevertheless, this essay is helpful for gaining a better understanding of his earlier work.

17. Räisänen, *Beyond NT Theology*, 22.

18. N.T. Wright, Review of Heiki Räisänen, *Beyond New Testament Theology: A Story and a Programme*, *JTS* 43 (1992): 628-29.

19. Räisänen, *Beyond NT Theology*, 166.

Jesus.[20] Räisänen, however, not only denies the role of faith in the historical task but wants these texts to deliver the same information to Christians and non-Christians.[21] He thereby modernizes these texts by imposing modern readings over against ancient ones for the sake of perceived *contemporary* global needs. In addition, his hope that such neutral historical findings will enable global communicability is only possible if other cultures adopt his historical-critical paradigm—a conversion of worldviews that lacks verifiable grounds.

Consequently, when considering how to interpret a text such as Luke 23:34a, one should not assume that historical criticism offers an unbiased exegetical strategy, since all interpretive paradigms are founded on unverifiable assumptions. My point is not that there are no reasons why someone *might* practice historical criticism. Instead, the point is that one should be aware of the biases and assumptions within an interpretive paradigm, and question whether those biases and assumptions offer the best lenses for reading biblical texts.[22] We will return to this question in ch. 4 as we consider whether historical criticism offers a sufficient interpretative paradigm for readers whose assumptions about biblical texts are informed by their ecclesial location.

Authors/Texts

Just as there is no inherent reason for privileging the historical critical paradigm, so also there is no inherent reason for privileging authors, texts, or the socio-historical situation of the readers. However, even if one were to privilege such matters, there is often ambiguity about the intention of the text/author and much diversity within the socio-historical setting so that discovering *the* meaning of a text is far from guaranteed. Nevertheless, such appeals are common. For example, according to Stendahl, it is paramount to distinguish what a text "meant" from what it "means": "from the point of view of method it is clear that our only concern is to find out what these words meant when uttered or written by the prophet, the priest, the evangelist, or the apostle—and regardless of their mean-

---

20. In a similar vein, Barth would argue that any paradigm that fails to account for *die Sache* ("the subject matter"), which is God, is a paradigm that does not read the text as they were intended to be read (cf. Richard E. Burnett, *Karl Barth's Theological Exegesis: The Hermeneutical Principles of the Römerbrief Period* [WUNT 2/145; Tübingen: Mohr Siebeck, 2001], 79).

21. Räisänen is not alone in his assumptions about neutrality in interpretation. For Krister Stendahl, "[t]he distinction between the descriptive function as the *core* of all biblical theology on the one hand, and the hermeneutics and up-to-date translation on the other, must be upheld if there is to be any chance for the original to act creatively on the minds of theologians and believers of our time." Reversing this order—i.e., bringing theology into the descriptive task—must be avoided; allowing the canon to have a determine role in meaning making, for example, is disallowed: "as far as the descriptive task goes, the canon can have no crucial significance" ("Biblical Theology," 423, 428, italics my own).

22. Cf. Joel B. Green, "Reading Luke," in *Methods for Luke* (ed. Joel B. Green; New York: Cambridge University Press, 2010), 4-6.

ing in later stages of religious history, our own included." Although Stendahl recognizes that "every historian is subjective," he continues as if the reader plays no role in meaning-making, as evidenced in his claim that "this descriptive task can be carried out by believer and agnostic alike."[23]

I contend that closer attention to hermeneutical theory reveals the elusiveness of authorial intent in historiographical works like the Gospels and Acts. For instance, in the very title of his book, *History/Writing*, Albert Cook underscores one inevitable and fundamental paradox of historiography—namely, "the *Dinge an sich* of 'events' cannot be separated from the act of writing, or fused with it either."[24] In other words, though it seems tautological, it seems necessary to state that historiographies are only available to readers in their written form. There is no disembodied, text-free account of ancient historiography.

This may sound like a mild, self-evident claim, but it has at least two significant consequences for our study, which are developed by Elizabeth Clark in her *History, Theory, Text*.[25] First, the past is only accessible through documents that are mediated through language—a cultural product with inherent ambiguity regarding its referents. A word can have various definitions and nuances; with no access to the author's mind, the interpreter cannot guarantee that she has understood a word as the author understood it. Second, even if language were without ambiguity, the subjectivity of presentism is inescapable because the reader cannot approach the text detached, uninfluenced by her own perspective, questions, and interpretive framework.[26] Thus, regarding her own work with premodern texts, Clark writes:

> It recognizes (with Michel de Certeau) the foreignness of the past, that "dead souls" resurge only in present discourse…[and with Hans-Georg Gadamer] that since historians' "horizons" fuse with that of the text, they themselves comprise part of the phenomena to be studied…. It recognizes that writing

---

23. Stendahl, "Biblical Theology," 422. Returning briefly to the issue of the norms of reading, one must wonder why, in Stendahl's paradigm, the theologian would rather build theology on top of authorial intent rather than on the early church's readings of these texts. That is, why should the theologian be more interested in Luke's intention than early church interpretation, particularly since it was these early Christian readers—who often do not seem to read according to authorial intent—who preserved, passed down, and taught others to value these texts?

24. Albert S. Cook, *History/Writing: The Theory and Practice of History in Antiquity and in Modern Times* (Cambridge: Cambridge University Press, 1988), 7.

25. Elizabeth A. Clark, *History, Theory, Text: Historians and the Linguistic Turn* (Cambridge, MA: Harvard University Press, 2004).

26. Contra Räisänen, who, while maintaining that he avoids "universalistic [claims]," can in the same paragraph discuss "detached accounts" as though detachment were possible ("What I Meant," 414). The irony, of course, is that to be detached from one view—e.g., the supernatural as a causal factor—is to be attached to another view—in this case, rejection (or avoidance or neglecting) of the supernatural as a causal factor (see pages 32-33 above).

renders problematic the presumed centrality of authorial intention, both because readers in different times and places "collaborate" with texts to produce new meanings and because "high" texts themselves encourage the proliferation of meaning beyond authorial intention.[27]

In other words, the reader can only venture a best guess at the author's intentions, because of the ambiguity of language that is made further ambiguous by the socio-cultural distance between ancient texts and modern readers, and because readers cannot access the author's psyche (pace Schleiermacher).

Recognizing that our access to ancient history is textually mediated also has consequences for the reconstructive work that occupies much Jesus studies, particularly the attempt to sift the Gospels for "what really happened." One major problem is that the data from such siftings are inevitably placed into some new narrative framework that consequently offers its own subjective retelling. For example, after taking a minimalist approach to historical Jesus research, Luke Timothy Johnson lays out a handful of data that might be largely agreed to be historically verifiable about Jesus. Then—as would be expected from a book whose subtitle reads, *The Misguided Quest for the Historical Jesus and the Truth of the Traditional Gospels*—he intentionally problematizes his own research by rightly noting that such handfuls of "facts" about Jesus mean little without a narratival structure, a structure that historical inquiry cannot provide. Johnson writes:

> The patterns and pieces alike, without the framework provided by a sustained narrative, must remain as discrete items—things that "Jesus said and did." It is *not* legitimate on the basis of demonstrating the probability of such items to then connect them, arrange them in sequence, infer causality, or ascribe special significance to any combination of them. This is why the abandonment of the Gospel narratives throws open the door for any number of combinations. Once that narrative control is gone, the pieces can be (and have been) put together in multiple ways.... My point is, however, that whether plausible or implausible, all such constructions lack any real claim to historical probability once the given narrative framework has definitively been abandoned.[28]

Consequently, Johnson notes that, apart from the Gospels, one cannot know, e.g., where the baptism of Jesus by John the Baptist fits into Jesus' life, or at what point to locate an "incident in the Temple" in Jesus' ministry.[29] Johnson avers, "The placement *and* the meaning of the event are given by the narrative, and if we abandon the narrative we have no reason to place it here rather than there, or to make any statements about what the event might have meant for Je-

---

27. Clark, *History, Theory, Text*, 156-58.

28. Luke Timothy Johnson, *The Real Jesus: The Misguided Quest for the Historical Jesus and the Truth of the Traditional Gospels* (San Francisco: HarperSanFrancisco, 1996), 124-25 (italics original).

29. Ibid., 125.

sus."[30] Thus, the attempt to remove the biases of the *ancient* author only results in the introduction of the biases of the *contemporary* author.

In other words, when one forces the round peg of historiographies like Luke through the square hole of such sifting, the result may actually be less "historical." For instance, it is largely held that the evangelists reported sayings of Jesus in contexts wherein those sayings were not originally spoken. Whereas the sifting of Jesus studies wants to remove the secondary context from the saying, historiographical theory might suggest that the proper way to understand this saying is within the narrative context given by the historiographer. In other words, a saying of Jesus coupled with an ancient historiographer's narrative context might offer a more accurate depiction than a saying disconnected from its narrative context.[31] In the end, if one hopes to have more than scattered, disconnected bits of ancient historical data, it requires taking seriously the narrative framework of ancient historiographies.

In summary, it has been argued that there is no neutral reason for privileging the historical-critical paradigm and/or authorial intent; rather, such hermeneutical convictions are founded on viewpoints that surpass human ability to verify. Furthermore, meaning cannot be based solely on authorial intent because the gap between readers and authors inevitably produces equivocality.

Socio-Historical Situation

Thus far, I have argued against any notion of indisputably verifiable norms for reading and contended that the meaning of a text cannot be equated with authorial intent, given that readers inescapably contribute to the process by filling in gaps that arise from the ambiguity of language and the inevitable distance between author/text and reader. One might argue, however, that the gap between Luke and his turn-of-the-first-century audience would not have been large enough to allow for much ambiguity, that ambiguity is largely the result of the near two-thousand-year, socio-cultural divide separating early readers of Luke's Gospel and ourselves. For instance, Stendahl apparently believed that an original meaning could be pinpointed in a text, enabling one "to grasp the meaning of an OT or NT text in its own time."[32] It seems that an unstated assumption of Stendahl's is that rigorous historical investigation can discern a text's *Sitz im Leben*, which holds the key to unlocking a text's original meaning.

In what follows, I will show that the opposite is true—namely, that socio-cultural research suggests that even in the first century there would have been multiple ways for potential readers to interpret Luke 23:34a. I begin with the

---

30. Ibid., 126 (italics original).

31. Cf. Francis Watson's reading of Barth wherein "[Barth] postulates an 'intratextual realism' in which one regards the text in its final form as the irreducible witness to a divine-human history...which can only be known in its textual mediation" (*Text, Church and World: Biblical Interpretation in Theological Perspective* [Grand Rapids: Eerdmans, 1994], 230).

32. Stendahl, "Biblical Theology," 428.

potential intertextual echoes in Jesus' prayer before moving to Blum's and Flusser's claims about early crucifixion practices. Next, I examine Shelly Matthews' case that an understanding of Roman clemency might illuminate Luke 23:34a. Thereafter, we will look at the DSS and Philo, noting how some around the first century understood the issue of forgiveness for sins of ignorance, an issue thematically related to the prayer, "Father, forgive them, for they know not what they do." Along the way, I will suggest how such interpretive frameworks might influence potential readings of Luke, and how these multiple readings might each find additional support for their interpretation from Luke-Acts itself. We will look at this material again in greater detail in ch. 5, where I argue my own case for the most textually coherent reading of the verse in question. For now, we are simply noting how the text could lend itself to a variety of different readings in the first century, the goal being to demonstrate that socio-cultural work is by itself insufficient for discovering *the* meaning(s) that early readers could have heard in our text, particularly a text such as Luke's Gospel where there is little known about the distinctive makeup of his audience(s). In other words, since we only have access to some general information about Luke's audience (e.g., ca. 1st century, Greco-Roman socio-cultural milieu, some familiarity with OT),[33] who can know with certainty details that move beyond these generalities, such as the intertextual attentiveness of Luke's readers, or whether they would have drawn on concepts more like those of Philo, the DSS, Roman clemency, or some other interpretive schema? In what follows, we will survey several plausible interpretive schemas for reading Luke 23:34a in the first-century Greco-Roman world.

Intertextuality. Two OT texts are most frequently associated with Luke 23:34a: Isa 53:12 and Num 15:22-31. Regarding the former, several observa-

---

33. For a concise and convincing argument about the elusive task of determining the specific situation of the Lukan community that brings together the works of such scholars as Luke Timothy Johnson and Dale Allison, see Stephen C. Barton, "Can We Identify the Gospel Audiences?" in *The Gospels for All Christians: Rethinking the Gospel Audiences* (ed. Richard Bauckham; Grand Rapids: Eerdmans, 1998), 186-89. See also the essay by F. Scott Spencer, who rightly notes about mirror reading that "it does not follow that themes and characters in a narrative's internal world necessarily reflect *real* (not just realistic) issues and people in the author's and readers' external environment" (italics original). Spencer further writes that, "while Luke's narrative is a product of its originating historical and cultural milieu...we cannot presume that it directly aims to explain and interpret some *particular event* in 'recent history'.... An epic narrative like Luke-Acts...is not a transparently *occasional* document in the sense of a Pauline letter ("Preparing the Way of the Lord: Introducing and Interpreting Luke's Narrative: A Response to David Wenham," in *Reading Luke: Interpretation, Reflection, Formation* [ed. Craig G. Bartholemew et al.; Grand Rapids: Zondervan, 2005], 115, 119 [italics original]). For more on the debates about establishing the Gospel audiences, see Edward W. Klink III, "Gospel Audience and Origin: The Current Debate," in *The Audience of the Gospels: The Origin and Function of the Gospels in Early Christianity* (ed. Edward Klink III; New York: T&T Clark, 2010), 1-26.

tions have led some interpreters to find a connection between Luke 23:34a and Isa 53:12 MT: "...and [he] was numbered with the transgressors; yet he bore the sins of many, and made intercession for the transgressors." For instance, immediately prior to Jesus' prayer in Luke 23:34a, DeLobel notes that another potential echo to Isa 53:12 may exist between "numbered with the transgressors" and Jesus' being crucified between two evildoers (Luke 23:33).[34] If this was heard as an echo of Isa 53:12, then it might suggest that Jesus' subsequent prayer in v. 34a would be heard as an echo of this text as well. Crossan reveals evidence of two early potential links between these two criminals and Isa 53:12. First, in the beginning of the third century, Tertullian explicitly makes this connection with Luke 23:32-43, "Moreover two malefactors are crucified around him, in order that he might be reckoned amongst the transgressors" (*Against Marcion* 4.42.4 [ca. AD 208]).[35] Second, some mss. (e.g., L, Θ, sy[p.h.]) add the phrase, "And the scripture was fulfilled which says, 'He was reckoned with the transgressors'" after Mark 15:27, "And with him they crucified two robbers...."[36] To Crossan's observations could be added that earlier in Luke, Jesus alludes to Isa 53:12 by saying, "For I tell you, this scripture must be fulfilled in me, 'And he was counted among the lawless'" (Luke 22:37).

Regarding Luke 23:34a itself, the connection of Isa 53:12 with Jesus' prayer is understandable. For example, Isa 53:12 MT reads, "he bore the sins of many, and made intercession for the transgressors." Some object that hearing an echo with Luke 23:34a would take Isa 53:12 out of context, since, as many have noted, the servant makes intercession by bearing sins, and not by praying.[37] Nevertheless, the Targum interprets the intercession of Isa 53:12 as prayer: "...he will beseech [בעי] concerning the sins of many, and to the rebels it shall be forgiven [ישבק]."[38] Thus, there is obvious thematic overlap between the forgiveness prayer of Luke 23:34a and, at least, the Targum of Isa 53:12. Again, the argument is not what Luke intended, but how Luke's text might have been heard by his readers.[39] Given the potential echoes of Isa 53 in Luke's passion account (two criminals and intercession), the direct reference to Isa 53:12 in Luke 22:37 (cf. the quotation of Isa 53:7-8 in Acts 8:32-33), and the thematic link between Jesus' forgiveness prayer and the Targumic translation of Isa

---

34. Delobel, "Crux," 33n29; cf. Schmithals, *Lukas*, 225.

35. John Dominic Crossan, *The Cross That Spoke: The Origins of the Passion Narrative* (San Francisco: Harper and Row: 1988), 165.

36. Ibid., 165.

37. Nolland, *Luke*, 1146; Carras, "Numbers 15:22-31 and Luke 23:34," 612.

38. English translation of the Targum comes from Bruce D. Chilton, *The Isaiah Targum: Introduction, Translation, Apparatus and Notes* (The Aramaic Bible 11; Wilmington, DE: Michael Glazier, 1987), 105.

39. Thus, as argued in ch. 5, even though this echo requires the MT whereas Luke characteristically uses the LXX, some of Luke's readers may have been more familiar with the MT or Targum.

53:12, it seems possible that an early reader of Luke would hear Jesus' prayer as an echo of Isa 53:12 as it occurs in the MT or Targum.

George Carras is the primary advocate for the theory that Luke 23:34a echoes Num 15:22-31.[40] In Num 15, the Lord instructs Moses to tell the people that a distinction is made between intentional sins (ἐν χειρὶ ὑπερηφανίας, lit., "with a hand of arrogance" [15:30]) and unintentional sins (ἀκουσίως [Num 15:24, 27, 28, 29]). Carras recognizes that the vocabulary does not parallel that of Luke 23:34a ("they know not" [οὐ οἴδασιν]), so he argues for a "thematic" link.[41] If Carras had noticed the verbal link between sins of "ignorance" (ἄγνοια and ἀγνοέω) in Acts 3:17 and 17:30 and the sins of "ignorance" in Lev 5:18 (ἄγνοια and ἀγνοέω in the same verse), he might have built a stronger argument for thematic and linguistic similarities in the parallel Levitical text on unintentional sin. Nevertheless, Carras is correct to note the thematic similarities; and it would seem likely that an early reader would have connected the Pentateuchal laws on unintentional sin with Jesus' prayer, particularly given the familiarity of these laws evidenced in the first century (see below on Philo and the DSS; see also references to sins of ignorance in 1 Tim 1:13-16 and esp. Heb 5:2). Even Shelly Matthews, who argues that Luke intended no intertextual echoes, nevertheless writes, "It is possible that readers of Luke might hear echoes of atonement provisions, or affirmations of the suffering servant's gentleness in these prayers. Origen provides a relatively early instance of one who connects Levitical provisions for inadvertent sins and the dominical clause, 'for they know not what they do.'"[42] Specifically, in his *Homilies on Leviticus* (ca. AD 240), when Origen comes to the matter of involuntary sins of the congregation (Lev 4:13-21), he explains that the entire congregation can in fact sin in ignorance, because "[the] Lord also confirms this in the Gospels when he says, 'Father, forgive them for they do not know what they do'" (2.1.5 [FC]).

In sum, without access to Luke's mind, one cannot be certain whether Luke intended Luke 23:34a to echo Israel's Scriptures. Nevertheless, one can see evidence that the text would lend itself to at least two intertextual echoes. Regarding Isa 53:12, the volume of potential echoes of Isa 53 near Luke 23:34a, and in Luke-Acts as a whole, suggests that an attentive reader could well have heard this text echoed in Jesus' prayer. As for the Pentateuchal texts on unintentional sins, the thematic and verbal links, as well as Origen's early connection of these texts, suggest that an early reader might have interpreted Luke 23:34a with reference to Lev 5 (or Num 15). Consequently, even in the singular issue of intertextuality, it is unlikely that early readers would have uniformly heard the same (if any) echoes in Luke 23:34a, thereby making it problematic to determine a text's solitary meaning by appeal to early readers.

Agents of Crucifixion. As mentioned earlier, Blum and Flusser assume that only the Roman soldiers would have been allowed to carry out the crucifixion

---

40. Carras, "Numbers 15:22-31 and Luke 23:34a," 604-16.
41. Ibid., 616.
42. Matthews, "Clemency as Cruelty," 130.

and, thus, would have been those on whose behalf Jesus asks forgiveness. Regarding Jewish authority to impose capital punishment in general, the evidence is mixed, with some examples of Jews carrying out the death penalty (e.g., the stoning of Stephen [Acts 6:8-7:60]) and other examples of the Jews having to go through Roman authorities (e.g., "We are not permitted to put anyone to death" [John 18:31]).[43] According to Brown's weighing of the evidence: "The Romans permitted the Jews to execute for certain clear religious offenses.... Beyond this specified religious sphere the Jewish authorities were supposed to hand over cases to the Romans, who would decide whether or not to pass and execute a death sentence."[44] With regard to whether the Jews practiced crucifixion, the evidence is also disputed.[45] Nevertheless, though some acknowledge that Jews did crucify, it seems largely recognized that crucifixion "remained a predominantly Roman mode of execution in Judea."[46] In light of this, Blum and Flusser may be correct that early readers would have assumed that the Roman soldiers are in mind in our text. The uncertainty on this matter, however, might suggest that Blum and Flusser have placed too strict limits on whom the reader might have imagined.[47]

Clemency. Shelly Matthews offers evidence from both Luke's Gospel as well as early Christian readers to argue that Jesus' prayer for forgiveness should be interpreted in light of the Roman virtue of clemency. Matthews describes clemency as a form of "self-mastery" wherein one of higher power shows mercy

---

43. For a concise survey of evidence on this matter, see Brown, *Death*, 1:363-72.

44. Brown, *Death*, 1:371. Similarly, Catchpole writes, "The lack of final proof...makes it unwise to make argument at this point.... All the present writer would claim is that the balance of probability favours the view that the Jews could at that time pass capital sentences, but were prevented from executing them" (David R. Catchpole, "The Problem of the Historicity of the Sanhedrin Trial," in *The Trial of Jesus: Cambridge Studies in Honour of C.F.D. Moule* [ed. Ernst Bammel; Naperville, IL: SCM, 1970], 59).

45. Fitzmyer argues that certain Qumran texts point to crucifixion being carried out by Essenes (Joseph A. Fitzmyer, *To Advance the Gospel: New Testament Studies* [2d ed.; Grand Rapids: Eerdmans, 1998], 129-35); in contrast, Paul Winter proffers evidence to claim that the Jews did not carry out crucifixion (*On the Trial of Jesus* [2d. ed.; Berlin: Walter de Gruyter, 1974], 90-96); and Hengel claims that Jews did carry out crucifixions *until* "the beginning of direct Roman rule" (Martin Hengel, *Crucifixion in the Ancient World and the Folly of the Message of the Cross* [Philadelphia: Fortress, 1977], 84-85).

46. John T. Carroll and Joel B. Green, *The Death of Jesus in Early Christianity* (Peabody, MA: Hendrickson, 1995), 203; cf. Brown, *Death*, 1:857.

47. Nevertheless, even if Blum and Flusser are correct that the Romans are the agents of crucifixion (and I believe they are correct), I will argue in ch. 5 that attentive readers of Luke-Acts will notice that the Jewish leaders and Jerusalem inhabitants are primarily indicated as those who carry out the crucifixion. More specifically, I will show how the Jewish leaders and Jerusalem inhabitants are described as those who crucify Jesus through the hands of others: e.g., "you crucified (προσπήξαντες) and killed (ἀνείλατε) [Jesus], by the hands (διὰ χειρός) of those outside the law" (Acts 2:23).

to one expecting revenge or punishment.[48] Importantly, in the emperor's case, his display of mercy is often a show, having little consequence for its recipients. For Matthews, "while clemency does not perfectly mirror Lukan forgiveness" it is a "useful discourse" that helps make sense of the seeming discrepancy between Jesus' prayer of forgiveness on the one hand, and the impending desolation of Jerusalem on the other (e.g., Luke 21:20), which suggests the prayer was ineffective.[49] Thus, her proposed solution is to see the prayer as "first and foremost—if not solely—a celebration of [virtue]," so that the reader is not truly expecting mercy, but instead focuses on the virtue and authoritative status of the speaker.[50] To make her case, she notes various early Christian readings of Jesus' prayer (and Stephen's parallel prayer in Acts 7:60) where the readers' focus is on the speaker's virtue rather than on the effects of his prayer.[51] Most notably, she cites Irenaeus as "able to celebrate both the compassion Jesus demonstrates through praying for his crucifiers [*Haer.* 3.18.5] and the certainty that those crucifiers receive no compassion [*Haer.* 4.28.4]."[52] Although Matthews' proposed reading may or may not align with Luke's intention, she does reveal 1) a seeming tension in Luke's text, 2) an early reader of Luke's text (Irenaeus) who retains this tension, and 3) a plausible explanation for how a Greco-Roman reader might hold together this tension. Thus, her research may suggest another possible reading within the socio-cultural milieu of early Lukan readers.

Dead Sea Scrolls and Philo. Gary Anderson has detailed how the Pentateuchal laws on unintentional and intentional sin were understood in the DSS, with particular attention to the *Community Rule* and the *Damascus Document*.[53] Anderson, building on the earlier work of E. Quimron,[54] reveals a key aspect of the sect's teaching on the subject: the DSS distinguish between the "revealed" (נגלה) law—i.e., the written law of Moses—and the "hidden" (נסתר) law—i.e., "the newer revelations stemming from the community itself."[55] On the basis of this distinction, intentional sin is defined as any violation of the revealed law, and unintentional sin as violation of the hidden law. In other words, since the *revealed* law was "public knowledge for all Israel, any sin against these norms would invariably fall under the category of 'intentional sin'"; whereas the *hidden* law "could not be known to those outside the sect, and even within the sect [these laws] were continually evolving, [so that] greater leniency had to be

---

48. Matthews, "Clemency as Cruelty, 142-43.

49. Ibid., 145.

50. Ibid., 121.

51. Ibid., 140.

52. Ibid., 140-41.

53. Gary A. Anderson, "Intentional and Unintentional Sin," 49-64. Anderson's work will be examined in more detail in ch. 5.

54. E. Quimron, "Al Shegagot u-Zdnonot bi-Mgillot Midbar Yehuda: Iyyun ba-Munahim ha-Meshamshim le-Tsiyyunam," in *Proceedings of the Tenth World Congress of Jewish Studies* (Jerusalem: World Union of Jewish Studies, 1990), 103-10.

55. Anderson, "Intentional and Unintentional Sin," 51, 54-55.

shown toward those who disobeyed them."[56] Throughout Philo's works, one finds a related idea about the connection between unintentional sin and lack of special discernment (e.g., *Ebr.* 125; *Fug.* 116-18). We will examine relevant texts from Philo in ch. 5. For my present purpose, it is enough to observe that, in Philo, we have first-century evidence that early readers could have understood sins of ignorance as stemming from lack of revelation. Given such observations in Philo and the DSS, and given Lukan texts such as Luke 24:45 ("Then [Jesus] opened their minds to understand the Scriptures") and Acts 8:31 ("How can I [understand what I am reading] unless someone guides me"), it would seem that attentive readers of Luke-Acts could draw a similar connection between ignorance and unillumined minds and unillumined readings of Scripture. Once again, Jesus' prayer in Luke 23:34a would seem amenable to another plausible first-century reading—in this case, one in which the ignorance of the offenders is understood as resulting from lack of revelation, such as lack of illumined readings of Scripture.

Summary. Luke's *intent* may have specific meaning(s), but Luke's *text* lends itself to several possible readings within the socio-cultural milieu of his potential first-century readers:

- The thematic links and volume of echoes of Isa 53 make it plausible that Luke's readers would interpret Luke 23:34a as Jesus embodying the Suffering Servant.
- The thematic and verbal links with—and Origen's early connection of Luke 23:34a to—Pentateuchal laws on sins of ignorance evidence another possible framework for understanding Jesus' prayer.
- The tension in Luke's text between Jesus' prayer and Jerusalem's impending punishment could find its resolve in something akin to Roman clemency.
- The DSS explaining sins of ignorance via appeal to unenlightened readings of Scripture could find potential overlap in texts such as Luke 24:45 and Acts 8:31.
- The evidence for crucifixion practices suggests that Jesus' prayer could be understood as referring to the Roman soldiers.
- Yet, as mentioned in ch. 2, Nathan Eubank details how the earliest extant readings consistently interpreted the prayer as referring to the Jews, not the soldiers.[57]

These multiple possible readings evidence that an appeal to early readers is insufficient for determining a solitary meaning in the text.

---

56. Ibid., 55.

57. See n. 49 in ch. 2. In ch. 6, we will also see how Luke 23:34a lent itself to a variety of readings among the Fathers in the first five centuries. Given that such Greco-Roman readers would presumably have more extensively shared presupposition pools with Luke and his audience(s) than we would, their differing readings could serve as further evidence that early readers would interpret this text diversely.

Conclusion

To summarize, I have argued, first, that no indisputably verifiable norms privilege any reading strategy, with the result that all interpretive paradigms contain biases and assumptions; second, that an appeal to texts/authors is incapable of determining *the* meaning of a text, due to the ambiguity of language and the inescapable presentism of the reader; and third, that an appeal to the interpretive schemas of early readers of Luke 23:34a is likewise unable to definitively establish *the* meaning of our text, because of the diversity of plausible interpretive frameworks available to Luke's early readers of whom we have limited information. What is true of Luke 23:34a would seem true of other biblical texts as well, evidenced by the myriad of articles and commentaries that dispute a text's interpretation based on conflicting appeals to the author, text, and socio-historical situation.

How does one determine proper readings? That depends on how one defines "proper." If we take seriously the argument earlier that 1) readers play a role in meaning making, and 2) there are no definitively verifiable rules that dictate proper reading, then the interpreter must appeal to some unverifiable starting point that will guide her reading. Those who privilege the text might define proper readings as those that seem to make the most sense of the text *in its entirety* (which, as I will argue in ch. 5, would problematize the aforementioned readings of Matthews and Marshall). Those who privilege the historical-critical paradigm might define proper readings according to Räisänen's notions of historical veracity so that they might, for example, further the work of Blum by attempting to determine both the agents of Jesus' crucifixion and whether this Lukan prayer is authentic and/or in its proper context of origin. Those who privilege readers might define proper readings according to, for example, the interpretation's effect, as occurs in Flusser's essay.[58] Whatever the case, one's subjective starting point guides one's determination of "right" readings.

Recognizing subjectivity, however, does not necessitate that "anything goes" in interpretation. As Umberto Eco writes, "To privilege the initiative of the reader does not necessarily mean to guarantee the infinity of reading. If one privileges the initiative of the reader one must also consider the possibility of an active reader."[59] Taking Eco one step further, privileging the reader could mean privileging the reader's (subjective) interpretive paradigm. Given that there is no certainly verifiable starting point, I would suggest that for *Christians*, the starting point for evaluating interpretation should not be identical to the starting point of the historical-critical paradigm; rather, *the starting point should be an ecclesially informed interpretive approach*. Hence, in the following chapter, I describe what an ecclesially informed interpretive paradigm might look like.

---

58. See especially where Flusser notes how interpreting the prayer as referring to the Jews has had both positive (e.g., Jerome using the prayer as a missional invitation for the Jews [*Epistle* 120.8]) and negative effects (e.g., placing blame upon Jews) (Flusser, "Sie Wissen Nicht," 403-10).

59. Eco, *Limits of Interpretation*, 51.

4

Ecclesially Located Exegesis

Introduction

Having argued in the previous chapter that all interpretive paradigms are found-ed on unverifiable assumptions and biases, I closed by suggesting that, for *Christians*, the starting point for evaluating interpretation would be an *ecclesial-ly* informed interpretive approach. The goal of this chapter is not to offer an apologetic for Christian protocol, but to describe how it might inform a reading of Scripture. As Aquinas explains, "[S]acred doctrine does not argue to establish its first principles (the articles of faith) but advances from them to prove some-thing else," so that if one "believes nothing of what has been divinely revealed, no way lies open for proving the articles of faith" (*Summa Theologiae* 1.1.8; cf. 1.1.6).[1] In order to articulate what an ecclesially informed reading strategy might look like, I will highlight several principles from Augustine's *De Doctrina Christiana* (*DDC*) for insight into hermeneutical matters concerning authors, readers, polysemy, and interpretive guides and delimiters.[2] After looking at *DDC*, I will suggest how Augustine's insight—and the insight of others who share some of Augustine's theological convictions—might inform our conversa-tion in ch. 3, particularly regarding the proper statuses of authorial intent and historical criticism within an ecclesially informed interpretive approach. I will conclude by noting how some of Augustine's strategies for delimiting interpreta-tion combine the strengths of the strategies of numerous contemporary theologi-cal interpreters. To be clear, what follows is neither a wholesale apologetic of the principles in *DDC*,[3] nor a claim that Augustine's exegetical principles match

---

1. Translations of *Summa Theologiae* in what follows are from Thomas Aquinas, *Summa Theologiae* (ed. Brian Davies and Brian Leftow; Cambridge: Cambridge Univer-sity Press, 2006).

2. As Bonner notes, "The most important feature of Augustine's biblical exegesis is its ecclesial quality. The Bible must be read and understood within the framework of the life and doctrine of the Christian community" (Gerald Bonner, "Augustine as Biblical Scholar," in *The Cambridge History of the Bible*, vol. 1: *From the Beginnings to Jerome* [Cambridge: Cambridge University Press, 1970], 561).

3. For example, some of Augustine's discussion about typology—especially, nu-merology—is difficult to view as exemplary. As Bonner writes, "This numerical interpre-tation represents Augustine at his most extravagant, and most readers will recoil before an exegetical ingenuity so subtle and fecund and, withal, so laboured and unconvincing" (Ibid., 560).

his practice.[4] Rather, it is a chance to listen for how an ancient Christian exegete might speak to a contemporary question. As I hope to show, Augustine's *DDC* is particularly helpful in this task, because it offers a way to hold together complicated hermeneutical and theological concerns.

De Doctrina Christiana

> There are certain rules for interpreting the scriptures which, as I am well aware, can usefully be passed on to those with an appetite for such study.... It is my intention to communicate these rules to those with the will and wit to learn. (Augustine, *DDC*, preface)[5]

To avoid confusing the means with the end, it is necessary to state up front what is, for Augustine, the ultimate purpose of reading Scripture. Specifically, he teaches that the goal of reading Scripture is "faith, hope and love" so that one "who holds steadfastly to [these three] has no need of the Scriptures except to instruct others" (*DDC* 1.39).[6] He immediately reiterates this with language borrowed from 1 Tim 1:5: "the aim of the commandment is love from a pure heart, and a good conscience [i.e., hope[7]], and genuine faith" (*DDC* 1.40). Keeping this interpretive goal in mind, we now turn to *DDC* to learn how an ecclesially located exegesis might deal with interrelated hermeneutical matters concerning authors, readers, polysemy, and interpretive guides and delimiters. Specifically, this investigation will reveal that Augustine's ecclesially located reading strategy 1) requires humble and submissive readers; 2) allows for a single text to have multiple meanings that go beyond the human author's intent; 3) bounds polysemy by appeal to the rule of faith, clearer canonical texts, and the love of God and neighbor; and 4) makes discerning authorial communicative intent a priority.

Readers

For Augustine, the proper attitude when reading scripture is one characterized not by neutrality, but by fear of God, humility, and submission. As he writes,

---

4. After listing several of the same Augustinian exegetical principles that will be noted below, Bernard L. Ramm writes, "[It] is disheartening to realize how far short in so many instances Augustine came. There is hardly a rule he made which he did not frequently violate" (*Protestant Biblical Interpretation: A Textbook of Hermeneutics* [3d ed.; Grand Rapids: Baker Book House, 1970], 37; also quoted by Howard J. Loewen, "The Use of Scripture in Augustine's Theology," *SJT* 34 [1981]: 222).

5. English translations of *DDC* in what follows are from Augustine, *De Doctrina Christiana* (ed. R.P.H. Green; OECT; Oxford: Clarendon Press, 1995). In this edition of *DDC*, Green offers a helpful introduction for those with further interest in the date, context, and structure of *DDC* (ix-xxiii).

6. Bonner, "Augustine as Biblical Scholar," 548, 562.

7. Augustine clarifies that "good conscience" relates to "hope" (*DDC* 1.95).

> It is necessary above all else to be moved by the fear of God towards learning his will.... After that it is necessary, through holiness, to become docile, and not contradict holy Scripture—whether we understand it...or fail to understand it (as when we feel that we could by ourselves gain better knowledge or give better instruction)—but rather ponder and believe that what is written there, even if obscure, is better and truer than any insights that we may gain by our own efforts. (*DDC* 2.7; cf. 2.41)

Just as the reader's posture when reading is important for proper perception, so is his character: "[O]ur minds must be purified so that they are able to perceive that light...through goodness of purpose and character" (*DDC* 1.10).[8] Even such virtuous readers, however, must recognize that proper perception is not always within their power but God's, so that it is "paramount and absolutely vital to pray for understanding" (*DDC* 3.37).[9]

Polysemy

For Augustine, the polysemic nature of Scripture is not only the result of different readers but also of Scripture itself. Regarding the former, certain readers might interpret a text differently from others, depending on their circumstances: "[F]or example, a man who has embraced a life of celibacy...might maintain that any instructions given in the sacred books about loving or governing one's wife should be taken not literally but figuratively.... We must understand that some instructions are given to all people alike, but others to particular classes of people" (*DDC* 3.27). Regarding the latter, the Spirit's work in producing Scripture also allows Scripture to communicate multiple meanings through a single text: "Sometimes not just one meaning but two or more meanings are perceived in the same words of Scripture.... Certainly the Spirit of God who worked through the author foresaw without any doubt that it would present itself to a reader or listener.... Could God have built into the divine eloquence a more generous or bountiful gift than the possibility of understanding the same word in several ways?" (*DDC* 3.27). The polysemic, and sometimes, ambiguous nature of Scripture raises the issue of guidelines and delimiters for interpretation.

---

8. John Webster describes a similar posture recommended by Calvin—namely, "the insistence that right use of Scripture is for spiritual profit; the requirement for the consent of conscience (*conscience*/*conscientia* being, of course, not a function of deliberative acts of the human will but of conformity of mind and will to given truth); submission, obedience and affection as primary in human reception of the Word; and, undergirding all else, a sense that encountering Scripture is encountering 'truth come down from heaven'" (*Holy Scripture: A Dogmatic Sketch* [Cambridge: Cambridge University Press, 2003], 78).

9. Cf. Loewen, "Scripture in Augustine's Theology," 214.

Delimiters and Guidelines

Four recurring delimiters and guides are found in *DDC*. First, ambiguities in punctuation must be limited by the rule of faith, which here, and elsewhere, appears akin to the Apostles' and Nicene Creeds (*DDC* 3.2; cf. 1.5).[10] Not only does this apply to ambiguities in punctuation, as is the case in *DDC* 3.2, but apparently to all interpretation, since "[Scripture] asserts nothing except the catholic faith" (*DDC* 3.10).[11] Second, interpretations must accord with the twofold commandment of loving God and neighbor. Augustine makes this particularly clear by claiming, "The chief purpose of all that we have been saying…is to make it understood that the fulfillment and end of the law and all the divine Scriptures is to love the thing which must be enjoyed and the thing which together with us can enjoy that thing" (*DDC* 1.35).[12] In other words, "anyone who thinks that he has understood the divine Scriptures or any part of them, but cannot by his understanding build up this double love of God and neighbor, has not yet succeeded in understanding them" (*DDC* 1.36). For Augustine, loving one's neighbor is no easy rule, for it entails loving another person "more than our own bodies," loving "the person to whom an act of compassion is due" even if he is an enemy, and having the same compassion for others as God had for oneself (*DDC* 1.27, 30). Third, the more ambiguous canonical texts are to be interpreted in ways consistent with clearer canonical texts: "[A]fter gaining a familiarity with the language of divine Scriptures, one should proceed to explore and analyze the obscure passages, by taking examples from the more obvious parts to illuminate obscure expressions" (*DDC* 2.9; cf. 3.28).[13] Thus, when dealing with multiple meanings, the interpreter "[may] carve out from the words another meaning which does not run counter to the faith, using the evidence of any other passage of the divine utterances" (*DDC* 3.27). Fourth, authorial communicative intent guides interpreters, a topic to which we now turn.

Authors

For Augustine, the interpreter's focus should frequently be on discerning the author's communicative intent.[14] Thus, when discussing polysemy, he writes,

---

10. See also Augustine's *De Fide et Symbolo* (*Faith and the Creed*), where he expounds on articles in a creed akin to the Apostles' Creed. Finbarr G. Clancy refers to it as "an amalgam of the Nicene and Romano-Milanese creeds" ("*Fide et Symbolo, De*," in *Augustine through the Ages: An Encyclopedia* [ed. Allan D. Fitzgerald; Grand Rapids: Eerdmans, 1999], 360).

11. Cf. Loewen, "Scripture in Augustine's Theology," 205-8, 215.

12. As laid out in Book 1 of *DDC,* the being that is to be enjoyed is God, and the being that can share that joy is one's neighbor; cf. Thomas Williams, "Biblical Interpretation," in *The Cambridge Companion to Augustine* (ed. Eleonore Stump and Norman Kretzmann; Cambridge: Cambridge University Press, 2001), 67.

13. Elsewhere, Augustine explains that ambiguous texts contain "virtually nothing" (*nihil fere*) that is not in the clearer texts (*DDC* 2.6).

14. In *DDC*, Augustine's references to authorial intent are best understood as referring to what Stephen Fowl calls authorial communicative intent ("Authorial Intention,"

"The person examining the divine utterances must of course do his best to arrive at the intention of the writer through whom the Holy Spirit produced that part of Scripture" (*DDC* 3.27; cf. 1.36). Seeking the author's communicative intent is aided by knowledge of the original biblical languages (*DDC* 2.11, 13; 3.1, 3), recognition of subgenres and rhetorical devices (e.g., parables, irony, allegory [*DDC* 3.29]), and familiarity with socio-cultural conventions (*DDC* 3.12-15). Of particular importance when interpreting is a text's cotext: "It often happens that by thoughtlessly asserting something that the author did not mean an interpreter runs up against other things which cannot be reconciled with that original idea. If he agrees that these things are true and certain, his original interpretation could not possibly be true" (*DDC* 1.37; cf. 3.2-4).[15]

Comparing Augustine with Räisänen and Stendahl

To summarize the previous section, Augustine calls for interpreters to approach Scripture prayerfully, with a spirit of humility and submission. Such readers should seek the author's communicative intent while being aware that some texts have multiple meanings. These multiple meanings are not limitless, however, but are guided and bounded by the rule of faith, the double love of God and neighbor, and the clearer texts of the canon. Such an interpretive paradigm clashes with the paradigms of both Räisänen and Stendahl, which we surveyed in the previous chapter.

Regarding the former, one fundamental difference stands out between the ecclesially located reading proffered by Augustine and the historical-critical paradigm set forth by Räisänen. Specifically, Räisänen calls interpreters to approach the text from a neutral standpoint (by which he apparently means the standpoint of modern historical analysis), whereas Augustine calls for interpreters to come to the text from the standpoint of faith.[16] Three examples suffice to illustrate this difference. First, Augustine approaches Scripture humbly and

---

73-77), since Augustine's concern is not with the author's psyche, but with textual matters (e.g., language, rhetorical devices, and cotext). Regarding Augustine's exegetical presumptions in *Confessions*, Thomas Williams writes, "[The] ability to get at the author's intention is limited. Moses is not around for us to ask him questions, and any difficult text might bear more than one plausible and defensible interpretation" ("Biblical Interpretation," 64-65).

15. Ibid., 69.

16. As Loewen writes, "[I]t is clear that Augustine perceived the authoritative function of Scripture to exist in the framework of a rather robust doctrine of the Church…. Within this context biblical authority was an interpreted authority, reflected in the faithful and widely held Catholic interpretation and teaching of its saving message" (Loewen, "Scripture in Augustine's Theology," 205; cf. 206-10); so also Gordon J. Hamilton, "Augustine's Methods of Biblical Interpretation," in *Grace, Politics and Desire: Essays on Augustine* (ed. Hugo A. Meynell; Calgary, Alberta: University of Calgary Press, 1990), 113-14; Bonner, "Augustine as Biblical Scholar," 553, 557.

submissively,[17] with the *a priori* belief that the Scriptures will conform to the rule of faith and the twofold commandment of love. Second, whereas Räisänen disallows the canon in interpretation, Augustine finds the canon essential for guiding exegesis. Third, for Räisänen, the goal of interpretation is the descriptive task of amassing information, whereas, for Augustine, the goal of interpretation is transformative progress in faith, hope, and love.

Thus, the primary difference between Augustine's interpretive paradigm and Räisänen's can be stated as follows: Räisänen founds his reading on modern historical criteria whereas Augustine founds his on ecclesially located theology. As Webster writes, within a "Christian theological account of Scripture," the problem with an interpretive strategy that makes historical naturalism foundational is "the denial that texts with a 'natural history' may function within the communicative divine economy, and that such a function is ontologically definitive of the text."[18] For contemporary interpreters, deciding between such interpretive options is a theological matter. If, on the one hand, the reader does not regard Scripture from an ecclesially informed position, then ecclesial theology should not guide interpretation. If, on the other hand, these texts are read from an ecclesial location, then such theology is necessary, making it insufficient to interpret Scripture through a paradigm, such as historical criticism, that does not have room for certain ecclesial convictions (e.g., allowing for the supernatural). In other words, for ecclesial readers, "In comparing the integrally related functions of faith and reason, Augustine himself says that 'prior to reason, there must be some knowledge in us which reason itself uses as a starting point' (*Magnitude of the Soul* 26; cf. *Instruction* 1.34, 38).... Reason, therefore, is in need of faith to be fully operative. It is not to be taken in isolation from the illuminating activity of God."[19]

Regarding authorial intent, as mentioned in ch. 3, it is a common assumption that a text's meaning is determined by the original author or redactor. To quote Stendahl again: "[F]rom the point of view of method it is clear that our only concern is to find out what these words meant when uttered or written by the prophet, the priest, the evangelist, or the apostle—and regardless of their meaning in later stages of religious history, our own included."[20] In contrast,

---

17. In contrast, "teachableness and naiveté...are generally considered ill-adapted for the critical task," resulting in interpreters who place themselves over—rather than "with or under"—the text and, thus, outside of an ecclesial location (Webster, *Holy Scripture*, 103-6).

18. Ibid., 19. Webster goes on to write, "[T]he assumption that biblical writings are instances of the natural class of texts [is] to be resisted.... The biblical text *is* Scripture; its being is defined, not simply by its membership of the class of texts, but by the fact that it is *this* text—sanctified, that is, Spirit-generated and preserved—in *this* field of action—the communicative economy of God's merciful friendship with his lost creatures" (29, emphasis original).

19. Loewen, "Scripture in Augustine's Theology," 217; cf. 216-21.

20. Stendahl, "Biblical Theology," 422.

although Augustine holds authorial intent in high regard, he allows for Scripture to have meanings that go beyond human authorial intent. He grounds this in 1) the dialogical nature of reading whereby the circumstances of the reader can influence meaning, and 2) the Spirit's co-authorship of Scripture. Augustine's allowance for polysemy fits well in an ecclesially informed interpretive paradigm, as can be seen in conversation with Stephen Fowl's work, "The Role of Authorial Intention in the Theological Interpretation of Scripture."

To begin, the NT writers frequently read the OT in ways that go beyond the human author's communicative intent. For example, the author of Hos 11:1 ("out of Egypt I called my son") likely intends his words to refer to the past exodus of corporate Israel, whereas in Matthew's Gospel, these words refer to Mary and Joseph's escape to and return from Egypt with Jesus (Matt 2:15). If Hos 11:1 is limited to the meaning of human authorial intent, then it would seem impossible to reconcile Matt 2:15 with Hos 11:1.[21] The reader familiar with the NT's use of the OT is aware that the same is true not only elsewhere in Matthew (e.g., interpreting Rachel's weeping for her children [Jer 31:15] as referring to Herod's killing infants [Matt 2:16-18]) but also throughout the NT such as in the writings of Paul (e.g., the allegorical reading of Sarah and Hagar [Gal 4:21-31]), Luke (e.g., reading "Let another take his office" [Ps 109:8] as referring to choosing a replacement for Judas [Acts 1:20]), and John (e.g., reading the casting of lots for clothes [Ps 22:18] as fulfilled at Jesus' crucifixion [John 19:24]). While the OT readings in these NT examples might not contradict the original authorial intent, they certainly go beyond what the human author was likely communicating to his audience. Therefore, as Fowl points out, "A single meaning determined by authorial intention will either force Christians into rather implausible arguments about the communicative intent [of the OT author] or lead them to reduce the christological aspect of these passages into a subsidiary or parasitic role."[22] For those who might assume that such reading strategies should no longer be practiced by contemporary Christian exegetes, Richard Hays convincingly argues otherwise:

> [Such a position] cuts the lifeline between Paul's time and ours...[and grants] hermeneutical veto power to a modern critical method of which Paul himself was entirely innocent. From the perspective of faith it is not clear why this should be so. Besides...the 'apostolic faith and doctrine' cannot be extricated so cleanly from apostolic exegesis.... Scripture interpretation is the theologi-

---

21. "The reference to God's son being called from Egypt in 11:1 would not have conveyed this [i.e., Matthew's] sense to Hosea's own generation.... [Matthew portrays] a different significance for 11:1 than that intended by Hosea for his generation, but [demonstrates] a coherence with divine activity" (J. Andrew Dearman, *Hosea* [NICOT 28; Grand Rapids: Eerdmans, 2010], 280); cf. Douglas Stuart, *Hosea-Jonah* (WBC 31; Waco, TX: Word, 1987), 178; A.A. Macintosh, *Hosea* (ICC 28; Edinburgh: T&T Clark, 1997), 437-38.

22. Fowl, "Authorial Intention," 81.

cal matrix within which the kerygma took shape; removed from that matrix, it will die.... There is no possibility of accepting Paul's message while simultaneously rejecting the legitimacy of the scriptural interpretation that sustains it.... [If] his material claims are in any sense true, then we must go back and learn from him how to read Scripture.[23]

Hays' comments regarding Paul's exegesis would seem relevant regarding other NT authors as well.

Second, an appeal to human authorial intent is insufficient for determining crucial tenets of Christian theology. Thus, as Fowl notes, one struggles to debate an Arian reading of John's prologue (1:1-18) if appeal can only be made to the theological framework of the first-century author. Rather, "one needs to invoke such things as the *skopos* of Scripture, the rule of faith, and theological doctrines about Christology and about how humans might be saved."[24] Or, for example, when Paul in Phil 2:7 refers to Jesus' having been found in "human likeness" (ὁμοιώματι ἀνθρώπων) and "human form" (σχήματι ὡς ἄνθρωπος), an ecclesially informed exegesis cannot oppose docetic readings merely on the basis of authorial intent. Fowl rightly notes that "grammar, syntax, and semantics alone [i.e., tools for determining authorial intent]...support neither a docetic nor orthodox account of Christ's humanity." Rather, ecclesially informed readings preserve orthodoxy by appealing to theological grounds wherein Christ must necessarily be fully human in order to save humanity.[25] Even the canonization process itself depended, in part, on prior theological parameters (e.g., the rule of faith), precisely because there needed to be criteria outside of texts to help discern the various texts' normative statuses.[26]

Certainly, one might level the charge that such a reading strategy is anachronistic as it allows texts from the first century and earlier to be interpreted through the lenses of theological convictions ironed out centuries later. One theological response to this accusation has been put forward in Matthew Levering's *Participatory Biblical Exegesis*. Levering argues that such an interpretive framework as described above is only anachronistic according to a linear-historical model. Unlike the atomism of a linear-historical model, Levering proposes a participatory-historical model that is grounded in a theosistic, patristic-medieval metaphysics wherein all creation, and thus all history, participates in

---

23. Richard B. Hays, *Echoes of Scripture in the Letters of Paul* (New Haven, CT: Yale University Press, 1989), 180-82.

24. Ibid., 81-82.

25. Stephen E. Fowl, *Philippians* (THNTC 11; Grand Rapids: Eerdmans, 2005), 98.

26. "A basic prerequisite for canonicity was conformity to what was called the 'rule of faith'...that is, the congruity of a given document with the basic Christian tradition recognized as normative by the church" (Bruce M. Metzger, *The Canon of the New Testament: Its Origin, Development, and Significance* [Oxford: Clarendon Press, 1987], 251-53).

the divine and is therefore interrelated within God.[27] In other words, since all creation participates in God, and since all history is bound in creation, then all history is simultaneously present within God with the result that it is not anachronistic to interpret God's revelation in the first century in light of God's revelation in the fourth century because these events are ever-present within God.

Although there is clear logic buttressing Levering's participatory-historical model, its limitation rests in its debatable theological claim that one must view creation as a "finite participation in divine being."[28] Though this may not pose problems for some Christian traditions, it may for those whose theology would suggest, for example, that creation, specifically fallen creation, does not participate in the divine. This leads me to Fowl's third point that offers a more ecumenical basis for reading texts in an allegedly anachronistic manner.

Through interaction with Thomas Aquinas' *Summa Theologiae*, Fowl explains that, if one takes seriously that God is the author of Scripture, there is no problem with concluding that God might intend multiple meanings that extend beyond the human author's intent. Thus, pneumatology becomes the scarlet thread that unites past, present, and future divine revelations. Since the Spirit worked alongside biblical authors to communicate divine revelation, then it is not anachronistic to interpret a first-century revelation of the Spirit in light of a subsequent revelation of the *same* Spirit. To deem this move as anachronistic is to put anthropological limitations on a supra-anthropological text.[29] As Aquinas writes, "[because] the author of sacred Scripture is God (who comprehends everything all at once in his understanding), it is not surprising, as Augustine observes [*Confessions* 12.31], that many meanings are present even in the literal sense of one passage of Scripture."[30]

By following Aquinas' lead and consulting *Confessions* 12, one finds Augustine contemplating the various meanings of a single text and wondering whether the human author was privy to the various ways that God would communicate to his people (12.24, 32). When discussing the numerous interpretations of the phrase "in the beginning God created the heaven and the earth,"[31]

---

27. Matthew Levering, *Participatory Biblical Exegesis: A Theology of Biblical Interpretation* (Notre Dame, IN: University of Notre Dame Press, 2008), 1-3.

28. Ibid., 3.

29. Nor is this a docetic move, as Kevin Vanhoozer suggests, for it does not ignore the human element but merely understands that God could enhance it ("Four Theological Faces of Biblical Interpretation," in *Reading Scripture with the Church: Toward a Hermeneutic for Theological Interpretation* [by A.K.M. Adam et al.; Grand Rapids: Baker, 2006], 137).

30. *SummaTheologiae* 1.1.10 (also quoted by Fowl, "Authorial Intention," 83-84).

31. E.g., "[The author] could have thought about the very start of God's creative action when he said, 'In the beginning.' He could have wished that the words 'heaven and earth' in this passage be interpreted not as meaning a nature already formed and perfected, whether spiritual or corporeal, but as meaning both as just started and still unformed" (12.24). Translations of *Confessions* in what follows are from Augustine, *The Confessions of Saint Augustine* (trans. John K. Ryan; New York: Doubleday, 1960).

Augustine remarks, "See now how stupid it is, amid such an abundance of true meanings as can be taken out of these words, rashly to affirm which of them Moses chiefly meant" (12.24-25).[32] Augustine prefers to accept numerous orthodox interpretations as true because "the one God has adapted the sacred writings to many [humans'] interpretations, wherein will be seen things true and also diverse" (12.31). Though one might think that this violates the anthropological element of Scripture, Augustine imagines that if he were the human author, he would desire for God to use his words with similar richness and diversity (12.31). But, even if the human author intended one meaning, Augustine would rather hear the meaning God intends for him to hear rather than what the human author intended for his audience to hear: "Lord, you point out either [the author's] meaning or such other true meaning as pleases you. Hence, whether you uncover the same meaning to us as to that servant of yours [the author], or some other meaning ...you will still nourish us and error will not delude us" (12.32).[33]

One way to make sense of Augustine's simultaneous appeal to two authors is to adapt Eco's Model Reader so that it includes not only the readers and presupposition pools anticipated by the human author, *but also* those anticipated by the divine author—thus, a kind of ecclesial Model Reader. Thus, the model reader of Scripture may interpret Scripture in light of the ecclesially informed presupposition pools already mentioned, such as the rule of faith and other canonical texts. This allows one to move beyond the human author's presupposition pool so that, for example, one can interpret individual texts in light of other canonical texts.[34] At the same time, Augustine would value human authorial intent by trying to be a Model Reader of the human author, as evidenced, for example, in his aforementioned teaching on the importance of shared verbal and socio-cultural communication pools (e.g., language and rhetorical devices). This twofold notion of reading would seem to fit with Webster's claim:

---

32. As Pamela Bright notes about *Confessions* 12, Augustine's belief in the "insufficiency of the self" and in Scripture's "depth" means that "truth cannot be 'grasped' or possessed in a single unfaltering glance (at least in the human condition); neither can it be possessed by the individual interpreter." In other words, "[t]he proud, solitary interpreter holding to a singleness of truth is revealed as an empty and boastful liar" ("Augustine: The Hermeneutics of Conversion," in *Handbook of Patristic Exegesis: The Bible in Ancient Christianity* [2 vols.; by Charles Kannengiesser; Leiden: Brill, 2004], 2:1221, 1225-27, 1232-33).

33. See also Carol Harrison, *Beauty and Revelation in the Thought of Saint Augustine* (Oxford: Clarendon Press, 1992), 83-84; Williams, "Biblical Interpretation," 65-67.

34. Cf. Vanhoozer's "implied canonical reader" where the Model Reader is the one envisioned by the whole canon and not the single text ("The Apostolic Discourse and Its Developments," in *Scripture's Doctrine and Theology's Bible: How the New Testament Shapes Christian Dogmatics* [ed. Markus Bockmuehl and Alan J. Torrance; Grand Rapids: Baker Academic, 2008], 199; idem, "Imprisoned or Free? Text, Status, and Theological Interpretation in the Master/Slave Discourse of Philemon," in *Reading Scripture with the Church: Toward a Hermeneutic for Theological Interpretation* (by A.K.M. Adam et al.; Grand Rapids: Baker, 2006), 70-71.

Talk of the biblical text as *Holy* Scripture thus indicates a two-fold conviction about their place in divine revelation. First, because they are sanctified, the texts are not simply 'natural' entities, to be defined and interpreted exhaustively as such. They are fields of the Spirit's activity in the publication of the knowledge of God. Second, because sanctification does not diminish creatureliness, the text's place in the divine economy does not entail withdrawal from the realm of human process.[35]

Thus, the Model Reader of this divine-and-human text recognizes, on the one hand, that interpretations may extend beyond the human author's intent as the text is read through lenses such as the canon, the love of God and neighbor, and the revelation of Christ; and on the other hand, that the communicative intent of the human author, when discernable, functions as an additional guide illuminating one's hearing for the present. As mentioned earlier, Augustine clearly values human authorial intent, but realizes that it is not only elusive, but also that it might not be the most necessary message for one's context. Thus, he can write: "If I should say that which your minister intended, I will say what is right and best. For this should I strive, and if I do not attain to it, I would still say that which your Truth willed by his words to say to me, which also spoke to him what it willed" (Augustine, *Confessions* 12.33).[36]

To summarize, in dialogue with Fowl it has been argued that an allowance for polysemy works well in an ecclesially informed interpretation because of the NT's use of the OT, the inability of *sola scriptura* to determine crucial theological doctrines, and the authorship of the Spirit who transcends human limitations. To these could be added Augustine's correct observation that a reader's circumstances can lead to different interpretations. Consequently, if one takes communication to be a dialogical process between authors and readers, one should not be surprised if the Scriptures are heard differently by the diverse ecclesial members in the varying contexts of the diasporic church.[37]

Boundaries for Polysemy

Among theological interpreters, much diversity revolves around determining what principles and constraints, if any, should guide interpretation in such a way that allows for both orthodoxy and polysemy. In this section I will survey a vari-

---

35. *Holy Scripture*, 27-29 (italics original).

36. James J. O'Donnell, commenting on *Confessions*, writes, "[W]hen faced generally with the polysemy of scripture, hermeneutics runs the risk of floundering in the '*opaca frutecta*' [shady thickets] (12.28.38) and never getting out of the woods. The willingness to cease hunting the unicorn of author's intention and to settle for (mere!) truth is the key to delimiting interpretation and connecting it to life" (*Augustine Confessions III: Commentary on Books 8-13* [Oxford: Oxford University Press, 1992], 342).

37. Cf. Joel B. Green, "Afterword: Rethinking History (and Theology)," in *Between Two Horizons: Spanning New Testament Studies and Systematic Theology* (ed. Joel B. Green and Max Turner; Grand Rapids: Eerdmans, 2000), 239-41.

ety of strategies for regulating polysemy and suggest how Augustine's *DDC* contains many of the strengths these strategies offer. Specifically, I will look at how and whether the various strategies 1) account for the NT's use of the OT, 2) offer suitable parameters for ecclesially informed orthodoxy, 3) allow Scripture enough autonomy to challenge and inform ecclesial readers,[38] and 4) are such that the global church could practice them.[39]

For Max Turner, authorial communicative intent functions as an interpretive "benchmark," a "relatively 'determinate' meaning" by which to evaluate polysemic interpretations, particularly when reading the genre of letter, though this principle largely applies to narratives as well.[40] He grounds this in Eco's notion of Model Reader wherein a text anticipates certain readers who share a particular presupposition pool with the human author.[41] The advantages of Turner's approach are numerous. For example, it allows the text to have a voice that is not completely hijacked by hermeneutical theories where meaning is determined solely by the reader. Similarly, it honors the anthropological element of Scripture and the canonization process because it resists harmonization and reductionism in favor of listening for the communicative intent of the texts.[42] Moreover, this strategy recognizes that the church, throughout the centuries, has acknowledged the importance of Scripture's authors.

Like Turner, Augustine's *DDC* places high value on authorial communicative intent. Turner's approach, however, does not fully account for three issues. First, it downplays the aforementioned elusiveness of authorial communicative intent, which is problematic if this is to serve as a benchmark. Second, uncovering this benchmark requires an expertise that seems to exceed that of most

---

38. "If the church is constituted by the Word, and by Holy Scriptures as the Word's servant, then Scripture is an aspect of the church's stability only in so far as that stability is grounded *extra ecclesiam*.... Scripture is as much a de-stablising feature of the life of the church as it is a factor in its cohesion and continuity.... Through Scripture the church is constantly exposed to interruption. Being a hearing church is never, therefore, a matter of routine, whether liturgical or doctrinal" (Webster, *Holy Scripture*, 46-47).

39. Given that the church has existed amidst various cultures, and given that the current church is becoming increasingly nonwestern and third-world (see e.g., Justo L. González, *The Changing Shape of Church History* [St. Louis, MO: Chalice, 2002]), then an ecclesially informed strategy for delimiting readings should be accessible to others besides contemporary western biblical scholars. Moreover, it would seem proper that such a strategy should also be accessible to pastors of local congregations who have been charged with teaching and guiding their congregations.

40. Turner, "Historical Criticism and Theological Hermeneutics," 44-70. Turner's view is not far from Vanhoozer's, who wants authorial communicative intent to function as the delimiter of polysemy. For Vanhoozer, "our task is to discern what the Spirit is saying by means of what the human authors of Scripture have said"; and therefore, the appropriate context for interpretation is "the historical, literary, and canonical settings of biblical discourse" ("Imprisoned or Free," 60-61; idem, "Four Faces," 137).

41. Turner, "Historical Criticism and Theological Hermeneutics," 45-49.

42. Ibid., 54-57, 69.

scholars and, consequently, would seem to exceed that of most pastors and non-western third-world readers with limited access to such scholarship. Third, Turner's paradigm does not adequately address the issues raised earlier, particularly the NT writers' use of the OT, wherein human authorial intent does not appear to be the interpretive benchmark.

The particular difficulty of applying this type of strategy can be seen in a recent article by Murray Rae.[43] Rae proposes that polysemic interpretations "need not be the same as but should rather be congruent with the intentions of the author."[44] To illustrate this, he offers several distinct interpretations of Isa 53 that he deems congruent with the original communicative intent. The difficulty comes when he concludes that NT christological interpretations of Isa 53 are congruent with authorial intention. To do so, in my opinion, requires him to expand his definition of "congruency" beyond the point where it can serve as a sufficient delimiter. As Rae himself seems aware, a christological reading of Isa 53 is not self-evidently congruent with the author's intention, unless one already reads from a Christian perspective. When Rae delimits interpretations of Isa 53, he does not appeal to incongruence with authorial intent, as much as he appeals to incongruence with the divine economy to which Scripture ultimately testifies—something akin to a rule of faith. Presumably, his concept of authorial congruency has been extended too broadly for it to function as a sufficient delimiter.[45]

Another strategy for delimitation occurs in separate articles, where Joel Green and Richard Hays advocate the polysemic nature of Scripture while simultaneously prioritizing a hermeneutic that takes seriously a close reading of the text.[46] Thus, Hays can write on the one hand, "theological exegesis is committed to the discovery...of *multiple senses* in biblical texts," and on the other hand, "the more we know about the Mediterranean world of Greco-Roman antiquity, the more nuanced will be our understanding of the ways in which the NT's epistles summoned their readers to a conversion of the imagination."[47] Similarly for Green, the interpreter should utilize socio-historical and linguistic tools in order to discern how "[the text] itself engages in theological discourse."[48] The result, for both Green and Hays, is akin to a Barthian approach "to stand where these [biblical] witnesses stand and look where they point."[49]

Their approach has the advantages attributed above to Rae and Turner, though it is to be preferred insofar as its foundation for polysemic readings is not the narrower ledge of authorial communicative intent, but the broader base of

---

43. Rae, "Texts in Context."

44. Ibid., 40.

45. Ibid., 43-45.

46. Green, "Scripture and Theology"; Hays, "Reading the Bible."

47. Hays, "Reading the Bible," 12, 14.

48. Green, "Scripture and Theology," 41.

49. Hays, "Reading the Bible," 13; cf. Burnett, *Barth's Theological Exegesis*, 59, 193, 284.

authorial theological discourse. In other words, it is easier to find congruency between the author's theological discourse and polysemic interpretations of Isa 53 than it is between the author's communicative intent and polysemic interpretations. Moreover, readers who stand beside the biblical witnesses can hardly be detached but instead stand in a position to be transformed by the Spirit and are consequently in a better position to hear Scripture.[50] Like Green and Hays, Augustine recognizes the importance of authorial communicative intent, theology, and transformation. A seeming limitation of Green's and Hays' approaches, however, is that they still seem to interpret Scripture primarily through socio-historical lenses, whereas these lenses cannot fully account for the NT writer's use of the OT.[51] Moreover, it seems as if the only interpreters capable of doing the socio-cultural and grammatical work necessary for reading-beside-the-witnesses well are those with rare intellects such as Green and Hays, rather than, for instance, the average pastor of the local congregation. This seems problematic if one assumes that an ecclesially informed interpretation should be accessible for the teachers of local ecclesial communities. Further, the pastors of the growing population of third-world churches have limited access to the interpretive tools necessary for such socio-historical research.

In both his *Philippians* commentary and in the aforementioned article, Stephen Fowl claims that the task of theological interpretation primarily requires transformed communities whose readings correspond to the rule of faith.[52] This strategy, like Augustine's, certainly allows for polysemy, is tangible for both pastors and lay persons, and can accommodate the use of the OT in the NT, while also acknowledging the Spirit's transformative role in Christian exegesis.[53] A potential disadvantage of Fowl's strategy is that Scripture can theoretically be reduced to nothing more than, or everything not at odds with, the rule of faith. Of course, Fowl's recognition of the need for transformed readers would certainly offer a great help in this matter. Nevertheless, it would seem that his strategy could be helped by some notion of authorial communicative intent in order to give transformed communities an external standard by which to judge proper transformation.[54] For example, Augustine recognizes that some readers

---

50. For the role of transformation in exegesis, see below.

51. It is not clear to the author how Hays' comments above regarding Paul's exegesis of the OT fit into Hays' article here on "The Practice of Theological Exegesis."

52. Fowl, "Authorial Intention," 86-87; idem, *Philippians*, 206, 224. For a more thorough account, where Fowl's views on this matter seem to have remained consistent, see Fowl, *Engaging Scripture: A Model for Theological Interpretation* (Oxford: Blackwell, 1999); cf. idem, *Theological Interpretation of Scripture* [Eugene, OR: Cascade, 2009]).

53. Fowl, "Authorial Intention," 86.

54. Similarly, in *Text, Church and World*, Watson proffers a dialogical interpretation model that entails a cyclical and reciprocal approach wherein the *world* informs the *church's* theological reading of the *text*, the *text* informs the *church's* theology and identity within the *world*, and the *church* informs the *world* about the God mediated in the *text*. In practice, however, the reciprocity of Watson's dialogical approach is not evident. In

allow their cultures too much influence in determining what actions correspond to love of God and neighbor (*DDC* 3.10), whereas Augustine's own aforementioned emphasis on authorial communicative intent functions as a helpful corrective and guide for defining love of God and neighbor.

Like Augustine, A.K.M. Adam recognizes the reader's role in meaning making. Adam, however, wants to make readers the primary meaning-makers of texts. For Adam, "texts do not possess characteristics that promote or resist various interpretations"; rather, the reader largely determines a text's meaning.[55] The only valid constraints for interpretation are those set by the local community because no universal norms for interpretation exist. The only hindrances from bizarre or self-serving interpretations are "the consequences of alienating everyone who deems our readings as nonsensical."[56] Though Adam's proposed exegesis allows for polysemy, it seems capable of making Scripture a lifeless puppet whose voice can be controlled by individuals and local communities. This seems to run counter to the biblical picture wherein some communally accepted readings are simply wrong (e.g., the wrongful "annulling" [ἀκυρόω] of the command to honor one's father and mother [Exod 20:12; Deut 5:16] by appealing to the tradition of Corban [Mark 7:10-13][57]).[58] Further, such exclusive privileging of local interpretation would seem counter to ecclesial protocol wherein some readings of Scripture are *universally* heretical and some are *universally* orthodox.[59] Therefore, while Adam rightly notes that, in the real world, interpretations are largely governed by local communities, it does not follow that all interpretations should be considered valid by the church. For ecclesially informed interpretation, neither the local community nor the local church are sufficient to function by themselves as the authoritative interpretive community.

---

particular, the text seems to become a largely silent partner such that the "plain meaning of certain texts must be resisted and rejected," in favor of readings determined by contemporary ethical standards and the "gospel" (236). Consequently, his program seems to offer no strategy for hearing any normative voice(s) in the text beyond what is permitted by one's culture and one's definition of the gospel (which seems inescapably determined by what one's culture deems as appropriate or non-offensive). Cf. James Andrews' critique of Fowl in conversation with *DDC* ("Why Theological Hermeneutics Needs Rhetoric: Augustine's *De Doctrina Christiana*," *IJST* 12 [2010]: 196-200).

55. Adam, *Faithful Interpretation,* 14, 138.

56. Ibid., 14.

57. Cf. the devil's misuse of scripture (γέγραπται) when tempting Jesus (Matt 4:6, quoting verbatim Ps 90:11-12 [LXX]; cf. Luke 4:10-11).

58. Though my argument is circular (justifying a reading theory via a text read according to a reading theory), even according to Adam's reading criteria, it still seems that most local communities would struggle to make the texts say something other than that Mark 7:10-13 and Matt 4:6 are examples of improper readings.

59. Vanhoozer helpfully comments, "I doubt that Adam's inclusivity extends as far as Arians, Deists, or Scientologists. But why not? Do not they have criteria too?" ("Four Faces," 139).

The works of Fowl and Adam require us to look closer at Augustine's appeal to clearer teachings of Scripture. An examination of this topic in *DDC* will reveal that Augustine's thoughts are far from naive and are actually quite fitting for twenty-first century dialogue on theological interpretation. Before dealing with the clearer teachings of Scripture, Augustine advises readers to first become familiar with all of Scripture, "to know these books; not necessarily to understand them but to read them so as to commit them to memory or at least make them not totally unfamiliar" (2.9).[60] Next, Augustine directs one to interpret the "obscure" texts in light of the teachings "clearly expressed" (2.9). This immediately, and rightly, raises a red flag about the criteria for determining clearer teachings. Augustine never offers criteria but apparently assumes that some teachings are clear. He is, however, careful to note that even these clear teachings must be examined "carefully and intelligently" (2.9).[61]

In light of the sectarian outgrowths following the Protestant Reformation, Augustine's appeal to the clear teachings of Scripture may still seem overly optimistic. Nevertheless, Augustine's words have a ring of truth to them. After all, if God is to communicate through his Scriptures in a way capable of guiding and challenging his church, then it seems to follow that Scripture is neither wholly unclear nor entirely reader-determined.[62] For two reasons, I would argue that the genius of Augustine's strategy for determining clearer readings is that one must begin by familiarizing herself with *all* of Scripture. First, such an approach might enable one to discover clearer teachings not simply in an assortment of proof-texts but within the recurring themes and overarching narrative of Scripture. For Augustine, the scope of Scripture is unmistakably love of God and love of neighbor,[63] and his christocentric[64] metanarrative of Scripture might be described as "the history of God's saving work for man in the past, the present, and the future, until the Second Coming of Christ."[65] This larger christocentric and soteriological framework for interpreting Scripture, along with the twofold love commandment and the rule of faith, would guide canonical interpretation. Thus, one cannot simply appeal to "clear" proof-texts to make Scripture say anything, for the meanings of these canonical witnesses are themselves constrained by an interpretive framework.[66] Although there might be multiple ways

---

60. A potential benefit of this approach is that one may be transformed by encountering the living Word, even without comprehension, and consequently come to a better position to hear the Spirit speaking (see below).

61. As mentioned above, he is aware that clear ethical teachings might be culturally specific and therefore not applied literally to all contexts.

62. See n. 38, above.

63. Cf. Bright, "Augustine," 1233.

64. Loewen, "Scripture in Augustine's Theology," 213.

65. Bonner, "Augustine as Biblical Scholar," 553.

66. See the commentary below in ch. 6 on Augustine's *Sermon* 317, where Augustine brings canonical texts into conversation in such a way that prioritizes love for one's enemies.

in which an enigmatic text could be illuminated by other canonical texts, this canonical dialogue would seem to work best in our Augustinian-informed hermeneutical framework if the resultant interpretation 1) strengthened love of God and neighbor, 2) conformed to the rule of faith, 3) fit within the metanarrative of God's salvific work, and 4) made for a textually coherent reading of the enigmatic text in question.

Second, turning to Eco's notion that a text shapes its Model Readers in the acts of reading, by reading and re-reading Scripture (i.e., becoming familiar with all of Scripture), a reader is continuously shaped into a Model Reader who can better read Scripture.[67] Thus, one can begin to see how the comprehension of Scripture is a cycle wherein one reads Scripture within the scope of the rule of faith, the double commandment of love, and Scripture's recurring themes and overarching narrative, which results in clearer understanding of certain obscure passage, which then results in greater comprehension through which to interpret increasingly more obscure texts, and so on. Even so, the interpreter must be humble and open to learn from the insight of others. As Pamela Bright writes on Augustine's hermeneutics: "The properly partial and refracted mode of knowing in our human condition is what draws us together and therefore establishes our need for each other."[68]

Clearly, this strategy assumes a fundamental harmony within the canon. Augustine, who recognizes that the Spirit's intentions may exceed that of the human author, can assert, "Even if the writer's meaning is obscure, there is no danger here [with polysemy], provided that it can be shown from other passages of the holy scriptures that each of these interpretations is consistent with the truth" (3.27).[69]

Lastly, Richard Briggs brings up the role of virtue in interpretation,[70] a topic related to virtue epistemology. Just as there is no single definition for theological interpretation, neither is there is only one definition for virtue epistemology.[71] Without unnecessarily delving into complex epistemological arguments,

---

67. Umberto Eco, *The Role of the Reader: Explorations in the Semiotics of Texts* (London: Hutchinson, 1981), 7-8. Similarly, Trevor Hart notes how the Spirit collapses the historical distance by bringing the reader into the world of the text thereby enabling her to better encounter God within the story ("Tradition, Authority, and a Christian Approach to the Bible as Scripture," in *Between Two Horizons: Spanning New Testament Studies and Systematic Theology* [ed. Joel B. Green and Max Turner; Grand Rapids: Eerdmans, 2000], 203).

68. Bright, "Augustine," 1233.

69. See also Harrison, *Augustine*, 84.

70. Briggs, *Virtuous Reader*.

71. For a concise and shrewd analysis of the field, see Jason Baehr, "Four Varieties of Character-Based Virtue Epistemology," *SJP* 46 (2008): 469-502, where he distinguishes "responsibilist" virtue epistemology that focuses on character traits (e.g., open-mindedness) from "reliabilist" virtue epistemology that focuses on personal faculties (e.g., eyesight) before offering four further nuances of responsibilists virtue epistemology.

the primary commonality of the various approaches to virtue epistemology is that one takes seriously the role the *personal agent* plays in attaining knowledge. As this pertains to theological interpretation, it raises the question about whether "virtue" is necessary for interpreting Scripture. The "yes" to this question is made plain by Webster, who writes, "[W]e do not read well, not only because of technical incompetence, cultural distance...or lack of readerly sophistication, but also and most of all because in reading Scripture we are addressed by that which runs clean counter to our will. Reading Scripture is thus a moral matter; it requires that we become certain kinds of readers."[72]

For insight into which virtues are necessary for Scripture's readers, Briggs turns to OT narratives, looking for what virtues are anticipated for the implied reader, because Briggs is interested in "what role Scripture might have in shaping our understanding of the virtues."[73] As mentioned above, Augustine also recognizes the importance of virtue (or character) for interpretation, calling for readers to approach humbly, submissively, and with purified minds. Taking a different direction than Briggs, whose case study looks at the virtues presupposed in OT narrative, Augustine emphasizes that *the starting point for the interpreter's character formation is Jesus*: "[T]his process of cleansing" is "progress towards the one who is ever present.... This we would be unable to do, if wisdom itself had not deigned to adapt itself to our great weakness and offered us a pattern for living; and it has done so actually in human form because we too are human" (*DDC* 1.10-11).[74] Thus, like Briggs, Augustine recognizes that proper interpretation rests not simply on the *hermeneutic*, but also on the *hermeneut*, to which Augustine would add that such a hermeneut is firstly conformed to the pattern of Christ. Of course, growing in virtue is not something that completely happens prior to reading Scripture, but is actually a cyclical process wherein "virtue" illumines a reading → while reading shapes a more virtuous reader → who is enabled to better hear a reading → that better transforms her → and so on (cf. *DDC*, 2.7).

To summarize, Augustine's strategy for delimiting polysemy combines many of the strengths found in those strategies offered by contemporary theological interpreters: like Turner, Green, and Hays, Augustine places a high value on the authorial communicative intent of Scripture; at the same time, like Fowl, Augustine provides a way for Scripture to speak beyond authorial communicative intent; like Adam, Augustine leaves room for Scripture to speak to different readers, although he limits such readings by appeal to such bounds as the rule of faith (as does Fowl) and virtue (as does Briggs).

---

72. Webster, *Holy Scripture*, 87.

73. Briggs, *Virtuous Reader*, 30.

74. Webster warns against any notion that the acquisition of such virtues are within the "sphere of unaided human competence"; rather, they are the Spirit's working in the reader (*Holy Scripture*, 87-91).

Conclusion

Having argued in ch. 3 that no interpretive paradigms are without bias, I turned in this chapter to Augustine's *De Doctrina Christiana* for an example of an ec-clesially informed interpretive approach. The survey of *DDC* revealed a herme-neutic with *a priori* theological convictions that resulted in an exegesis that 1) approaches Scripture humbly, submissively, and virtuously; 2) places authorial communicative intent in high regard; 3) allows for multiple meanings; and 4) delimits polysemy by the rule of faith, the twofold love commandment, and clearer canonical texts. This interpretive paradigm was shown to clash with the hermeneutics of Räisänen and Stendahl. Regarding the former, Räisänen's foun-dation of modern historical criteria was not compatible with Augustine's foun-dation of ecclesially informed faith. Regarding the latter, Stendahl's exclusive privileging of authorial intent did not fit well within an ecclesially informed hermeneutic, because it could not account for such matters as the NT writers' use of the OT and the inability of *sola scriptura* to determine crucial theological doctrines. Finally, contemporary strategies for delimiting polysemy were com-pared with the strategies of *DDC*, with the conclusion that Augustine's insight offers a way to hold together many of the strengths offered by contemporary theological interpreters.

In the following chapters, I offer an example of how an Augustinian-informed, ecclesially located exegetical strategy might be applied to a reading of Luke 23:34a. Thus, in ch. 5, I offer a proposed reading of the authorial commu-nicative intent of the text, noting how the verse functions in its context in Luke's Gospel. In ch. 6, I survey how the Fathers read Luke 23:34a, which not only allows us to learn how the text was heard by those teachers who acted as spiritu-al guides during the foundational years of the church, but also gives an oppor-tunity to critique readings that might go beyond the ecclesially informed param-eters for which I have contended. In ch. 7, I conclude my work by summarizing the finding of the previous chapters, then showing how Martin Luther King Jr.'s sermon on Luke 23:34a is a helpful example of a contemporary ecclesially lo-cated reading —one in which a man of virtue reads along with the biblical au-thor, interprets via the church's faith-informed hermeneutical lenses, and simultaneously listens for the Scriptures to build up love for one's enemies in his context.

5

Textual Coherency and Luke 23:34a

Introduction

In the previous two chapters, we focused on historiographical and hermeneutical theory. At this point, the focus will move from theory to reading. In the last chapter, I suggested that an ecclesially informed reader is concerned with hearing the authorial communicative intent,[1] though such a reader does not assume that the authorial communicative intent is either the only voice or the determinative voice informing ecclesial interpretations. Further, it should be clear that the attempt to hear the authorial communicative intent is neither foolproof nor uninfluenced by the reader, though such a reader strives for the most textually coherent reading. As Umberto Eco writes:

> Thus it is possible to speak of text intention only as the result of a *conjecture* on the part of the reader. The initiative of the reader basically consists in making a conjecture about the text intention.... How to prove a conjecture about the *intentio operis?* The only way is to check it against the text as a coherent whole. This idea, too, is an old one and comes from Augustine (*De doctrina Christiana* 2-3): any interpretation given of a certain portion of a text can be accepted if it is confirmed and must be rejected if it is challenged by another portion of the same text. In this sense the internal textual coherence controls the otherwise uncontrollable drives of the reader.[2]

Consequently, in what follows, we will be asking what interpretation of Luke 23:34a makes the most sense of the text—i.e., *Which reading best evidences textual coherence?*

With this goal in mind, we now turn to Luke 23:34a itself, to see if the text of Luke-Acts guides its attentive readers to interpret Jesus' prayer in more specific ways, particularly regarding the questions about the prayer's referent(s), intertextual background, and nature of the misunderstanding. As we saw in ch. 1, several answers have been proffered for these questions. Regarding the pray-

---

1. Listening for the authorial communicative intent offers a way for the ecclesial reader to take seriously the human element of the divine communication in Scripture, while simultaneously allowing the text enough autonomy to challenge the church (see ch. 4).

2. Eco, *Limits of Interpretation*, 58-59 (italics original).

er's referents: for example, Blum and Flusser maintain that Jesus' forgiveness is directed only to the Roman soldiers;[3] Carras claims that the prayer is on behalf of "the Jerusalem religious establishment";[4] and between these two extremes is Raymond Brown who allows for "both the Romans and the Jews" to be the prayer's referents.[5] Regarding intertextuality: for example, George Carras avers that Luke 23:34a should be read in view of the Pentateuchal laws on unintentional sin (esp. Num 15:22-31);[6] in contrast, I. Howard Marshall, apparently relying on the MT, sees the primary intertextual link to be Isa 53:12, wherein the prayer of Jesus "exemplifies the statement of Isa 53:12 that the Servant makes intercession for the transgressors."[7] Regarding the nature of the misunderstanding: for example, Blum argues that "not know" refers to lack of information whereas Carras interprets "not know" as "lack of understanding."[8]

Given that Luke-Acts is a historical writing, and given that historical writings are narratives and that Luke claims his own work to be "narrative" (διήγησις [Luke 1:1]),[9] it would seem wise to seek the authorial communicative intent of Luke-Acts with some type of *narrative* analysis. Specifically, I will employ a type of discourse analysis, a methodology particularly appropriate for examining the textual coherence of historiography, as it allows one to use tools of narrative analysis (e.g., an awareness of sequence, structure, characterization, and intertextuality[10]) while simultaneously paying attention to the text's socio-historical context (e.g., through synchronic analysis of language and thought). In other words, when investigating the coherence of historiography's authorial communicative intent, discourse analysis is especially fitting because, as Eco notes about texts, "[a] text is a place where the irreducible polysemy of symbols is in fact reduced because in a text symbols are anchored in their context"—both "textually" and socio-historically.[11]

---

3. See also Schmithals, *Lukas*, 225.

4. Carras, "Numbers 15:22-31 and Luke 23:34," 609; see also Fitzmyer, *Luke*, 1503-4.

5. Brown, *Death*, 973. For a similar reading, see Nolland, *Luke*, 1146. Schneider understands the prayer as directed also to the mockers, given the present tense of ποιοῦσιν (*Lukas*, 483]). Crump reads the prayer as even more far-reaching, referring to "the entire scene and all its actors" (*Intercessor*, 86).

6. Carras, "Numbers 15:22-31 and Luke 23:34a," 605-16.

7. Marshall, *Luke: Historian and Theologian*, 172; see also Flusser, "Sie Wissen Nicht," 395-96; Bock, *Luke*, 1849; contra Nolland, *Luke*, 1146.

8. Blum, *Denn Sie Wissen Nicht*, 53; Carras, "Numbers 15:22-31 and Luke 23:34," 613.

9. On historiography as narratival, in contrast with chronicles, see Cook, *History/Writing*, 57.

10. Cf. Mark Allan Powell, "Narrative Criticism," in *Hearing the New Testament: Strategies for Interpretation* (ed. Joel B. Green; 2d ed.; Grand Rapids: Eerdmans, 2010), 245-49.

11. Eco, *Limits of Interpretation*, 21.

Analysis of Luke 23:34a

In order to argue for the textual coherence of my proposed reading, we will look at 1) the language, repetition, and order of events in the surrounding pericope; 2) other Lukan texts whose subject matter closely overlaps that of Luke 23:34a; and 3) how Philo and the DSS show that my proposed intertextual reading would have been at home in Luke's first-century world. By means of this investigation, it will be shown, first, that the "not know[ing]" of Luke 23:34a is essentially a *misperception* of Jesus' paradoxical identity and ministry— exemplified by the cross; second, that such misperception in Luke-Acts is linked not only with untransformed minds and untransformed exegesis but also with the fulfillment of God's purposes; third, that the most likely intertextual echo is to the Pentateuchal laws on unintentional sin; and fourth, that the primary referents of Jesus' prayer are the Jewish leaders and the Jerusalem inhabitants, with the Roman actors being less emphasized. Throughout this investigation, I will suggest why other proposed interpretations of v. 34a might be less textually coherent.

The Immediate Cotext: Luke 23:32-43

It seems clear that a new pericope begins in Luke 23:32-33a, as marked by the introduction of new characters (two other criminals [v. 32]) and a geographic change (the Skull [v. 33a]); the pericope apparently ends in v. 43, given the change of time in v. 44 (sixth hour) and the subsequent absence of most characters who were present in vv. 32-43. Consequently, an interpretation of Jesus' prayer in v. 34a should cohere especially well with its cotextual details in vv. 32-43. In what follows, I will show how the cotextual details of this pericope guide a textually coherent reading, in particular by making clear that the "not know[ing]" of v. 34a is not simply a lack of information or generic misunderstanding, but is a specific misperception of Jesus' *salvific* work and his consequent identity as *Christ* and *king*. Such a reading differs from those such as Blum's where "not knowing" is interpreted as "not having information" (and thus, connected to the Roman soldiers who would presumably know less about Jesus and his ministry).[12]

Three interrelated repetitions occur in the pericope of Luke 23:32-43— derision, titles for Jesus, and σῴζω—all of which support the claim that "not

---

12. Blum, *Denn Sie Wissen Nicht*, 36. It is noteworthy that Taeger concludes his study of Lukan anthropology by claiming that Luke attempts to portray Christianity as reasonable, obvious, and appropriate for all people ("einsichtig, naheliegend und dem Menschen angemessen" [228]), a conclusion that would seem to fit Blum's idea that lack of information rather than misperception is the issue in Luke 23:34a (i.e., if the Christian message is reasonable and obvious, then misperception is not a factor). Nevertheless, even Taeger acknowledges that misperception ("verkannt') and not simply lack of information is the issue in Luke 23:34a (Jens-W. Taeger, *Der Mensch und sein Heil: Studien zum Bild des Menschen und zur Sicht der Bekehrung bei Lukas* [SNT 14; Gütersloh: Gütersloher Verlagshaus Gerd Mohn, 1982], 81-82).

knowing" refers to a misperception of Jesus' salvific work and identity. Regarding derision, the rulers "scoff" (ἐκμυκτηρίζω [v. 35]), the soldiers "mock" (ἐμπαίζω [v. 36]), and the criminal "derides" (βλασφημέω [v. 39]). The theme of mockery, set within a crucifixion scene, might bring to mind texts such as Luke 18:32-33 where Jesus predicts his being "mocked" (ἐμπαίζω [see v. 36 above]), flogged, killed, and raised. Noteworthy is the immediately following verse, which states that "[the twelve] understood nothing about all these things; in fact, what he said was hidden from them, and they did not grasp what was said (18:34)."[13] We will look at these other verses in more detail later; for now it is worth noting the potential parallel between these texts that link misunderstanding and Jesus' seemingly shameful death.

The specific mockeries that take the form of σώζω and titles for Jesus are key clues for interpreting v. 34a, given their recurrence in our pericope: σώζω [4x], χριστός [2x], and βασιλεὺς τῶν Ἰουδαίων [2x]. The "king-" language (βασιλ–) serves to highlight the misperception of the mockers and the unexpected insight of the confessing criminal. On the one hand, the soldiers jeer, "If you are the king (βασιλεύς) of the Jews, save yourself" (v. 37), and above Jesus an inscription satirically reads, "King (βασιλεύς) of the Jews" (v. 38). On the other hand, one of the criminals acknowledges Jesus' kingship by requesting of him, "Remember me when you come into your kingdom (βασιλεία)" (v. 42).[14] Somehow, the criminal understands what those around him cannot. A closer look at βασιλ– language in Luke reveals the misunderstood connection between being king and being least.

At the Passover feast with his disciples, Jesus alludes to his death with reference to the bread ("This is my body, which is given for you" [22:19]) and wine ("this cup that is poured out for you is the new covenant in my blood" [22:20]).[15] Just as Jesus' prediction of his "betrayal" (παραδίδωμι) in 9:44 was

---

13. See also the disciples' response in Luke 9:45 following Jesus' passion prediction: "But they did not understand this saying, its meaning was concealed from them, so that they could not perceive it."

14. Cf. Robert J. Karris, *Luke: Artist and Theologian: Luke's Passion Account as Literature* (New York: Paulist, 1985), 102; Carroll and Green, *Death of Jesus*, 72. Also tying together the criminal's confession and the mockers' derisive comments is the language of "saving" (σώζω), which we will return to below.

15. Further evidence that the Passover scene foreshadows Jesus' death is found in v. 22, where Jesus refers to the Son of Man going as it is determined—language that is repeatedly connected with Jesus' suffering and death (e.g., 9:22, 44; 24:7). The absence of Luke 22:19b-20 in D it might suggest the text's unoriginality (via Western noninterpolation). Nevertheless, "the overwhelming preponderance of external evidence supporting the longer form"—i.e., the text's presence not only in other Western representatives, but in every Greek mss. besides D—points to the text's originality, with its omission likely stemming from a scribe's wrestling with Luke's cup-bread-cup account (Metzger, *Textual Commentary*, 148-50); contra Bart D. Ehrman, "The Cup, the Bread, and the Salvific Effect of Jesus' Death in Luke-Acts," in *SBL Seminar Papers, 1991* (*SBLSP* 30; Atlanta: Scholars Press, 1991), 576-91; also contra G.D. Kilpatrick, who

immediately followed by the disciples' inability to understand, exemplified in their dispute over who was the greatest (9:45-46), so also Jesus' reference to his body, blood, and "betrayal" (παραδίδωμι) at the Passover meal is misunderstood by the disciples, evidenced by yet another dispute over who was the greatest (22:22-24). In the same way that Jesus spoke against such disputes in 9:47 by claiming that the least is the greatest, so also at the Passover meal Jesus compares such ways of thinking to "the kings (βασιλεύς) of the Gentiles," whereas he explains to his disciples that "the greatest among you must become like the youngest, and the leader like one who serves" (22:25-26). In these parallel passages, it is clear that Jesus is proffering a teaching that is misunderstood, even by those closest to him. Moreover, this teaching is misunderstood even after repeated teachings, thereby showing that the disciples are not lacking information, but the interpretive categories to comprehend such information. Thus, in our pericope, those who mock Jesus as king are likely not merely lacking information about Jesus; rather, they are operating with the wrong definition of "king." They are blind to the truth that Jesus, acting as the least, could actually be the greatest. A closer look at the terms χριστός and σώζω further attests that such is the nature of the scoffers' misperception.

βασιλεύς is connected with the other repeated title of mockery, χριστός, in Luke 23:2: "We found this man...*saying that he himself is the Messiah, a king*" (λέγοντα ἑαυτὸν χριστὸν βασιλέα εἶναι). This close connection suggests these terms' overlapping definitions and consequent overlapping misunderstandings. As with βασιλεύς, Luke ties the notion of χριστός closely to the idea of Jesus' suffering and death. Immediately after Peter claims that Jesus is χριστός, Jesus teaches, "The Son of Man must undergo great suffering, and be rejected by the elders, chief priests, and scribes, and be killed, and on the third day be raised" (9:20-22). Once again, the disciples are given information they cannot understand, evidenced by their subsequent arguing about who was the greatest (9:46). Similarly, after the resurrection Jesus makes two analogous comments: "Was it not necessary that the Messiah (χριστός) should suffer these things and then enter into his glory?" (24:26), and, "Thus it is written, that the Messiah (χριστός) is to suffer and to rise from the dead on the third day" (24:46). Not surprisingly, Jesus makes these comments in response to those who misunderstand messiahship (e.g., "our chief priests and leaders handed him over to be condemned to death and crucified him. But we had hoped that he was the one to redeem Israel" [24:20-21]). Responding to such misperception, Jesus comments, "Oh, how foolish you are, and how slow of heart to believe all that the prophets have declared!" (24:25). As with Jesus' concept of king, Jesus' definition of "messiah" is so contrary to the apparent definitions of others that even when he plainly lays out the information, it is misunderstood.

The language of the leaders' taunt in 23:35 ("He saved [σώζω] others; let him save [σώζω] himself if he is the Messiah [χριστός] of God") and of the

---

essentially discounts external evidence (*The Eucharist in Bible and Liturgy* [New York: Cambridge University Press, 1983], 28-42, esp. 29-30).

criminal's taunt in 23:39 ("Are you not the Messiah [χριστός]? Save [σῴζω] yourself and us!") is antithetical to the announcement of the angel of the Lord to the shepherds ("To you is born this day in the city of David a Savior [σωτήρ] who is the Messiah [χριστός], the Lord" [2:11]). From the very outset of the narrative, then, Luke's readers know that Jesus is Messiah and savior. As "savior" (σωτήρ), he holds the key to the proper understanding of "saving" (σῴζω), in contrast to the scoffers.

Throughout our pericope, the irony of the mockery should be noticeable: although taunted as "king of the Jews," the reader knows that Jesus is, in fact, king of the Jews (e.g., 19:38; 23:3); although ridiculed as "Messiah," the reader knows that Jesus is, indeed, the Messiah (e.g., 2:11, 26; 4:41). Consequently, when the reader encounters the fourfold repetition of σῴζω, she is inclined to find irony in this term as well, recognizing that the mocking statements actually contain truth.[16] This doubly ironic reading is confirmed by recalling Jesus' words at the Passover meal (22:14-23). His opening words at the meal are: "I have eagerly desired to eat this Passover with you before I suffer" (v. 15). By placing suffering at the head of Jesus' comments, Luke guides the reader to interpret Jesus' subsequent passion sufferings in light of Jesus' Passover comments. Specifically, Jesus explains his "body given" and "blood poured out" as done "for you" (ὑπὲρ ὑμῶν [2x; vv. 19-20]).[17] Consequently, when the reader comes to the fourfold use of σῴζω in our pericope, she knows that, by not *saving* himself, Jesus is actually *saving* others.[18] Thus, in light of the irony surrounding our pericope and the Passover teaching of Jesus' suffering "on your behalf," it would seem likely that the most textually coherent reading of σῴζω

---

16. So also Crump, *Intercessor*, 87; Johnson, *Luke*, 380; Karris, *Luke: Artist and Theologian*, 100-101.

17. Cf. I.J. Du Plessus, who suggests that, in Luke 22:1-20, Jesus' death seals the new covenant in which Jesus is the authorized forgiver of sins ("The Saving Significance of Jesus and His Death on the Cross in Luke's Gospel—Focusing on Luke 22:19b-20," *Neot* 28 [1994]: 523-40, esp. 537). On text-critical matters related to 22:19b-20, see n. 15, above.

18. To be clear, I am referring to "saving" as it is defined in the Lukan narrative, not according to a Pauline definition that might not capture the Lukan soteriology of Jesus' death (Du Plessus, "The Saving Significance of Jesus," 524-25). For a concise overview of why redaction critics have often downplayed the soteriology of Jesus' death in Luke-Acts, see H.C. van Zyl, who notes such issues as the absence of λύτρον in Luke 22:27 (cf. Mark 10:45) and the claim that Luke 22:19-20 seems like a "mechanically" borrowed tradition largely unrelated to Luke's soteriology elsewhere ("The Soteriological Meaning of Jesus' Death in Luke-Acts: A Survey of Possibilities," *Verbum et Ecclesia* 23 [2002]: 533-36). In contrast, our reading strategy seeks to attend to the Lukan text as a coherent whole, so that texts such as Luke 22:19-20 cannot simply be dismissed from Luke's theology. Further, as was demonstrated above, the irony that permeates Luke 23:32-43 suggests that Jesus' death does indeed have soteriological (i.e., saving [σῴζω]) significance.

is an ironic reading, wherein the mockers cannot perceive the truth that Jesus is reversing their expectations once again: saving by suffering and dying.[19]

In summary, having established the parameters of our pericope, I have contended that the language and repetition of vv. 32-43 underscore the link between misperception and Jesus' salvific suffering and consequent identity. Specifically, through irony and repitition Luke highlights the scoffers' distorted worldview wherein suffering and least-ness are incompatible with their notions of saving (σώζω), kingship (βασιλεύς), and messiahship (χριστός). Based on this evidence, the most textually coherent reading of "know not" in v. 34a would *not* seem to be a simple lack of information, but an inability to perceive the truth about Jesus, based on antithetical definitions of the aforementioned issues. This same motif of misperceiving the cross occurs throughout Luke,[20] as will be developed more fully below under the heading: *Misperception (οἶδα)*.

One final observation from our pericope is noteworthy insofar as its fits with the proposed reading. As mentioned in ch. 2, some have suggested that v. 34a seems out of place in its present location in the pericope. If one takes seriously my proposed reading, the placement of Jesus' prayer actually works quite well. Specifically, if the issue is a misunderstanding of Jesus' suffering and lowness, then it makes perfect sense that a prayer of forgiveness for misunderstanding immediately follows a depiction of Jesus at a seeming low point—namely, when undergoing the shameful death of crucifixion and hanging between two criminals (v. 33).

The Prayer's Referents (αὐτοῖς)
Regarding the referents of Jesus' prayer, a consideration of other Lukan texts will reveal that the Jewish leaders and the Jerusalem inhabitants are the primary referents, though the ubiquity of misperceiving Jesus throughout the pericope, and the narrated culpability of nearly everyone at the crucifixion scene, would suggest the prayer extends to others as well, including the Roman actors.[21]

The ambiguous object of the prayer (αὐτοῖς) are those forgiven for "what (τί) they do (ποιέω)." Although τί and ποιέω themselves have ambiguous referents, the likelihood that they refer to the crucifixion is evidenced by the nearest preceding verb in the previous sentence ("...they crucified [σταυρόω] Je-

---

19. As Johnson notes, the prayer of forgiveness, in itself, is an ironic act of saving (*Luke*, 380); also Joel B. Green, *The Gospel of Luke* (NICNT 42; Grand Rapids: Eerdmans, 1997), 812; cf. Jack Dean Kingsbury, *Conflict in Luke: Jesus, Authorities, Disciples* (Minneapolis: Fortress, 1991), 67-68.

20. E.g., the disciples are so unable to grasp Jesus' repeated teachings about the necessity of his sufferings that they even use swords to prevent Jesus from being taken (22:49-51) (Kingsbury, *Conflict in Luke*, 130-31).

21. Bock comes to a similar conclusion, though he does so on grounds that I find less convincing (e.g., via comparison with Stephen's prayer in Acts 7:60, and "a conceptual tie to Isa 53:12" [*Luke*, 1849]).

sus" [v. 33]).[22] The subject of the verb σταυρόω, however, is not mentioned, so that one is forced to look elsewhere in Luke-Acts to determine which subject for this verb would offer the greatest textual coherency in Luke's narrative. Even if Blum and Flusser are correct, that in the first century the Roman soldiers (and not the Jews) performed crucifixions, this does not mean that Luke's narrative could not depict others as the primary actors in the crucifixion.[23] In fact, a brief survey will make clear that, in Luke-Acts, the Jewish leaders (ἄρχων) are most frequently depicted as the subjects of verbs related to the crucifixion. After the Jewish leaders, the Jerusalem inhabitants (κατοικέω) are most frequently mentioned as the subjects of crucifixion verbs. Furthermore, when the Roman actors are mentioned, they are mentioned as agents/instruments of the verbs, rather than as subjects. Thus, it will be argued that the primary subjects for the verb σταυρόω in v. 33 are the Jewish leaders and the Jerusalem inhabitants, who would then be the primary referents of the prayer in v. 34a.

Closely related to Luke 23:34a are two texts that also connect the *crucifixion* with *misperception*: Acts 3:17 and 13:27-28. In both, Luke identifies the Jewish people and their leaders as the subjects of verbs of crucifixion.[24] Acts 3:17 reads, "I know that you [the people present in Jerusalem][25] acted (πράσσω) in ignorance as did also your rulers (ἄρχων)." Clearly, their "action" refers to the crucifixion as is evidenced in the immediate cotext, where they are

---

22. Contra Crump who argues, "Since the action which precipitates Jesus' prayer is left indeterminate…the prayer serves to cover any actions in the narrative which would require God's forgiveness" (*Intercessor*, 86). My primary reason for rejecting Crump's indeterminate reading is shown below, where one sees the ignorance excuse twice connected with the crucifixion.

23. It is noteworthy that the agents who lead Jesus away (v. 26), who crucify him (v. 33), and who divide up his clothes (v. 34b) are not specified by Luke. In fact, the soldiers are not mentioned until v. 36. Green, commenting on v. 26, rightly notes that the ambiguity "signifies the concord of Rome, Jewish leaders, and Jewish people" (*Luke*, 814, 819-20; cf. Richard P. Carlson, "The Role of the Jewish People in Luke's Passion Theology," in *SBL Seminar Papers, 1991* [SBLSP 30; Atlanta: Scholars Press, 1991], 97). Nevertheless, subsequent Lukan texts will reveal that the primary emphasis lies on the Jewish leaders and the Jerusalem inhabitants.

24. Cf. J. Bradley Chance who, having creatively argued that the Jewish people are not implicated in Jesus' death until Acts, works to find some measure of authorial consistency between Luke and Acts on this subject ("The Jewish People and the Death of Jesus in Luke-Acts: Some Implications of an Inconsistent Narrative Role," in *SBL Seminar Papers, 1991* [SBLSP 30; Atlanta: Scholars Press, 1991], 50-81). The simpler solution is to recognize that Chance's reading of the Lukan passion narrative is *too* creative, not making sense of Luke-Acts as a whole or of the Lukan passion narrative itself (e.g., the "people" [λαός] in Luke 23:13 would seem included in the "all-together" [παμ–πληθεί] shouting to release Barabbas and take away Jesus [23:18]). For a helpful reading of the people's role in Luke's passion narrative, see Carlson, "The Role of the Jewish People," esp. 94-96.

25. Specifically, the "you" refers to "all the people" (πᾶς ὁ λαός [2x; Acts 3:9, 11]) present at the temple.

also subjects of the verb (e.g., "you killed [ἀποκτείνω] the Author of life" [Acts 3:15]). A similar text appears in Acts 13:27-28, which also links misperception, crucifixion, and the activity of the Jewish leaders and Jerusalem residents: "For the inhabitants (κατοικέω) in Jerusalem and their leaders (ἄρχων) did not recognize him, they fulfilled the words of the prophets... condemning (κρίνω) him...and they asked Pilate to have him killed (ἀναιρέω)."[26] When Pilate is mentioned, he seems to function as the agent of the leaders and the crowd, with ἀναιρέω occurring as a passive verb (ἀναιρεθῆναι). Consequently, given the repeated statements narrating the Jewish rulers and the Jerusalem inhabitants as the actors of the crucifixion, and given that these statements (Acts 3:17; 13:27-28) have content closely paralleled with Luke 23:34a (i.e., collocating crucifixion and ignorance), it follows that *in the Lukan narrative*, the "them" in Jesus' prayer who "know not what they do" focuses more on the Jewish leaders and the Jerusalem inhabitants than on the Roman rulers or soldiers.[27]

Beyond these closely related texts, other Lukan texts confirm what is argued above insofar as they primarily emphasize the action of the Jewish leaders and the Jerusalem inhabitants, whereas the Romans function largely as the instruments of their will. Thus, the Emmaus road disciples say that "our chief priests and leaders (ἄρχων) handed him over to be condemned to death and crucified (σταυρόω) him" (Luke 24:20).[28] In his address to the "people of Judea" (ἄνδρες Ἰουδαῖοι) and the "inhabitants (κατοικέω) of Jerusalem," Peter proclaims that "you crucified (προσπήγνυμι) and killed (ἀναιρέω) [Jesus], by the hands (διὰ χειρός) of those outside the law" (Acts 2:14, 23).[29] *For Luke, the subject of the verb "kill" (and the nominative participle "fasten") is not identified with those whose "hands" (χείρ) carry out the crucifixion, but with those whose actions led to the crucifixion.*[30] Similarly, when Peter and the apostles were before the Sanhedrin addressing the high priest—who himself claimed that the apostles were placing the guilt of Jesus' blood upon them (Acts 5:28)—the

---

26. Translation mine.

27. Similarly, Wolter writes, "dies beiden Texte [i.e., Acts 3:17; 13:27] machen es zudem wahrscheinlich, dass Lukas die Vergebungsbitte auf die Jerusalemer Juden und nicht auf die römischen Soldaten bezogen wissen wollte" (*Lukasevangelium*, 757); contra Carras, who, for an unidentifiable reason, disallows the parallel texts of Acts from helping identify the prayer's referents, thereby leading him to exclude the Jerusalem inhabitants as referents ("Numbers 15:22-31 and Luke 23:34, 609-11).

28. Similarly, Wolter reads Luke 24:20 as accentuating the Jewish leaders' responsibility and minimizing Pilate's (*Lukasevangelium*, 781).

29. "Die Heiden sind als Handlanger bzw. Werkzeuge verstanden" (Gerhard Schneider, *Die Apostelgeschichte I. Teil: Einleitung. Kommentar zu Kap 1:1-8:40* [HTKNT 5; Freiburg: Herder, 1980], 272 n.70). The reference to ἄνομος also indicates that the soldiers were Roman, not Jewish; cf. Carlson, "The Role of the Jewish People," 99; contra Paul W. Walaskay, "Trial and Death of Jesus in the Gospel of Luke," *JBL* 94 (1975): 92.

30. See also Carras, "Numbers 15:22-31 and Luke 23:34," 609.

apostles name these Jewish leaders as those who not only "kill" (διαχειρίζω) Jesus, but also "hung (κρεμάννυμι) him on a tree" (Acts 5:30).[31]

To summarize, this survey draws attention to the way Luke consistently portrays the Jewish leaders and the Jerusalem inhabitants as the subjects of verbs related to Jesus' crucifixion, even when acknowledging that it was carried out "by the hands" of others.[32] Moreover, Acts 3:17 and 13:27-28 make plain that an excuse of ignorance applied both to the Jewish leaders and the Jerusalem inhabitants with regard to the crucifixion.[33] Consequently, in Luke 23:34a, the αὐτοῖς who "know not what they do"—i.e., those who imperceptibly "crucify" Jesus (v. 33)—would primarily be the Jewish leaders and the Jerusalem inhabitants; however, the prayer would seem to extend to others as well—such as the soldiers, Pilate, and ἄνομοι—given both their narrated implication in the crucifixion as well as their own apparent misperception within the pericope of Luke 23:32-43 (e.g., the Roman mockery), which suggests an ignorance excuse might apply to them as well.[34] However, *since neither Luke 24 nor Acts emphasize the Romans' role in the crucifixion nor explicitly apply the excuse of ignorance to their part in the crucifixion*, it seems likely that they would be in the background and not the foreground of Jesus' prayer in Luke 23:34a.[35]

Misperception (οἶδα)

Having established earlier that "not know" in v. 34a most likely refers to a misperception of Jesus' seeming lowliness and consequent identity, typified in the crucifixion, we turn elsewhere in Luke-Acts for help in further clarifying the nature of the aforementioned misperception (οἶδα). Regarding the nature of misperception, other texts in Luke-Acts will show that misunderstanding of the cross is particularly tied to unillumined minds and unillumined readings of Scripture, and that such misunderstanding is corrected when Scripture is interpreted according to the reading proffered by the Resurrected One. Further, misperception is also linked with God's purposes being fulfilled. This insight into misperception will come into play in the subsequent section where I argue for the intertextual echo that best coheres with the Lukan narrative. In what follows we will focus on those texts that deal with misperception and subsequent percep-

---

31. For more examples, see also Carras, "Numbers 15:22-31 and Luke 23:34a," 609.

32. For a similar argument with further examples of the responsibility of the Jewish leaders and Jerusalemites in Acts, see Matera, "Responsibility for the Death of Jesus," 77-93.

33. So also Brown, *Death*, who further notes the likelihood that the nearby verb ποιέω in 23:31 almost certainly implies the "Jewish antagonists" as its subject (973).

34. For a similar conclusion about responsibility for the crucifixion in Luke that is derived from a close literary reading of Luke-Acts, see Carroll and Green, *Death of Jesus*, 194-98.

35. "Therefore, in Luke 23:34a the 'they' for whom Jesus is praying includes both the Romans and the Jews *in proportion* to their respective roles in Jesus' death" (Brown, *Death*, 973, italics mine).

tion of the significance of the cross and Jesus' suffering. Thus, we will look at the related texts of Luke 9:45; 18:34; 24:1-49; Acts 3:17; 13:27.

Luke 9:45 and 18:34. In both Luke 9:45 and 18:34, Jesus offers a passion prediction that his disciples cannot comprehend. Both texts have ambiguous passive verbs (παρακεκαλυμμένον, κεκρυμμένον), making the precise reason for their misunderstanding unclear.[36] The text provides a clue about the cause of their misunderstanding in the disciples' subsequent actions. In 9:46, the disciples argue about who was the greatest, to which Jesus responds with a lesson about welcoming children—i.e., teaching them to act as if those of seemingly lower status (the children) are of higher status than themselves (vv. 47-48). A similar blunder of the disciples occurs immediately after Jesus' passion prediction in 18:34. For example, in 18:39, those in the front (προάγοντες) of the crowd "rebuked" (ἐπιτιμάω) the low-status blind beggar who was calling out to Jesus (18:39). It may be that "those in front" are the disciples, who only a few verses earlier committed a similar error—namely, they "rebuked" (ἐπιτιμάω) those bringing children to Jesus (18:15).[37] This portrait of the disciples' concept of greatness also fits the aforementioned reaction of the disciples at the Passover meal wherein Jesus' prediction of suffering was followed by another argument about who would be the greatest.

One sees a pattern emerging in Luke 9:45 and 18:34, a pattern that is re-peated again at the Passover meal: Jesus predicts his suffering, the disciples re-spond by arguing over who was the greatest and possibly by acting as if they were greater than others. This suggests that their misperception of Jesus' suffer-ing is intimately related to their definitions of greatness and status—definitions that even Jesus' repeated teaching and actions have been unable to redefine even as far as Luke 22. This, of course, fits well with our discussion of 23:32-43, in which the concepts of king, messiah, and saving are wrongly understood as be-ing antithetical to suffering.

Luke 24:1-49. The disciples' inability to understand Jesus' specific teach-ings on suffering and status raises the question of how one could possibly under-stand. The answer lies in Luke 24, where the ability to perceive is made possible through Jesus' opening of minds and Scripture *after* the resurrection—an event capable of confirming Jesus' teachings and redefining his followers' worldview.[38] The disciples' enabled perception in Luke 24 is especially helpful in guiding our reading of Luke 23:34a, given not only its close proximity but also its repetitive motif of an initial misperception followed by subsequent per-ception of Jesus' suffering and status.

---

36. O'Toole might be correct that these verbs are divine passives (Robert F. O'Toole, "Luke's Message in Luke 9:1-50," *CBQ* 49 [1987]: 82-83); nevertheless, the disciples' actions (and Jesus' later censure of others' slowness to believe [Luke 24:25]) suggest that the disciples also play some role in their own misperception.

37. Green, *Luke*, 664 n. 173.

38. Ibid., 834-35.

Luke 24 contains three accounts where the necessity of Jesus' suffering is made perceptible to the women followers (vv. 1-12), the Emmaus road disciples (vv. 13-35),[39] and the Jerusalem disciples (vv. 36-49). The last account offers helpful clues for understanding the former two, so we will start there. Despite the testimony from the women and the Emmaus road disciples, an inability to understand persists.[40] Thus, when Jesus appears, they think (δοκέω) he is a ghost, questions (διαλογισμός) arise in their hearts, and they disbelieved (ἀπιστέω) and wondered (θαυμάζω) because of their joy (vv. 37-38, 41). Jesus then demonstrates that he truly was resurrected and was not simply a spirit by showing them his hands and feet and eating fish. Having done so, Jesus turns to Scripture and says, "'These are my words that I spoke to you while I was still with you—that everything written (γράφω) about me in the law of Moses, the prophets, and the psalms must be fulfilled.' Then he opened their minds to understand the scriptures (γραφή), and he said to them, 'Thus it is written (γράφω), that the Messiah is to suffer and to rise from the dead on the third day'" (vv. 44-46).

Three observations about perception are important from this text. First, proper perception requires Scripture, as evidenced in the repetitive scriptural language in vv. 44-46, particularly in the related terms γράφω (2x) and γραφή. Second, Scripture by itself is insufficient without the deliberate action of Jesus actively "opening their minds in order to understand" (διήνοιξεν αὐτῶν τὸν νοῦν τοῦ συνιέναι [v. 45]).[41] Third, given that Jesus has earlier taught repeatedly about his suffering without the disciples' resultant understanding, it would seem possible that his teaching on the same subject is more capable of redefining the disciples' worldview *after* his authority is confirmed by the resurrection.

---

39. On Augustine's reading of Luke 24:13-35, see Finbarr G. Clancy, "St Augustine's Commentary on the Emmaus Scene in Luke's Gospel," StPatr 43 (2006): 51-58.

40. Although Joseph Plevnik rightly notes that these Jerusalem disciples already had faith in Jesus' resurrection (Luke 24:34 [note that the participle λέγοντας specifies the Jerusalem disciples' belief and not the Emmaus road disciples'), he overstates his case by suggesting that that this pericope is not concerned with overcoming doubt, but only with the disciples' understanding of the bodily nature of Jesus' resurrection and with their being empowered as witnesses ("The Eyewitnesses of the Risen Jesus in Luke 24," *CBQ* 49 [1987]: 97-103). Such a reading does not make sense of 24:44-46 where Jesus opens their mind to "understand" (συνίημι) the Scripture's teaching about *the necessity of the Messiah's suffering, death, and resurrection*. Thus, much like earlier in the Lukan narrative when Peter makes a rightful, but misinformed, confession of Jesus as Christ (9:20-22), it would seem here that the Jerusalem disciples' belief in the resurrection is partly right, but not fully illumined.

41. On διανοίγω, see below on the Emmaus road disciples, as well as Acts 16:14 where the Lord *opened* Lydia's heart to give heed to Paul's words. Kingsbury rightly notes, "If the disciples are blind to the truth that God saves the world through a crucified Messiah, it is not, to Luke's way of thinking, that they are simply lacking in information. It is rather that, of themselves, they are incapable of seeing this" (Jack Dean Kingsbury, "Luke 24:44-49," *Int* 35 [1981]: 172).

This is hinted at through the focus on both the resurrection and Jesus' authority in vv. 36-43, and would seem further confirmed in vv. 13-35, to which we now turn.[42]

As with the disciples in vv. 36-49, the disciples on the Emmaus road show signs of misperception: e.g., looking sad (v. 17); they *were* hoping he was the one to redeem Israel (v. 21); Jesus replies, "Oh, how foolish you are and how slow of heart to believe" (v. 25). Also similar is that Jesus "opens" (διανοίγω) and interprets Scripture to evidence the Messiah's needing to suffer: "...how slow of heart [you are] to believe all that the prophets have declared.... Then beginning with Moses and all the prophets, he interpreted (διερμηνεύω) to them the things about himself in all the scriptures.... Were not our hearts burning within us...while he was opening (διανοίγω) the scriptures to us?" (vv. 25, 27, 32).

Unlike the disciples of vv. 36-49, Jesus opened the Scriptures *before* they had such strong evidence of the resurrection. In fact, their eyes were not "opened" (διανοίγω) until he broke bread, at which point they recognized him (vv. 30-31).[43] The actions of these disciples suggest that it was only *after* recognizing the resurrected Jesus that the previous opening of Scripture was fully internalized.[44] Specifically, by itself, Jesus' opening of Scripture did not convince these disciples of the urgency to bear witness, which suggests they were still unconvinced. Thus, after his opening of Scriptures, they were content to stay in the village; as they say in their own words, "it is almost evening and the day is now nearly over" (vv. 28-29). In contrast, after perceiving Jesus' identity, they departed the "same hour" (αὐτῇ ὥρᾳ) for Jerusalem and witnessed to the eleven (vv. 33-34). It would seem that Jesus' opening of Scripture—even when

---

42. On Jesus' interpretive authority being emphasized, see Brent Laytham, who notes, e.g., the repetition of Jesus' resurrection prediction ("Interpretation on the Way to Emmaus: Jesus Performs His Story," *JTI* 1 [2007]: 103-4).

43. For a convincing argument that the breaking of bread was eye-opening because it recalled a "pattern" of Jesus' prior actions in Luke, both his hosting and his breaking bread, see Laytham, "Interpretation on the Way to Emmaus," 110-11; see also Robert C. Tannehill, *The Narrative Unity of Luke-Acts: A Literary Interpretation*, vol. 1: *The Gospel according to Luke* (Philadelphia: Fortress, 1986), 289-90.

44. Cf. Kingsbury, *Conflict in Luke*, 134-35.

it "burns the heart" (v. 32)—contrasts so greatly with their worldview,[45] that the evidence of the resurrection is necessary to reorient their hermeneutical lenses.[46]

Of the three groups of Jesus' followers in Luke 24, the women appear the least slow to comprehend matters, though Luke's account of them also narrates similar elements found in the other two accounts—namely, misperception, Jesus' teaching on the necessity of his death, and evidence of the resurrection. Regarding misperception, they were "perplexed" ($\dot{\alpha}\pi o\rho\acute{\epsilon}\omega$[47]) by the empty tomb, and the angels asked, "Why do you look for the living among the dead?" (vv. 4-5). Regarding Jesus' teaching of the necessity of his suffering, the angels state, "Remember how [Jesus] told you...that the Son of Man must be handed over to sinners, and be crucified, and on the third day rise again" (vv. 6-7). Although Scripture is not explicitly mentioned, it is likely implicit, given that similar texts typically tie the necessity of his suffering to Scripture.[48] Regarding the resurrection, the angel specifically declares, "He is not here, but has risen" (v. 5). As with the others, the women followers knew of Jesus' teachings on his suffering and rising, but such teachings were apparently incompatible with their worldview.[49] After the angels remind them of Jesus' words and testify to his resurrection, the women seem to grasp the situation, and respond by bearing witness to the disciples (vv. 8-9).[50]

---

45. "Prior to this, they lack the categories of thought, they lack an imagination adequate to correlate what Jesus holds together in his passion predictions: his exalted status and his impending dishonor" (Joel B. Green, "Learning Theological Interpretation from Luke," in *Reading Luke: Interpretation, Reflection, Formation* [ed. Craig G. Bartholomew et al.; Grand Rapids: Zondervan, 2005], 69-72); see also Richard B. Hays, "Reading Scripture in Light of the Resurrection," in *The Art of Reading Scripture* (ed. Ellen F. Davis and Richard B. Hays; Grand Rapids: Eerdmans, 2003), 229-32; Robert J. Karris, "Luke 24:13-35," *Int* 41 (1987): 60-61; Tannehill, *Narrative Unity*, 282.

46. As Laytham writes, "[Jesus'] interpretation of Scripture 'opens' the text to a crucified, risen Messiah, and his revelation of resurrection requires Scripture thus opened. In other words, the two openings are mutually informing. The exegesis enables the epiphany, and the epiphany enables the full understanding of the exegesis" ("Interpretation on the Way to Emmaus," 109). Similarly, Johnson notes, "The 'opening of the eyes' to see the texts truly and the 'opening of the eyes' to see Jesus truly are both part of the same complex process" (*Luke*, 399); see also, Green, "Learning Theological Interpretation," 70.

47. On $\dot{\alpha}\pi o\rho\acute{\epsilon}\omega$ as "perplexed," see Acts 25:20, where this term describes Festus' uncertainty as to what to do with Paul.

48. See especially the language in the aforementioned, closely related texts of Luke 24:26-27 (e.g., Moses, the prophets, scripture) and 24:44-46 ("everything written about me in the law of Moses, the prophets and psalms," scriptures, "it is written"); see also 18:31-33 ("everything that is written about the Son of Man by the prophets").

49. As Johnson remarks about their ability to perceive: "Before there can be new sightings, there must be the cleansing of vision" (Luke Timothy Johnson, "Luke 24:1-11," *Int* 46 [1992]: 60).

50. For more on the belief of the women, see Plevnik, "The Eyewitnesses of the Risen Jesus," 92-93.

To summarize, Luke narrates three separate accounts in which followers of Jesus misperceive his suffering and crucifixion, but are enabled to perceive when Jesus' scriptural teaching is combined with the authorizing and worldview-altering experience of the resurrection.

Acts 3:17 and 13:27. Another facet of the Lukan ignorance motif becomes clear in Acts 3:17 and 13:27. The NRSV of Acts 13:27 reads: "Because the residents of Jerusalem and their leaders understood neither him nor the words of the prophets that are read every sabbath, they fulfilled those words by condemning him" (Acts 13:27). The Greek text however, is imprecise so that "the words of the prophets" may not be the object of the verb "understood" but only of the verb "fulfill": οἱ γὰρ κατοικοῦντες ἐν Ἰερουσαλὴμ καὶ οἱ ἄρχοντες αὐτῶν τοῦτον ἀγνοήσαντες καὶ τὰς φωνὰς τῶν προφητῶν τὰς κατὰ πᾶν σάββατον ἀναγινωσκομένας κρίναντες ἐπλήρωσαν. Even if one does not take "words of the prophets" as the explicit object of "understood," the message may be similar. Thus, Luke Timothy Johnson, not taking "words" as the object of "understood," nevertheless writes, "The point, of course, is ironic: they had listened to the prophets' utterances every week, yet did not 'recognize' the one of whom the prophets had spoken; thus in rejecting him they fulfilled the very texts foretelling his rejection!"[51] Such an interpretation fits well with my proposed reading of Luke 24 where misinterpretation of Scripture is connected with misperceiving Jesus.

I would proffer two reasons for concluding that Acts 13:27 emphasizes their *fulfilling* the words of the prophets rather than their *misunderstanding* these words. First, the parallel text of Acts 3:17-18 reads: "And now, friends, I know that you acted in ignorance, as did also your rulers. In this way God fulfilled what he had foretold through all the prophets, that his Messiah would suffer." The parallel language between Acts 3:17-18 and 13:27 (ἄγνοια and ἀγνοέω, ἄρχων and ἄρχων, προφήτης and προφήτης, πληρόω and πληρόω) implies similarity of thought.[52] The much simpler Greek of Acts 3:17-18, where the prophets' words are clearly fulfilled and not misunderstood, suggests that such is also the case in Acts 13:27. Second, as we will look at in more detail below, Philo's writings on the Pentateuchal laws on sins of ignorance reveal that such laws could be connected not only with unillumined minds and unillumined exegesis, *but also with God's working out his will through the offences of the ignorant.*[53] Given that these two texts in Acts both connect ignorance (ἄγνοια

---

51. Luke Timothy Johnson, *The Acts of the Apostles* (SP 5; Collegeville, MN: Liturgical, 1992), 234. See also Codex D, which apparently attempts to make clear that they misunderstood Scripture by replacing τοῦτον ἀγνοήσαντες καὶ τὰς φωνὰς with μὴ συνιέντες τὰς γραφὰς.

52. See also, Epp, "Ignorance Motif," 58.

53. For the Lukan motif of the divine necessity of the crucifixion, as seen, e.g., in the language consistently attached to this event (e.g., δεῖ, μέλλω, γράφω, πληρόω, ὁρίζω, βουλή, πρόγνωσις), see Robert L. Mowery, "The Divine Hand and the Divine

and ἀγνοέω) with fulfillment of prophecy, and given that parallel language occurs between these texts and the Pentateuchal laws on sins of ignorance (e.g., ἄγνοια and ἀγνοέω both occur in Lev 5:18), it would seem possible that a similar intertextual echo occurs in these verses in Acts, a topic to which we will turn shortly.

Three observations are important from Acts 3:17-18 and 13:27. First, and most importantly, these Lukan texts witness that *God fulfills Scripture through the offenses of the ignorant who crucify Jesus.*[54] Second, as Johnson notes, the irony of these texts continues the aforementioned theme that links misperception with misreading Scripture. Third, one learns that, in Luke-Acts, the matter of sins of ignorance is not one-dimensional, but is multifaceted.

Intertextuality

Two echoes have been proposed for Luke 23:34a—namely, Isa 53:12 and the Pentateuchal laws on unintentional sin. Beginning with the former, an echo of Isa 53:12 would not seem coherent with the Lukan text, largely because the necessary echo in Luke 23:34a would only seem to make sense via the MT ("he bore the sin of many, and *made intercession* [פגע] for the transgressors") or Targum ("...he will *beseech* [בעי] concerning the sins of many, and to the rebels it shall be forgiven [קשבק]"[55]), rather than the LXX ("he was *handed over* [παραδίδωμι] because of their sins"). It would be uncharacteristic for Luke to allude to the OT in such a way, since he typically alludes through the LXX.[56] Not only

---

Plan in the Lukan Passion Narrative," in *SBL Seminar Papers, 1991* (*SBLSP* 30; Atlanta: Scholars Press, 1991), 558-75.

54. Carroll and Green, *Death of Jesus*, 78.

55. English translation of the Targum comes from Chilton, *The Isaiah Targum,* 105.

56. Wilcox may be correct that "we have no right to assume that the one NT writer will have always used the same OT textual tradition in his works" (Max Wilcox, "Text Form," in *It Is Written: Scripture Citing Scripture: Essays in Honour of Barnabas Lindars* [ed. D.A. Carson and H.G.M. Williamson; Cambridge: Cambridge University Press, 1988], 194). Nevertheless, as will be shown, the Lukan tendency when citing Isa 53 is to follow the LXX. For more, see, e.g., Fitzmyer's chart of Luke's OT quotations and allusions, which leads him to claim that "Luke quotes the Old Testament almost always in a form either corresponding to the LXX or close to it, and not according to the Hebrew MT" (Fitzmyer, *To Advance the Gospel*, 304-6). Cf. Bock's claim that none of Luke's OT quotations and allusions "required the LXX for the *conceptual* framework of [Luke's] argument" (Darrell L. Bock, *Proclamation from Prophecy and Pattern: Lucan Old Testament Christology* [JSNTSS 12; Sheffield: Sheffield Academic Press, 1987], 271, italics original). For a shrewd survey of research on Luke's textual tradition, see François Bovon, *Luke the Theologian: Fifty-five Years of Research (1950-2005)* (2d ed.; Waco, TX: Baylor University Press, 2005), 108-19. Based on Luke's preference for the LXX, Wolter also deems it unlikely that Isa 53:12 is echoed at Luke 23:34a (*Lukasevangelium,* 757-58).

is this the case with his OT allusions throughout his passion narrative,[57] but it is also the case for his verbatim and near-verbatim LXX allusions elsewhere to Isa 53 (e.g., Luke 22:37 [Isa 53:12]; Acts 8:32-33 [Isa 53:7-8]).[58] In fact, Luke's familiarity with the παραδίδωμι language of the LXX at Isa 53:12 is suggested by the *fivefold* occurrence of παραδίδωμι in the very chapter in which Luke cites Isa 53:12 (vv. 4, 6, 21, 22, 48). Given this evidence, it is unlikely that, at the textual level, intertextuality exists between Isa 53:12 and Luke 23:34a.

If there is an intertextual echo in Luke 23:34a, the most textually coherent one would come from the Pentateuchal laws pertaining to forgiveness for unintentional sins[59] given 1) common vocabulary and themes, and 2) that such Pentateuchal laws were read in the first century in a way congruent with my proposed reading—specifically, insofar as first-century readers linked these texts with a) lacking illumined minds and illumined readings of Scripture (cf. Luke 24:1-49), and b) God accomplishing his purposes by means of ignorant offenders (cf. Acts 3:17 and 13:27).[60]

Shared Vocabulary. Of the various Pentateuchal texts dealing with unintentional sins, the one that stands out most for its verbal overlap is Lev 5:18b:

> And the priest shall make atonement for him concerning his ignorance (ἄγνοια), of which he was ignorant (ἀγνοέω), and did not know (οἶδα) himself; and it shall be forgiven (ἀφίημι) him. (LXX [NETS])

It has already been mentioned above that Acts 3:17 and 13:27—texts clearly similar to Luke 23:34a—share the terms ἀγνοέω and ἄγνοια with Lev 5:18. The terms ἀγνοέω and ἄγνοια are not prevalent in the LXX. Of its nine instances, ἀγνοέω twice occurs within Pentateuchal laws on unintentional sin (Lev 4:13, 5:18), with two other instances being Pentateuchal narration of sin-

---

57. Cf. especially the dividing of his clothes (διαμερίζω ἱμάτιον) and casting lots (βάλλω κλῆρος) for them (Luke 23:34b; Ps 22:18), and the verbatim vocabulary from Ps 31:5, (εἰς χεῖράς σου παρατίθεμαι τὸ πνεῦμά μου [Luke 23:46]).

58. As Holtz notes, in Acts 8:32-33, the wording and order of nearly 40 words are identical to the LXX of Isaiah 53:7-8. In Luke 22:37, the vocabulary and order is similar, although the prepositions differ: καὶ ἐν τοῖς ἀνόμοις ἐλογίσθη (Isa 53:12); καὶ μετὰ ἀνόμων ἐλογίσθη (Luke 22:37). For evidence that Luke's source in 22:37 is the LXX, Holtz notes, e.g., that the use of λογίζομαι suggests LXX origin, given that the typical Greek translation of the corresponding Hebrew verb (מנה ["to number"]) is ἀριθμέω (Traugott Holtz, *Untersuchungen über die Alttestamentlichen Zitate bei Lukas* [TUGAL 104; Berlin: Akademie-Verlag, 1968], 31, 41-43).

59. Cf. Gottfried Schille who also notes the possibility that such Pentateuchal texts are in the background of Acts 3:17 (*Die Apostelgeschichte des Lukas* [THKNT 5; Berlin: Evangelische Verlagsanstalt, 1983], 128).

60. Cf. Carras' argument that Luke 23:34a echoes one such Pentateuchal text (Num 15:22-31); however, his case is underdeveloped, for he only contends for an echo at the "thematic level" and not at the "contextual level, genre nor at the level of linguistic similarities" ("Numbers 15:22-31 and Luke 23:34," 616).

ning unintentionally (Gen 20:4; Num 12:11). Of the seventeen occurrences of ἄγνοια, two occur within Pentateuchal laws on unintentional sin (Lev 5:18; 22:14), with another being a Pentateuchal narration of sinning unintentionally (Gen 26:10).

To this evidence could be added the shared vocabulary between Lev 5:18 and Luke 23:34a itself—namely, οἶδα appearing closely beside ἀφίημι. Although ἀφίημι is a familiar verb in Luke-Acts and in the LXX, it is noteworthy that of its seventy-six appearances in the entire LXX, eleven of these—10 percent—are massed within a mere thirty-seven verses devoted to unintentional sins (Lev 4:20-5:18 [9x]; Num 15:25-36 [2x]). Also noteworthy is that the only Levitical instance of οἶδα is at 5:18.

In sum, the shared vocabulary between Lev 5:18 and Luke 23:34a is significant, particularly when one notes the further shared vocabulary between Lev 5:18 and the closely related Lukan texts of Acts 3:17 and 13:27. This observation gains further significance in light of how, in the LXX, three of these four terms are concentrated in the Pentateuchal laws pertaining to forgiveness for sins of ignorance. What increases the likelihood of this proposed echo, however, is the way other circa-first-century readings of such Pentateuchal texts correspond with the nature of misperception in the cotext of Luke 23:34a (and Acts 3:17 and 13:27). Specifically, a survey of the Scrolls and Philo will reveal that Pentateuchal texts on unintentional sin were interpreted with reference to the perpetrators' untransformed minds and untransformed exegesis, and also with reference to the fulfillment of God's purposes.

The Scrolls. As mentioned in ch. 3, Anderson notes the scholarly agreement that the Scrolls distinguish between the "revealed" (נגלה) law—i.e., the written law of Moses—and the "hidden" (נסתר) law—i.e., "the newer revelations stemming from the community itself."[61] On the basis of this distinction, Anderson argues that intentional sin is defined as any violation of the revealed law, and unintentional sin as violation of the hidden law. In other words, since the *revealed* law was "public knowledge for all Israel, any sin against these norms would invariably fall under the category of 'intentional sin'"; whereas the *hidden* law "could not be known to those outside the sect, and even within the sect [these laws] were continually evolving, [so that] greater leniency had to be shown toward those who disobeyed them."[62] To illustrate this distinction, Anderson offers 1QS V 11-12 as evidence:

> For [evil men] are not reckoned among [those of] his covenant because they
> do not search out or interpret his statutes so as to discern the hidden laws
> [נסתר]. For [in these matters] they have strayed so as to incur guilt. But to-
> ward the revealed laws [נגלה] they have acted in a high-handed [ביד רמה] fash-
> ion so as to raise up wrath for judgment and the executing of revenge accord-
> ing to the curses of the covenant. (translation Anderson's)

---

61. Anderson, "Intentional and Unintentional Sin," 51, 54-55.
62. Ibid., 55.

Besides describing Israel's "bold" departure from Egypt in Exod 14:8 and Num 33:3, the only other instance of "high-handed" (ביד רמה) in the OT is Num 15:30 where "high-handed" sins are contrasted with unintentional sins.[63] Thus, in 1QS V 11-12, a distinction is made between breaking the "revealed" law—i.e., the written law—and straying from "hidden" law—i.e., the new interpretations of Torah—with violations of the revealed/written law apparently being contrasted with unintentional sinning.

Hence, the Community Rule reveals that Pentateuchal language of intentional sinning was used to distinguish between sins against the written law and sins against new interpretations of the law. Although this observation by no means proves that Luke would have used such Pentateuchal texts similarly, it does suggest that my proposed reading of Luke 23:34a and related Lukan texts—i.e., that misperception is linked with unillumined readings of Scripture—would not have been out of place in the first century. That Philo connects such Pentateuchal texts with lack of revelation would seem to further this conclusion.

Philo. A close analysis of Philo's writings reveals that, for Philo, the Pentateuchal texts on unintentional sin can be understood 1) as God accomplishing his work—work that is beneath his holiness—through the hands of ignorant offenders, and 2) as resulting from the conscience's lack of the divine *Logos*. Although the details of Philo's writings on this subject have distinct differences from our Lukan texts on the matter, they nevertheless show how such Pentateuchal texts on unintentional sins were linked not only with God's carrying out his will (cf. Acts 3:17-18; 13:27), but also with the lack of an illumined conscience (cf. Luke 24:1-49).

Unlike the DSS that appear to focus on intentionality via the sacrificial laws of Lev 4:1-6:7 and Num 15:22-31,[64] Philo primarily discusses intentionality and sin by reference to the laws on unintentional manslaughter and places of refuge (e.g., Exod 21:12-14). Nevertheless, as shown below, when Philo does refer to intentionality in texts such as Lev 4:1-6:7, his views remain largely constant, thereby suggesting that Philo's thinking is essentially uniform on the topic of unintentional sins.

Beginning with *Fug.* 1.53-82, Philo turns to the laws on unintentional manslaughter and the places of refuge, with particular attention to Exod 21:12-14 that he quotes verbatim from the LXX:

> If a man smite another and he die, let him die the death. But he that did not intend it (ἐκών), but God delivered him into his hands, I will give thee a place to which the slayer shall flee. And if a man attack his neighbor to slay

---

63. For examples where "high-handed" is particularly used this way at Qumran, see ibid., 51.

64. See the parallel language (ibid., 51 n. 3, 52).

him by guile and he take refuge, from the altar shalt thou take him to put him
to death. (*Fug.* 1.53)[65]

In *Fug.* 1.65, Philo focuses upon the phrase, "not intentionally (οὐχ ἑκών), but
God delivered him" (v. 13). He sets οὐχ ἑκών in parallel with "unintentional"
(ἀκούσιος), a term that Philo perhaps knows from the OT where it primarily
appears in the context of the laws on unintentional sin (e.g., Lev 4:2) and in parallel texts on refuge for involuntary manslaughter (e.g., Deut 19:4). Regardless
of Philo's source behind the term ἀκούσιος, he defines by way of contrast the
meaning he has in mind: "intentional (ἑκούσιος) [acts] are from one's own purpose (γνώμη) and deeds (ἔργον), but unintentional (ἀκούσιος) [acts] are of
God (θεοῦ)" (1.65, translation mine).[66]

Philo clarifies how unintentional acts are "of God." Specifically, God uses
the unintentional killer as his instrument of "punishment" (κόλασις [1.65]).[67]
According to Philo, God assigns the task of punishing to his servants, since it is
"unbecoming" (ἀπρεπής) of God—whose "nature" consists of goodness and
grace (1.66)—to punish evil, because even though punishment is good, it has an
imitation of evil and therefore does not belong with God (1.74).[68] Unintentional
(ἀκούσιος) killers may therefore claim that their actions accord with God's will
(κατὰ θεόν), since God brought this change (τροπή) upon them (1.76).[69]

In *Spec.* 3.120, Philo paraphrases Exod 21:13 (God delivering the slain person into the hands of the unintentional killer) to reveal that the law "defends" the
unintentional killer. According to Philo's theological framework, the unintentionally slain was obviously guilty of a death-worthy crime that remained unde-

---

65. Unless otherwise noted, translations of Philo in what follows are from *Philo*
(LCL; 10 vols; trans. F.H. Colson and G.H. Whitaker; Cambridge, MA: Harvard University Press, 1929-62).

66. In what follows, in both *De Fuge et Inventione* and his other writings, Philo prefers the word ἀκούσιος, or its cognates, when referring to "unintentional" sins, and
ἑκούσιος or its cognates for "intentional" sins. Though the LXX does not describe intentional sins as ἑκούσιος, a term that nearly always refers to "freewill" offerings (e.g., Lev
7:16; Deut 12:6), perhaps Philo prefers this term for its nearness to ἀκούσιος.

67. This reading of Exod 21:13 also appears in *Sac.* 1.133.

68. Philo adds a reading of creation, focusing on the first person plural ("let us
make" [Gen 1:26]), to show that humans are more suitable for punishing, as their capaci-
ties for knowing good and evil were instilled by God's workers, not by God himself, who
apparently only creates the good (*Fug.* 1.68-72).

69. Perhaps this idea of God's bringing about the change is connected elsewhere
with Philo's teaching on the apparent uncontrollability or external causation of some
unintentional sins (e.g., unintentional [ἀκουσίως] sins happen "suddenly, without
thought...[or] time;" such sins are so bizarre that the unintentional sinner is left unable to
explain his motive behind the actions of which he is unaware [ἀγνοέω] [*Agr.* 176, 179];
also, in a reading of Num 6:9 [one suddenly dying near a Nazirite], Philo explains that an
unintentional [ἀκούσιος] act—being unplanned and seemingly caused by external
[ἔξωθεν] forces—temporarily "defiles" the soul [*Fug.* 1.115]; cf. also *Mig.* 1.225).

tected by humans, for the "merciful" God would not let an "innocent" person die (3.121). As a servant of God's justice, the unintentional killer is not guilty of murder, but only of a "little" misdeed that is pardonable (3.121). As before, Philo wants to distance God from any hint of evil. Hence he claims that God does not "show approval" of the unintentional killing, and that God uses those who commit "few" sins to carry out his punishment, rather than those who live their whole lives "stainless" (3.122).[70]

Next, one sees the relationship between unintentional sin and lack of illumination in Philo's merging of the divine *Logos* and the "conviction" (ἔλεγχος) of the "conscience" (σύνοιδα). Philo hints at the relationship between the conscience and intentional sin in a brief aside while discussing drunkenness, where he asserts that unintentional (ἀκούσιος) sins are half as evil and "lighter" (κοῦφος)[71] than intentional (ἑκών) sins, "since they have not upon them the sheer weight of convicting (ἔλεγχος) conscience (σύνοιδα)" (*Ebr.* 125). The nature of this relationship is further detailed in *Fug.* 1.116-18. Attempting to explain why the unintentional manslayer may return from exile after the high priest dies (Num 35:28), Philo suggests that the "high priest" represents the divine *Logos* (λόγον θεῖον [1.108]), which cannot be defiled (1.109) and which stands beyond unintentional (ἀκούσιος) error (1.115). As long as the high priest lives (i.e., as long as the divine *Logos* resides in the soul), it prevents unintentional (ἀκούσιος) errors because it cannot share in them (1.117a).[72] The *Logos* is then depicted as synonymous with conviction (ἔλεγχος [2x]), which allows no error of purpose (γνώμη) and functions as a judge over one's entire mind (1.118).[73]

---

70. The involuntary manslayer is exiled, but as an instrument of God, he is exiled for a limited time and to a special place, the sacred tribe of Levi (*Spec.* 3.123).

71. Similarly, after noting the irremediable consequence of Cain's sin (see below), Philo states that unintentional (ἀκούσιος) sins are "less weighty" (κοῦφος) than intentional sins (*Pos.* 1.11).

72. There is a text-critical problem in *Fug.* 117b, namely, when the high priest dies (i.e., when the divine *Logos* is removed from the soul), either sins of ἀκούσιος or those of ἑκούσιος reenter the soul. If ἀκούσιος is the original reading, it would suggest that, even if the *Logos* was at one time present, its absence makes it possible for one's subsequent sins to be "unintentional." If ἑκούσιος is original, it would suggest that all sins subsequent to the *Logos'* departure are "intentional," implying that the *Logos'* departure was desired with the result that the sinner is therefore inexcusable, having chosen ignorance (see F.H. Colson and G.H. Whitaker, notes on *Fug.* 117 [in *Philo*], 72 n. 3).

73. Our discussion will focus on the role of "conscience" only as it is described in our texts in question. For a more detailed discussion of the meanings of "conviction" (ἔλεγχος) and "conscience" (σύνοιδα) that deals with the complexities and ambiguities of Philo's thoughts, with particular attention to whether the conscience is immanent or transcendent, see the article and responses in Richard T. Wallis, *The Idea of Conscience in Philo of Alexandria: Protocol of the Thirteenth Colloquy 12 January 1975* (Berkeley, CA: The Center for Hermeneutical Studies in Hellenistic and Modern Culture, 1975), 1-28.

A similar idea appears in *Imm.* 127-35. After referring to Lev 13:11-13 (a person with partial leprosy is unclean, but one wholly covered in leprosy is clean), Philo allegorizes the text to teach that unintentional (ἀκούσιος) sins are "pure (καθαρός) and devoid of guilt" because they are not accused by the "conscience" (σύνοιδα), in contrast with intentional (ἑκούσιος) sins that are "convicted" (ἐλέγχω) by the judge of the soul and are therefore "impure" (ἀκάθαρτος) and unholy (127-28). In other words, the partially leprous person represents one who has the guide of λόγος[74] in his soul, but he ignores it and intentionally (ἑκούσιος) sins;[75] whereas the completely leprous person is like one with no power of λογίζομαι whatsoever, who can no more be blamed for falling into unintentional (ἀκούσιος) error than a blind person who trips over what is unseen (129-30). Philo furthers his point by referencing Lev 14:36,[76] which he reads as saying that the priest's entrance into a house would make the contents of that house unclean (131). For Philo, the priest represents the divine *Logos* (θεῖος λόγος); until the divine *Logos* enters the soul, one's unintentional sins are guiltless, for such sinners are so blind that they even consider their evil as good because they have not been admonished by the divine *Logos* who acts as their "guardian or father or teacher" (134). "But when the true priest, 'conviction' (ἔλεγχος), enters," it illumes the guilt of sins committed in ignorance and orders such guilty deeds to be carried away so that the soul's house may be healed (135). Thus, unintentional sins are not only those acts committed accidentally or even involuntarily; they are also acts that are done ignorantly, without the guidance of the conscience—which appears to refer to both "reason" and the divine *Logos*.

In sum, Philo's writings reveal that a first-century author could hold that unintentional sins were "of God" and can also be attributed to the absence of the "conviction" (ἔλεγχος) of the "conscience" (σύνοιδα)—an idea paralleled with the divine *Logos*. Although Luke clearly does not think Jesus is deserving of punishment, Philo's belief that unintentional manslayers are instruments "of God" might find some partial overlap in texts such as Acts 3:17-20, wherein Peter claims that Jesus' crucifiers were *ignorant*, that through their actions *God* fulfilled prophecy, and that they may *repent* and be forgiven.[77] Moreover, just as

---

74. The LCL translators, Colson and Whitaker, render λόγος in *Imm.* 129 as "reason," which fits the immediately following reference to "reasoning" (λογίζομαι [130]). Yet, as shown below, nearby references to the divine λόγος suggest that Philo in *Imm.* 129 may intend more than mere "reason."

75. See *Spec.* 1.235 where the "convicting" (ἐλέγχω) "conscience" (σύνοιδα) accuses those who have committed intentional (ἑκούσιος) sins.

76. "And the priest shall give orders to strip the house [that has leprosy] before the priest goes in to look at the attack, and whatever is in the house will not become unclean, and afterword the priest shall go in to examine the house" (Lev 14:36 LXX [NETS]).

77. In reference to Acts 3:18 ("In this way [οὕτως] God fulfilled what he had foretold through all the prophets, that his Messiah would suffer"), Mowery writes, "The words 'God fulfilled' are the subject and verb of the first main clause.... But what does

Philo explains unintentional sin via appeal to the absence of the guidance of the divine *Logos*, and just as the Scrolls explain it via appeal to ignorance of the new revelations of Scripture within the community, so also a similar idea can be found in Luke—namely, that a cause of misperception is unillumined minds and unillumined exegesis, wherein one's mind needs opening by something akin to the divine *Logos* (e.g., "Then [Jesus] opened their minds to understand the scriptures" [Luke 24:45]).

To conclude our study of intertextuality, the most likely echo in Luke 23:34a would be the Pentateuchal laws on unintentional sin (especially Lev 5:18) in light of 1) the verbal links between Lev 5:18 and Luke 23:34a, Acts 3:17-18, and 13:27; 2) the obvious thematic link between Jesus' prayer of forgiveness for "not knowing" and the Pentateuchal laws on forgiveness and atonement for unintentional sins; and 3) how Philo and the Scrolls reveal that circa-first-century persons could deal with such Pentateuchal texts in ways akin to the Lukan motif of forgiveness for sins of misperception. To put this in the language of Richard Hays' "seven tests": 1) an echo with the Pentateuch was *available*; 2) there is some *volume* of borrowed language; 3) there is probable *recurrence* in Acts 3:17-18 and 13:27 (and 17:30); 4) the *thematic coherence* is self-evident; 5) the *historical plausibility* is suggested by Philo and the Scrolls; 6) though not mentioned above, we will see in ch. 6 that, as early as Origen, the *history of interpretation* not only links Luke 23:34a with such Pentateuchal laws (*Homilies on Leviticus* 2.1.5), but also connects such misperception with uninformed readings of Scripture (*Treatise on the Passover* 43-47);[78] and 7) the suggested echo provides *satisfaction*, since "the proposed reading makes sense" of the Lukan texts in question.[79]

Other Proffered Readings of Luke 23:34a
In addition to those readings of Luke 23:34a that have been evaluated throughout this chapter, two other readings deserve mention, although I will suggest why they seem less textually coherent. One nagging issue remaining in my proposed reading concerns the criminal's insight into Jesus' identity, since the narrative records no instance where his mind or Scripture is opened (23:40-42).

---

this clause say God 'did' during the passion events? Although the passion references in Acts claim that Jesus' adversaries 'laid violent hands' on him (5:30)...and 'killed' him (2:23; 3:15...), Luke never made 'God' the subject of any of these verbs.... [T]he adverb 'in this way' [οὕτως] points back to the actions of Jesus' adversaries (3:13-15, 17), and this adverb indicates that God 'fulfilled' what God had 'foretold' through the repugnant actions of these adversaries" ("The Divine Hand," 569).

78. Specifically, in *Treatise on the Passover*, after alluding to our text ("the sacrificing of this lamb was carried out in ignorance [ἄγνοια] because they do not know what they do and that is why it is forgiven them"), Origen explains that ignorance results from "non-faith (ἀπιστία), [being] without full knowledge (οὐκ ἐγνωκότες) of the Scriptures" (47 [FC]).

79. Hays, *Echoes of Scripture in the Letters of Paul*, 29-32.

Crump suggests that the criminal's insight results from Jesus' prayer in v. 34a, but such a causal connection is not clear in the text.[80] In contrast, I would suggest that the criminal's insight is more related to his outsider status.[81] Not only would this fit the pericope of 23:32-43 wherein, as argued above, misperception is tied to issues of misunderstanding status, but it would also fit a motif throughout Luke where unexpected insight arises from low status individuals (e.g., the "sinful" woman [7:36-50], the bleeding woman [8:43-48], and Zacchaeus [19:1-10]).[82]

As mentioned in ch. 3, Shelly Matthews seeks to make sense of the seeming discrepancy between Jesus' prayer of forgiveness on the one hand, and the impending desolation of Jerusalem on the other (e.g., Luke 21:20) that suggests the prayer was ineffective. Her proposed solution is to see the prayer as "first and foremost—if not solely—a celebration of [virtue]," so that the reader expects "no effects on the prayer's objects," but instead focuses on the mercy of the speaker.[83] Such a reading, however, is not textually coherent in light of texts such as Acts 3:17-19 where forgiveness clearly is expected ("Repent therefore, and turn to God so that your sins may be wiped out"). That forgiveness and impending punishment are compatible, as Brown notes, is seen in the common coexistence of these two elements in the OT prophets.[84]

Conclusion

By means of investigating the language, structure, and socio-cultural context related to Luke 23:34a, I have suggested that the following conclusions represent the most textually coherent reading: first, the "not know[ing]" of Luke 23:34a is essentially a misperception of Jesus' paradoxical ministry and identity—exemplified by the cross; second, this misperception is linked with unillumined minds, unillumined readings of Scripture, and God fulfilling his purposes; third, the primary referents are the Jewish leaders and the Jerusalem inhabitants, though others such as the Romans would be included; and fourth, the most likely intertextual echo is the Pentateuchal laws on unintentional sin, especially Lev 5:18.

---

80. Crump, *Intercessor*, 86-88.

81. As Green notes with regard to the women (v. 26), the criminal (vv. 40-42), and the Gentile centurion (v. 47), "in the climatic scene of Jesus' death, sympathy toward Jesus or even recognition of and appropriate response to him are attributed to relative outsiders" (*Luke*, 812). This criminal recognizes his low position, confessing his guilt, thereby "presenting himself, according to the Lukan calculus, as a candidate for divine beneficence" (Ibid., 822).

82. The misperception of the first criminal could be explained as serving the narratival function of highlighting Jesus' shame "as persons of diminishing status—the religious leaders, the Roman soldiers, and an executed criminal—turn their derisive attention on Jesus" (Green, *Luke*, 818).

83. Matthews, "Clemency as Cruelty," 118, 121.

84. Brown, *Death*, 974.

In light of these conclusions, the prayer can be seen to have several functions. By recognizing that the primary referents include the Jewish leaders who are clearly a chief adversary of Jesus in Luke's Gospel, the prayer underscores Jesus' mercy and witnesses to his carrying out his own teaching about loving one's enemies (e.g., "Pray for those who abuse you" [Luke 6:28]).[85] By understanding that "not know" refers to *misperception* rather than simple lack of information, the prayer reminds the reader, particularly those early readers whose socio-cultural context would make venerating a crucified person problematic,[86] that the cross was misunderstood even though the ironic truth—as seen in the repeated mockery of our pericope—is that the cross actually testifies to Jesus' messianic and salvific identity. The possibility of an echo of the Pentateuchal laws on unintentional sin might offer the reader a clue as to how the persistent misperception of the cross will be resolved by foreshadowing the eye-opening effect of the Resurrected One's opening of minds and Scripture. Perhaps, the echo even hints at how God's purpose—i.e., the fulfillment of Christ's suffering[87]—is carried out apart from God forcing the crucifixion. To these various functions of the prayer could be added the prayer's role in preparing the reader for not only the ignorance excuse in texts such as Acts 3:17-19, but also the paralleled martyrdom of Stephen,[88] reminding the church of their call to follow Jesus.

With a text having as much ambiguity as Luke 23:34a, I do not presume to have offered a completely airtight case for a textually coherent reading. I do, however, hope to have offered a reading that has fewer "holes" than other possible readings—particularly with regard to the nature of misperception, the identity of the referents, and the most likely intertextual echo.

---

85. Carras rightly notes that this observation "is a telling corrective" to those who regard Luke as anti-Semitic since Jesus "has not given up on the Jewish leaders but prays for them" ("Numbers 15:22-31 and Luke 23:34," 615).

86. Bovon, *Lukas*, 462.

87. See also, Matera, "Responsibility," 78-88.

88. Delobel, "Crux," 34-35.

6

Patristic Readings of Luke 23:34a

Introduction

In ch. 4, an ecclesially located hermeneutic was put forward that prioritized *authorial communicative intent* while simultaneously allowing for a *theologically delimited polysemy*. Accordingly, in ch. 5, an attempt was made to hear the authorial communicative intent of Luke 23:34a by seeking the most textually coherent reading. This chapter offers an example of moving beyond authorial communicative intent in order to hear and delimit further readings of the text. The case study for doing so will be patristic readings of Luke 23:34a from the first five centuries.

The Fathers are chosen for two reasons. First, it seems wise for readers who are adopting an ecclesially located hermeneutic to learn how the text was heard by those persons who acted as spiritual guides during the foundational years of the church. Although my proposed reading strategy does not go as far as Robert Wall, who prioritizes those readings that occurred during Scripture's canonization,[1] I agree that it is worthwhile for *ecclesial* readers to learn how the Scriptures were interpreted when they were being discerned as *Scripture*. Second, given that our ecclesially located model recognizes the dialogical mode of reading wherein texts can be heard differently depending on the reader's situation, then it seems helpful to attend to those readers whose cultures are different than our own. As C.S. Lewis writes in his well-known preface to Athanasius' *Incarnation of the Word of God*:

---

1. As Wall writes, "I argue for the priority of the point of canonization in exegesis over the point of composition, precisely because it grounds the historical project more firmly into a text's ecclesial location for a theological reading. If we seek to read biblical texts as the church's Scripture then we should aim our historical work at that moment when the church originally recognized the text as sacred and started using it as canonical.... And if we approach Acts at its point of canonization, primarily for theological reasons...rather than at its point of composition, whenever that may have been, we will likely be more interested in the reading of Acts by Irenaeus, who was probably the first to read Acts as Scripture, than we are in a reading of Acts by Theophilus whom we do not know in any case" (Robert W. Wall, review of C. Kavin Rowe, *World Upside Down: Reading Acts in the Graeco-Roman Age* [paper presented at the Annual Meeting of the Society of Biblical Literature, Atlanta, 21 Nov 2010], 4).

Every age has its own outlook. It is [e]specially good at seeing certain truths and [e]specially liable to make certain mistakes. We all, therefore, need the books that will correct the characteristic mistakes of our own period. And that means the old books…. Where [the old books] are true they will give us truths which we half knew already. Where they are false they will aggravate the error with which we are already dangerously ill…. Two heads are better than one, not because either is infallible, but because they are unlikely to go wrong in the same direction.[2]

The chapter is divided into two sections: 1) a brief assessment of Blum's recent work on the history of interpretation of Luke 23:34a; and 2) a critical survey of patristic readings of our text where we attend to and delimit their readings of Luke 23:34a.

Recent Scholarship on the *Auslegungsgeschichte* of Luke 23:34a

In his monograph, *"Denn Sie Wissen Nicht, Was Sie Tun": Zur Rezeption der Fürbitte Jesu am Kreuz (Lk 23,34a) in der Antiken Jüdisch-christlichen Kontroverse*, Blum surveys nearly thirty texts that cite Jesus' prayer in Luke 23:34a (e.g., Hegesipuss, Irenaeus, Origen, Hippolytus, Gregory of Nyssa, Ambrose of Milan, John Chrysostom, Leo the Great, Apostolic Constitutions). The central focus of Blum's work is whether and how these ancient texts relate the prayer to Jews. This is not to say that he completely overlooks all other patristic usages of the prayer. For instance, Blum notes that the Fathers cite the prayer as evidence of Christ's abundant mercy (Ephraim the Syrian), his perfection (Irenaeus), his goodness (Leo the Great), and his exemplary character that the disciples should model (Pseudo-Clementine).[3] Nevertheless, as indicated by the subtitle of his book, Blum is chiefly concerned with anti-Semitism. For this reason, he not only underscores those writings wherein the referents are explicitly named, but also speculates about the assumed referent when the patristic author offers no explicit referent of the prayer. This forces Blum at times to turn to additional writings of an author in order to hypothesize whom the patristic writer had in mind as the prayer's referent. For instance, when Irenaeus alludes to Jesus' prayer in the third book of his *Against Heresies*, he does not specify the identity of the referents (3.16.9; 3.18.5); Blum must rely on Irenaeus' fourth book where he places blame on the Jews (4.28.3) in order to suggest that Irenaeus considers the Jews as the referents of Jesus' prayer mentioned in his third book.

Blum describes both positive and negative functions of Luke 23:34a when the Fathers apply the text to the Jews. For example, according to Blum's reading of the Fathers, Hippolytus connects the prayer to God's compassion on the Jews; Gregory of Nyssa's call to emulate Christ's patience would run counter to any

---

2. C.S. Lewis, introduction to Athanasius, *Incarnation of the Word of God* (New York: MacMillan, 1996), 6-7.

3. Blum, *Denn Sie Wissen Nicht*, 95, 119, 176, 124. See section 2 below for more detail on these citations.

anti-Semitic interpretations; Ambrose explains that the Jews were ignorant because they did not want to submit themselves to the truth, though God in his great mercy is still willing to forgive them; and Leo places guilt on the Jews in the death of Jesus, but he believes that Jesus' merciful prayer in Luke 23:34a made possible the conversion of the Jews on the Day of Pentecost.[4]

The present chapter departs from Blum in three respects. First, my reading of Luke 23:34a in ch. 5 suggests that the soldiers are not the sole referents of Jesus' prayer from the cross. Rather, it appears that the Jewish leaders and the Jerusalem inhabitants are the primary referents (e.g., Acts 2:36; 3:17). Consequently, when the Fathers refer this prayer to the Jews, I do not consider it anti-Semitic—or rather, I do not *a priori* consider it any more anti-Semitic than the Lukan author who, though placing a measure of guilt for Jesus' death on Jewish peoples, reports a story in which the hero, his closest followers, and his ministry were all Jewish.

Nevertheless, Blum is right to challenge anti-Semitic readings of Jesus' prayer. My second difference with Blum is our strategy for disallowing such readings. As already mentioned, Blum hopes that historical criticism is adequate to delimit anti-Semitic interpretations of Luke 23:34a. Because I do not find historical criticism sufficient for such a task, I will appeal to an ecclesially located exegetical strategy that limits harmful readings by recourse to the rule of faith, the double-commandment of love, and clearer canonical texts.

Third, Blum and I focus on different aspects of the reception history of Luke 23:34a. Whereas Blum comments on the prayer's function in Gnostic and other texts (e.g., *The First Apocalypse of James*), I am only concerned with the text's reception in the Church Fathers.[5] Moreover, Blum goes into great detail on both the Jewish-Christian content of the writings as well as historical-critical details behind the texts of the Fathers (e.g., he frequently speculates on the precise dating and geographic location of sources). As he has already done a thorough job in both respects, I will concentrate on the readings the Fathers derived from our prayer.

Patristic Treatment of Jesus' Prayer of Forgiveness from the Cross

In a case study that largely follows Blum's outline, we will look at how Jesus' prayer functions in writings of Fathers from the second century through the Council of Chalcedon in A.D. 451—namely, in the writings of Irenaeus, Origen, Gregory of Nyssa, Ambrose of Milan, John Chrysostom, Leo the Great, and Augustine.

---

4. Ibid., 115, 132, 151, 176, 179-82.

5. Despite the possibility of Origen's being anathematized at the Second Council of Constantinople, his writings are included in this survey because of the overall high respect they are given by the Fathers.

In ch. 4, it was proffered that an ecclesially located exegesis would delimit readings by appeal to the rule of faith, the twofold commandment of love,[6] and clearer canonical texts. Moreover, such an exegetical strategy recognizes both the ongoing value of authorial communicative intent and the importance of virtue in interpretation. Consequently, in what follows, we will be evaluating the aforementioned patristic readings according to their adherence to these criteria.

As will be seen below, some readings are easy to determine as valid or invalid, but others are much less clear; this raises the question of how to evaluate such readings. (It is perhaps obvious that there is no one-size-fits-all method for using the aforementioned criteria when evaluating readings.) Following Augustine's advice, it would seem that the interpreter must approach such a task humbly and prayerfully, because Scripture is unfathomably deep and humans are limited.[7] The interpreter, then, must practice discernment. This brings us back to the importance of virtue in biblical interpretation wherein those most transformed by the Spirit are those best able to discern the Spirit's working through Scripture. As Fowl notes:

> Given that Christians are called to interpret Scripture as part of their ongoing journey into ever-deeper communion with God, it is not surprising that those who have grown and advanced in virtue will tend to be masterful interpreters of Scripture.... [I]t simply stands to reason that those who have advanced in the Christian life will tend to offer the best interpretations for those whose primary aim is to advance in the Christian life.[8]

With no personal claim to virtue myself, the best I can offer in what follows is my own intuition.[9] Thus, borrowing Hays' caveat to his own work in NT ethics:

---

6. As was stated in ch. 4, for Augustine, loving one's neighbor is no easy rule, for it entails loving another person "more than our own bodies," loving "the person to whom an act of compassion is due" even if he is an enemy, and having the same compassion for others as God had for oneself (*DDC* 1.27, 30).

7. See ch. 4, n. 32.

8. Stephen E. Fowl, "Virtue," in *Dictionary for Theological Interpretation of the Bible* (ed. Kevin J. Vanhoozer; Grand Rapids: Baker Academic, 2005), 838.

9. As Robert W. Wall writes about his own proposed method of canonical reading, "How the intercanonical conversations are arranged and then adapted to a particular faith tradition is largely intuitive and depends a great deal upon the interpreter's talent and location, both social and religious" ("Canonical Context and Canonical Conversations," in *Between Two Horizons: Spanning New Testament Studies and Systematic Theology* [ed. Joel B. Green and Max Turner; Grand Rapids: Eerdmans, 2000], 182). Similarly, when writing on the seeming tension between James and Paul on the topic of faith and works, Childs closes his thoughts by suggesting that the louder voice of these two will ultimately depend on a community's situation as one "seek[s] to discern God's will...within changing historical contexts" and allows "the Word of God...freedom to address the continuing needs of the church in the world" (*New Testament as Canon*, 443).

"[W]e plunge ahead to the task, while acknowledging that our…reading of the texts will always be subject to critique or supplementation by other members of the community of faith who may teach us to see things more clearly."[10]

Irenaeus, Against Heresies 3.18.5 (ca. 2nd century AD)

> And from this fact, that he exclaimed upon the cross, *"Father, forgive them, for they know not what they do,"* the long-suffering, patience, compassion, and goodness of Christ are exhibited, since he both suffered, and did himself exculpate those who had maltreated him. For the Word of God, who said to us, "Love your enemies, and pray for those that hate you," himself did this very thing upon the cross; loving the human race to such a degree, that he even prayed for those putting him to death. If, however, any one, going upon the supposition that there are two, forms a judgment in regard to them, that he shall be found much the better one, and more patient, and the truly good one, who, in the midst of his own wounds and stripes, and the other [cruelties] inflicted upon him, was beneficent, and unmindful of the wrongs perpetrated upon him, than he who flew away, and sustained neither injury nor insult. (3.18.5 [*ANF*])

In his third book of *Against Heresies*, Irenaeus' quotation of Jesus' prayer should be understood in its cotext where Irenaeus is contending with false teachers who "understand that Christ was one and Jesus another; and they teach that there was not one Christ, but many. And if they speak of them as united, they do again separate them: for they show that one did indeed undergo sufferings, but that the other remained impassible…" (3.17.4 [*ANF*]).

Running throughout chapter eighteen of *Against Heresies* book three is the recurring motif that Christian salvation is dependent on *Christ's genuine humanity and suffering*. For instance, the chapter begins with Irenaeus explaining that Christ joined himself to humanity, even to humanity's suffering, in such a way necessary to save humans who were otherwise "conquered" by sin (3.18.1-2 [*ANF*]); and the chapter ends with Irenaeus' statement, "But if, not having been made flesh, he did appear as flesh, his work was not a true one…. God recapitulated in himself the ancient formation of man, that he might kill sin…and vivify man" (3.18.7 [*ANF*]). Between these brackets, then, Irenaeus cites several scriptural texts to prove his point. In 3.18.2-3, he cites a string of apparently mutually interpreting Pauline texts to illustrate that Christ indeed suffered (e.g., "And again: 'But now, in Christ, ye who sometimes were far off are made nigh by the blood of Christ' [Eph 2:13]. And again: 'Christ has redeemed us from the curse of the law, being made a curse for us…' [Gal 3:13]").

---

10. Richard B. Hays, *The Moral Vision of the New Testament: Community, Cross, New Creation: A Contemporary Introduction to New Testament Ethics* (New York: HarperOne, 1996), 189.

In 3.18.4-6, Irenaeus transitions from Paul's letters to the Gospels to cite evidence of Christ's suffering. He begins with Matt 16:13-21, focusing on how Peter's confession of Jesus as "Christ" was immediately followed with Jesus' prediction of his (i.e., Christ's) suffering: "He who was acknowledged by Peter as Christ...said that he must himself suffer" (3.18.4). Next, Irenaeus puts forward an argument grounded in reason, showing that several texts from the Gospel make no sense if Christ did not suffer. Thus, he begins by asking, if Christ did not truly suffer, "why did he exhort his disciples to take up the cross and follow him?" (citing as evidence, e.g., Matt 10:17-18, 28; 23:24). Then, Irenaeus argues that, if Christ did not truly suffer, he would be lesser than the one who prayed for his persecutors, "Father, forgive them, for they know not what they do" (3.18.5). Not only does Jesus practice his own teaching on love of enemies, but he carries this teaching out "to such a degree, that he even prayed for those putting him to death." Logically, then, unless Christ underwent genuine suffering on the cross, the human one who forgives his crucifiers would be superior to the one who "flew away and sustained neither injury nor insult." In addition, if Christ did not suffer, he would have "misled" his followers, instructing them to do that which he was only "seeming" to do (3.18.6 [ANF]). Furthermore, the followers who carry out the teachings that Christ avoided would be "even above the Master, because [they] suffer and sustain what [their] Master never bore or endured" (3.18.6 [ANF]). Thus, Irenaeus concludes his argument on the necessity of Christ's suffering by claiming that if Christ did not truly suffer as a human, then death has not been overcome, humanity has not been reunited with God or made a "partaker of incorruptibility," and Christian salvation is "unsecure" (3.18.7-3.19.1 [ANF]).

In sum, Irenaeus handles Jesus' prayer in a way that moves beyond its apparent witness to the great virtue of Jesus Christ—a point that Irenaeus makes earlier[11]—and reasons from it that Christ suffered, lest one assumes that the finite surpasses the infinite in greatness; this proof serves the larger argument wherein Christ's humanity is a necessary condition for Christian salvation.[12] While the Lukan author may not have envisioned such a use of Jesus' prayer, Irenaeus' reading should nonetheless be regarded as valid within an Augustinian-informed exegetical framework for three reasons. First, Irenaeus' use of the

---

11. In a string of other virtuous deeds of Jesus Christ, Irenaeus recalls how, "when he underwent tyranny, he prayed his Father that he would forgive those who had crucified him" (3.16.9).

12. Irenaeus' reading of Jesus' prayer fits well into his typical way of reading Scripture as summarized by Jourjon: "[S]ince all of Scripture is spiritual, it is necessary to take precise account of it in order to read it in the manner of Christ and to proclaim, teach, and transmit the faith just as the apostles do so, namely, in conformity with the Scriptures" (Maurice Jourjon, "Irenaeus's Reading of the Bible," in *The Bible in Greek Christian Antiquity* [ed. Paul M. Blowers; Notre Dame, IN: University of Notre Dame Press, 1997], 110); cf. Kevin M. Tortorelli, "Some Methods of Interpretation in St. Irenaeus," *VetChr* 30 (1993): 127.

prayer is not only in line with, but even affirms and reinforces the rule of faith, which Irenaeus earlier laid out: "The Church, though dispersed throughout the whole world...has received this faith: [She believes]...in one Christ Jesus, the Son of God, who became incarnate for our salvation" (1.10.1 [*ANF*]). Similarly, the Nicene Creed (325) attests to Jesus Christ's concurrent divinity, humanity and suffering, and the resultant salvation of humans: "[We believe] in *one* (ἑῖς) Lord Jesus Christ...very God of very God...who for us humans and our *salvation* (σωτηρία)...was made *human* (σαρκόω)...[and] *suffered* (πάσχω)...."[13] In contrast, the claim Irenaeus is attacking—i.e., that Christ did not suffer—cannot be reconciled with the *regula fidei* as it is witnessed in either Irenaeus' writings or the Nicene Creed. Second, Irenaeus' theologically informed use of the prayer finds support in other clear scriptural texts, which Irenaeus himself cites—e.g., Jesus' response to Peter's confession (Matt 16:13-21) makes it clear that the Christ will suffer (3.18.4). Third, Irenaeus' reading does not clash with the Lukan text, but finds coherence with the overall Lukan witness to both Christ's humanity and the "necessity" (δεῖ) of his "suffering" (πάσχω) (e.g., Luke 9:20-22; Acts 17:3; cf. Acts 26:23). The humanity and suffering of Jesus Christ are particularly noticeable in Luke 24:36-50 where the resurrected Christ has flesh (σάρξ [v. 39]), eats fish (v. 43), and shows from Scripture that Christ must suffer (πάσχω [v. 46]). Consequently, according to the hermeneutical framework of *DDC*, Irenaeus' reading is a good example of how an ecclesially located reader might hear a meaning that likely surpasses authorial communicative intent, but is nevertheless a good (better?) reading for his context (i.e., defending against heresy).

Origen (AD 185-253/54)
Jesus' prayer of forgiveness occurs twice in Origen's available works, once in *Treatise on the Passover* and once in *Homilies on Leviticus*. To begin with the latter, Origen writes:

> [It] is said of the sin of the congregation, "if they are ignorant and the word concealed from their eyes and they do one thing of all the commands of the Lord which they ought not do," then it is also apparent that "the entire congregation" can sin through ignorance [Lev 4:13]. The Lord also confirms this in the Gospels when he says, "Father, forgive them for they do not know what they do." (2.1.5 [FC])

Origen's *Homilies on Leviticus* is the earliest extant Christian writing on Leviticus and as such it represents the young church's struggle to adapt the teachings of the OT to the Christian community at a time when literal interpretations seemed impossible to harmonize with such matters as the destruction of the

---

13. Greek citations are from Philip Schaff, *The Creeds of Christendom: With a History and Critical Notes* (3 vols.; 6th ed.; Grand Rapids: Baker, 1985), 2:60.

temple.[14] Origen, who considers it heresy not to acknowledge the OT as Scripture (*Homilies on Leviticus* 13.4.2), turns in his second homily to an allegorical interpretation of the sacrificial prescriptions of Leviticus. When he comes to the matter of involuntary sins of the congregation (Lev 4:13), he offers a passing citation of our text to affirm that the entire congregation can in fact sin in ignorance: "[the] Lord also confirms this in the Gospels when he says, 'Father, forgive them for they do not know what they do'" (2.1.5 [FC]). Thus, Jesus' prayer functions as a further witness that sins of ignorance are carried out not only by individuals but also by entire communities. Such a use of Jesus' prayer works well in an ecclesial exegetical framework, where the reading of one text (Lev 4:13) is confirmed by another text (Luke 23:34a). Although there is ambiguity in Luke 23:34a, it is at least clear that sins of ignorance (οὐ...οἴδασιν) can be committed by a group of people (note the plurals: αὐτοῖς, οἴδασιν, ποιοῦσιν).

Turning to *Treatise on the Passover*, Origen writes:

> Therefore, those who heed the prophet will celebrate this Passover as strangers in his [Pharaoh's] land, as having come under his tyranny in a time of famine, because they received from their father that very old oath made to their father, Abraham, that his descendants would be sojourners. For the sacrificing of this lamb was carried out by them in ignorance because they do not know what they are doing—and that is why it is forgiven them. For it is good that one man die for all the people. For it is not permitted for a prophet to die outside Jerusalem. (43-44 [ACW])

This work is difficult to comprehend because of its typological nature, its missing fragments, and its assumption that the audience will recognize allusions and conversations that are no longer clear for today's readers. Further, as Robert J. Daly aptly comments: "This passage [*Treatise on the Passover* 43.7-47.27] is a striking example of Origen at his best, moving, in a kind of biblical-theological, midrash-like stream of consciousness from one image or idea or text to another, often without pausing to make the connections explicit."[15] Even so, two fundamental themes running throughout this work are discernable. First, Origen is opposed to typological readings that interpret the Passover as a type of Christ's passion. He explains that such readings are founded on an improper etymology that links the Passover (πάσχα) with the passion (πάθος), when in fact the proper etymological relationship derives from the Hebrew term for Passover, *fas* (פסח), that corresponds to the Greek word for "passage" (διάβασις [1-2]).[16]

---

14. Blum, *Denn Sie Wissen Nicht*, 102.

15. Robert J. Daly, introduction to *Origen: Treatise on the Passover and Dialogue of Origen with Heraclides and His Fellow Bishops on the Father, the Son, and the Soul* (ACW 54; New York: Paulist, 1992), 102n. 52.

16. "[The] Passover is indeed a type of Christ, but not of his passion" (13). Greek citations in what follows are from *Origène: Sur la Pâque* (ed. O. Guérand and P. Nautin; ChristAnt 2; Paris: Beauchesne, 1979).

Consequently, the true Passover that one should celebrate is the "passage" (ὑπέρβασις) through which Christ passed beyond "the limits (ὅρος)...of the disobedience of Adam," thereby overcoming death and creating a path for Christians to follow into salvation (47-48 [ACW]).[17]

The second theme—and the one that involves Luke 23:34a and, thus, will be the focus of our attention—revolves around the matter of ignorance versus understanding. For Origen, those who truly understand the Scriptures on the Passover read them according to the spiritual sense whereas those who only read the literal sense are in a state of ignorance.[18] For example, in a typological interpretation of the phrase, "eat the flesh roasted with fire" (Exod 12:8), Origen regards the "flesh" as the Scriptures that should not be consumed as "raw" (i.e., "just the letter" [μόναις ταῖς λέχεσιν]) but only after being cooked by the fire of the Spirit (26-29 [ACW]). Similarly, Origen writes, "For it is not in faith that they set out to celebrate the Passover, but in non-faith (ἀπιστία), without full knowledge (οὐκ ἐγνωκότες) of the Scriptures which the prophets proclaimed. As Scripture says, 'If you do not believe, neither will you understand'" (47 [ACW]).[19] Thus, one sees how, for Origen, ignorance results from lack of faith and incomplete knowledge of Scripture. Despite Origen's not making explicit connections, the cotext suggests that Origen sees the same type of scriptural and spiritual ignorance at work in the crucifixion when he writes, "For the sacrificing of this lamb was carried out by them in ignorance (ἄγνοια) because they do not know what they are doing and that is why it is forgiven them" (43 [ACW]). Jesus' prayer for his persecutors is, then, a plea for forgiveness on behalf of those who cannot rightly recognize him because of their lack of faith and their correspondingly insufficient (i.e., unspiritual) interpretive practices.[20]

---

17. See also Daly, who interprets Origen as regarding the Passover as a type "of Christ's passing over to the Father...and, by reason of our incorporation into Christ, of our own still ongoing passing over with Christ to the Father" (introduction to *Origen*, 6-7, 11).

18. For the importance and practice of literal and figurative readings in Origen's biblical exegesis, see Ronald Heine, "Reading the Bible with Origen," in *The Bible in Greek Christian Antiquity* (ed. Paul M. Blowers; Notre Dame, IN: University of Notre Dame Press, 1997), 131-45; cf. Hermann J. Vogt, "Origen of Alexandria," in *Handbook of Patristic Exegesis: The Bible in Ancient Christianity* (2 vols.; by Charles Kannengiesser; Leiden: Brill, 2004), 1:545-51.

19. See Daly, who clarifies that Origen is here referring to gnosis, the spiritual sense of Scripture (notes to *Origen: Treatise on the Passover*, 104, n.63). For Origen, the Spirit illuminates the full meaning of the Passover—namely, a salvific "passage" that Christ traveled and that Christians enter through baptism (4). As Heine writes, "The spiritual truth which has been buried in the Bible can be understood only by one in whom the same Spirit who was present and worked through the writers of the Bible dwells and works" ("Reading the Bible with Origen," 139).

20. To move beyond this ignorance, "it is necessary to have completely renounced creation and this world" and to clothe oneself in faith and good works (6, 44 [ACW]).

Though not (explicitly) grounded in Luke's cotext, Origen's apparent interpretation of the crucifiers' ignorance is similar to my reading in ch. 5. Particularly, I argued that misperception is linked to unillumined minds and unillumined reading of Scripture, whereas proper perception requires the opening of Scriptures and of minds by the Resurrected One. If one were to assume that Origen's reading is not grounded in Luke's cotext (and there is little evidence in this "midrash-like stream of consciousness" to determine if it was), then Origen might be akin to "a walker who leaves his path by mistake but reaches the destination to which the path leads by going through a field...[and who] must be put right and shown how it is more useful not to leave the path, in case the habit of deviating should force him to go astray or drift" (Augustine, *DDC* 1.36). Thus, on the one hand, Origen's reading is not, in itself, problematic. After all, it does not clash with the rule of faith or the twofold love commandment, and it coheres with the Lukan text. On the other hand, by leaving out the Lukan context of Jesus' prayer, Origen risks not only missing the benefit of attending to authorial communicative intent, but also proposing meanings that are problematic. To be certain, the exegetical framework of *DDC* does not make authorial communicative intent the gatekeeper of meaning; further, *DDC* provides additional parameters (e.g., rule of faith) that allow readings to go beyond authorial communicative intent while still being delimited. Nevertheless, *DDC* holds authorial communicative intent in high esteem. Consequently, Origen's reading of Luke 23:34a could be a valid reading, perhaps even the one most appropriate for his context; his reading strategy in this particular instance, however, should not be the *default* reading strategy of an Augustinian-informed, ecclesially located exegete because it does not evidence the practice of attending to authorial communicative intent.

Further, Origen's reading might be challenged in his seeming conflation of proper reading with his own method of spiritual exegesis, a method with the potential to neglect the importance of literal readings (μόναις ταῖς λέχεσιν). According to our ecclesial framework, literal readings *are* needed. As was discussed in greater detail in ch. 4, literal readings function as a means of both hermeneutical guidance and hermeneutical formation. Therefore, non-literal readings can have their place in Christian exegesis, but by no means at the exclusion of the literal.

Gregory of Nyssa (ca. AD 335–394)[21]

> Another color is patience which appears quantitatively in the 'image of the invisible God.' A sword, clubs, chains, whips, slaps in the face, the face spat upon, the back beaten, irreverent judgment, a harsh denial, soldiers mocking, the sullen rejection with jests and sarcasm and insults, blows from a reed, nails and gall and vinegar, and all of these terrible things were applied to him without cause, nay, rather, in return for innumerable good works! And how were those who did these things repaid? *"Father, forgive them, for they know not what they do."*[22] Was it not possible for him to bring the sky down upon them, or to bury these insolent men in a chasm of the earth, or to throw them down from their own mountains into the sea, or to inundate the earth with the depths of the ocean, or to send down upon them the Sodomitic rain of fire, or to do any other angry deed in revenge? Instead, he bore all these things in meekness and patience, legislating patience for your life through himself. (*On Perfection* 111)

In his treatise *On Perfection*, Gregory aims "to set before [the reader] an accurate description of the life toward which one must tend"—namely, a life that imitates Christ (95, 98-99).[23] Hence, this work is also known by its alternate title, *On What It Is Necessary for a Christian to Be*. To achieve his goal, Gregory expounds one-by-one on 30 Pauline names for Christ, since each name adds something unique to one's insight into the image of Christ (96-97).

Gregory quotes Jesus' prayer while reflecting on the name "image of the invisible God" (εἰκόνα τοῦ θεοῦ τοῦ ἀοράτου [Col 1:15]). His language drives home the idea that God is beyond "human comprehension" (ἀνθρωπίνης

---

21. References to *On Perfection* correspond to the page numbers in *Saint Gregory of Nyssa: Ascetical Works* (FC 58; Washington, D.C.: Catholic University of America Press, 1966). Greek citations in what follows are from *Gregorii Nysseni: Opera Ascetica* (ed. Wernerus Jaeger, Johannes P. Cavarnos, and Virginia Woods Callahan; Leiden: Brill, 1986).

22. Interestingly, Gregory uses the term συγχωρέω rather than ἀφίημι. Although Eubank's claim that this term should be translated "yield" is plausible (Eubank, "A Disconcerting Prayer," 531-32), "forgive" would seem to better fit the contrast that Gregory is making, which is also the translation choice of FC (above) and Blum (*Denn Sie Wissen Nicht*, 133); that "forgive" belongs to the semantic domain of συγχωρέω, see Diogenes Laertius, *Lives*, 1.45.

23. It is interesting to note the overlapping hermeneutical assumptions between Augustine's exegesis surveyed in ch. 4 and Gregory's exegesis as laid out by Everett Ferguson, "Some Aspects of Gregory of Nyssa's Interpretation of Scripture Exemplified in His *Homilies on Ecclesiastes*," StPatr 27 (1993): 29-33. For example, Ferguson writes, "consistency with Christian doctrine..., revelation through Christ, applicability to the people of his day, and the goal of Godliness [i.e., virtue] provide the guiding principles of Gregory's interpretation" (31). One can see especially how virtue—or, the "goal of Godliness"—informs his use of Jesus' prayer.

καταλήψεως): being "beyond knowledge (πάσης γνώσεως) and comprehension (κατάληψις), the ineffable (ἄφραστος) and the unspeakable (ἀνεκλάλητος) and the inexpressible (ἀνεκδιήγυτος)" (109-10). Yet, "because of his love for man," Christ took on the human image so that Christians might have something tangible to imitate (109-10).

Gregory then draws a comparison between "imitation" (μιμ– [6x]) and "painting" (ζωγραφ– [4x]), sticking with this analogy for the rest of the passage, with the final word being ζωγραφούμενος. As Gregory explains, just as beginning students learn to paint by looking at a "beautifully executed model" and trying to reduplicate it, so Christians, using "the pure colors of the virtues," should paint their lives according to the perfect model of Christ: "every person is the painter of his own life, and choice is the craftsman of the work, and the virtues are the paints for executing the image" (110).[24] The two virtuous colors that Gregory highlights are meekness (ταπεινοφροσύνη) and patience (μακ–ροθυμία), the latter of which is "quantitatively" (ποσῶς) exemplified in Jesus' prayer for his persecutors: "Father, forgive them, for they know not what they do." In particular, Gregory underscores Jesus' patience by narrating the shocking contrast between Jesus' divine capability (e.g., he could "bring the sky down" on his persecutors) and his graceful suffering (e.g., he prays for those mocking and beating him). By painting one's life with such patience, "each person becomes himself an 'image of the invisible God'" (111).

As regards an evaluation of Gregory's reading, it is noteworthy that Gregory's use of Jesus' prayer employs both a harmonization of the Gospels—e.g., struck with a reed (Matt 27:30; Mark 15:19)—and an ecclesially informed theology that recognizes Christ's divine power—e.g., Jesus' ability to call down Sodomitic fire upon his persecutors. Regarding the latter, Gregory's fleshing out the implications of Jesus' divinity is acceptable for ecclesial readers who assume that Scriptures "assert nothing except the catholic faith" (DDC 3.10). In other words, in an ecclesially located hermeneutic, recognizing that Jesus could call down Sodomitic fire is a natural consequence of reading Scripture through the lens of a regula fidei that asserts that Jesus is divine. Regarding the latter, i.e., Gregory's harmonization of the crucifixion, this is a practice that is better avoided in an ecclesially located exegesis for two reasons. First, harmonizations risk distorting and muffling the authorial communicative intent of the individual book, which we have already noted is important in our exegetical framework. Second, and related, the new narratives produced by harmonizations are not the canonical narratives of the Gospels, and hence cannot hold the same place in an ecclesially located exegesis as Matthew, Mark, Luke, and John; after all, "[t]he authoritative New Testament consists of the Gospels in four books (Matthew, Mark, Luke, John)" (DDC 2.8). In other words, since a narrative framework guides its model readers in how to interpret a text, a harmonized narrative

---

24. As Ferguson notes, such use of illustrations is typical for Gregory who "has a large rhetorical warehouse of contemporary illustrations" ("Gregory of Nyssa's Interpretation," 32).

framework guides readers to different interpretations than do the individual Gospels themselves. The canonization of four distinct narratives and not of their harmonization suggests that the individual narratives are to be given a distinct hearing.[25]

Consequently, the caveat I applied to Origen's reading beyond authorial intent is also true here of Gregory. However, I would contend that Gregory's reading is more palatable than Origen's. In particular, if love of God and neighbor is "the fulfillment and end of the law and all the divine Scriptures" (*DDC* 1.35),[26] and if loving one's neighbor entails loving "the person to whom an act of compassion is due" even if he is an enemy (*DDC* 1.30), then Gregory's reading is a good reading overall, especially insofar as it encourages the imitation of Jesus' enemy-loving patience.

Ambrose of Milan (ca. AD 335-397)
The prayer of Jesus for his persecutors occurs several times in the works of Ambrose, though we will focus on its appearance in *De Joseph* and *De Interpellatione Job et David*.[27] Beginning with the former, Ambrose writes:

> "And they came to him and he said, 'I am Joseph your brother whom you sold into Egypt. Now therefore be not grieved, and let it not seem to you a hard case, that you sold me here; for God sent me before you for life'" [Gen 45:4-5]. What fraternal devotion! What a good brotherly relation! He would even excuse his brothers' crime and say that it was God's providence and not man's unholiness, since He was not offered up to death by men but was sent by the Lord to life. What else is the meaning of that intervention made by our Lord Jesus Christ, who excelled all his brothers in holiness? When he was on the cross, he said in behalf of the people, "Father, forgive them; for they do not know what they are doing." (12.69 [FC])

Ambrose offers throughout this work a hyper-typological reading of the Joseph narrative wherein nearly all of Joseph's actions find their parallels in Jesus' life. As McHugh states, "In this work Joseph appears as a 'mirror of purity' [1.2] and a type-figure of Christ. Each action or event of his history, however slight, is

---

25. Cf. Eugene E. Lemcio, "The Gospels and Canonical Criticism," in *The New Testament as Canon: A Reader in Canonical Criticism* (by Robert W. Wall and Eugene E. Lemcio; JSNTSS 76; Sheffield: JSOT Press, 1992), 35-36.

26. Recall also from ch. 4: "anyone who thinks that he has understood the divine Scriptures or any part of them, but cannot by his understanding build up this double love of God and neighbor, has not yet succeeded in understanding them" (*DDC* 1.36).

27. For brief introductions to these works, see "Ambrose of Milan," in *Handbook of Patristic Exegesis: The Bible in Ancient Christianity* (2 vols.; by Charles Kannengiesser; Leiden: Brill, 2004), 2:1057, 1061.

invested with allegorical meaning."[28] For example, when Joseph invites his brothers, saying, "Come to me" (Gen 45:4), Ambrose links this to the way in which Jesus' incarnation invites people to come to him (12.68). This typological reading continues when Ambrose comes to Gen 45:4-5 where Joseph reveals his true identity to his brothers and ignores their crime against him by claiming that "God sent me before you to preserve life" (Gen 45:5). For Ambrose, Joseph's action corresponds to Jesus' prayer of forgiveness for his persecutors (12.69 [FC]). This typological reading, claims Ambrose, reveals "that we may know that He is the same who spoke before in Joseph and afterward in His own body" (12.70 [FC]).

It is difficult to evaluate Ambrose's typological reading. On the one hand, like the critique of Origen's *Treatise on the Passover*, the ecclesial reader wants to ensure a hearing for so-called literal readings of Scripture. On the other hand, Ambrose's christological framework reminds ecclesially located exegetes to take seriously that Jesus' life accords with Israel's Scriptures. Moreover, not only is Ambrose's reading in line with the rule of faith and the twofold love commandment, but also one finds similar typological readings in the NT canon (e.g., Paul's typological reading of Sarah and Hagar [Gal 4:21-31]). To requote Hays' claim: "There is no possibility of accepting Paul's message while simultaneously rejecting the legitimacy of the scriptural interpretation that sustains it."[29] Consequently, Ambrose's typological reading would seem valid insofar as the ecclesial reader also leaves room to attend to the authorial communicative intent of the Joseph narrative.[30] Unfortunately, as seen below, Ambrose's exegetical framework would not seem to value such literal readings.

In a collection of sermons known as *De Interpellatione Job et David*, Ambrose references Jesus' prayer for his persecutors three times, though only the first reference[31] will be examined in detail:

---

28. Michael P. McHugh, Introduction to *Joseph* (FC 65; Washington, D.C.: Catholic University of America Press, 1972), 188.

29. See ch. 4; Hays, *Echoes of Scripture in the Letters of Paul*, 182.

30. Cf. Christopher R. Seitz, who argues for a Christian exegetical approach to the OT that allows not only the NT's reading of the OT to speak to the church, but also the *per se* voice of the OT to speak to the church via interpretations that are restricted by the rule of faith and the overall canonical witness (*Word without End: The Old Testament as Abiding Theological Witness* [Grand Rapids: Eerdmans, 1998], 3-109). With regard to typological readings, Seitz primarily emphasizes how Israel and the church are types of "the selfsame reality" (8). For this reason, the *per se* voice of an OT text is not limited to any NT reading of it, but it can speak directly to the church from its own literary context.

31. In the second reference, Jesus' prayer is a fulfillment of his teaching to "bless those who curse you." This reference falls within a list of similar actions, such as King David's silence before Shemei's curses and Paul's writing in 1 Cor 4:12, "We are cursed and we bless" (2.6). In the third reference, Ambrose argues that Jesus' use of the title "Father" is text-critical proof that the title "Lord" is not original to Jesus' prayer in Luke 23:46 (6.24). Ambrose references Jesus' prayer for his persecutors in several other works as well. For instance, the prayer reveals Jesus' "great clemency" and also encourages

What are the mountains which God made to grow old [Job 9:5]? ...all the
books of the Old Testament. Jesus the Lord came; he brought the New Testament, and that which was, was made old. The Christian was brought in
new, the Jew grew old; grace was renewed, the letter grew old. God overturned the mountains and altered them. Yes, he overturned and subverted the
understanding according to the letter and established the comprehension that
is of the spirit. Therefore, that understanding of the law that is according to
the flesh has passed away, and the law has become spiritual.... And Jesus
made these mountains grow old, and the Jews know it not. Indeed, had they
known it, they would never have crucified the Lord of majesty.... They, then,
are the ones who know not. For this reason also the Lord Jesus says in the
Gospel, "Father, forgive them, for they know not what they are doing." But
they are not excused for their lack of knowledge, since they do not wish to
know what they should have known.... Granted, he [the Jew] did not know
previously whom he was persecuting. Nevertheless, he should have recognized [him]...[when] the elements trembled beneath him, the sky was darkened, the sun fled away, the earth split apart.... (1.5.13 [FC])

Here, Ambrose expounds on Job's words, "[The Lord] makes mountains to
grow old, and they know it not, and he overturns them in his wrath" (Job 9:5).
As seen in the quotation above, Ambrose makes it absolutely clear that the
"mountains that God made grow old" correspond with the OT and the literal
reading of Scripture (1.5.12 [FC]). The lack of spiritual understanding prevents
the Jews from recognizing whom they crucified and thus Jesus prays for their
forgiveness (1.5.12). Nevertheless, Ambrose avers that the excuse of ignorance
no longer covers their sins, because the events following the crucifixion (e.g.,
the earthquake and darkened sky [1.5.13]) make Jesus' identity unmistakable:
"[They] should have recognized that the one placed on the cross was the Lord of
all the elements. For all the elements trembled beneath him" (1.5.13 [FC]).
Those who do not grasp Jesus' identity are no longer excused because they
stubbornly "do not wish to know what they should have known" (1.5.13 [FC]).
Thus, Ambrose connects ignorance with lack of spiritual reading, and he declares that the excuse of ignorance only applied to the time before the earthquake and the darkening of the sun.

Within our Augustinian-informed exegetical framework, this passage from
De Interpellatione Job et David is problematic at several points. First, as was
claimed above with regard to Origen's *Treatise on the Passover*, the ecclesial
exegete does not devalue literal exegesis, but sees it as essential. Second, also
amiss is Ambrose's claim that the ignorance excuse of Luke 23:34a was not
applicable after the earthquake and darkening of the sun, based on his assumption that these events would make Jesus' identity obvious. Such a reading clash-

---

Christians to bless those who curse them, because an enemy's curse has no power when
one is protected by the "Author of blessing" (*On Valentinian*, 34 [FC]); also Jesus' prayer
fulfills and exceeds the description of love given in 1 Cor 13 (*Commentary on Luke*
5.77).

es with the Lukan account wherein even the disciples do not recognize Jesus' identity after these events (see ch. 5 on Luke 24:1-49). To requote Augustine's counsel: "It often happens that by thoughtlessly asserting something that the author did not mean an interpreter runs up against other things which cannot be reconciled with that original idea. If he agrees that these things are true and certain, his original interpretation could not possibly be true" (*DDC* 1.36). Third, the general tenor of Ambrose's reading is not one that builds up love of neighbor, particularly not love of one's Jewish neighbor. Commenting on this passage and one similar to it in Ambrose's *De Patriarchis* 2.9,[32] McHugh writes: "The tenor of this entire passage (2.9) is regrettable. Some might undertake a defense of Ambrose's attitude here by pointing out that the saint was a man of his time, and by citing evidence of similar passages in other Fathers; the present translator will not."[33] It is unfortunate that Ambrose, an important influence on Augustine, can read Jesus' merciful prayer in such a miserly way, a way that cannot be reconciled with an Augustinian-informed interpretive framework.

John Chrysostom (ca. AD 350-407)
Jesus' prayer in Luke 23:34a shows up in Chrysostom's eighteenth and sixtieth *Homily on Matthew*. The former reads:

> Hate not then the man that doeth thee wrong.... "But how," saith one, "is it possible for this to take place?" Having seen God become man and descend so far, and suffer so much for thy sake, dost thou still inquire and doubt, how it is possible to forgive thy fellow-servants their injuriousness? Hearest thou not him on the cross, saying, "Forgive them, for they know not what they do?" ...Seest thou not that even after the cross, and after he had been received up, he sent the apostles unto the Jews that had slain him, to bring them his ten thousand blessings...? But hast thou been greatly wronged? Nay, what hast thou endured like thy Lord, bound, beaten with whips, with rods, spit upon by servants, enduring death, and that death, which is of all deaths the most shameful...? (18.5-6 [*NPNF*[1]])

When Golden Mouth comes to the Sermon on the Mount in his *Homilies on Matthew*, he expects his audience to take literally Jesus' teaching of non-retaliation.[34] Consequently, while expounding on Matt 5:38-45 (esp. vv. 43-45:

---

32. A brief excerpt from *De Patriarchis* 2.9 will suffice: "And really, who is so stiff and insolent and abusive as the people of the Jews? ...when they could not deny [Jesus'] godlike works, they lashed him with scourges and fastened him with nails" [FC].

33. McHugh, notes on *De Patriarchis* (FC 65), 246-47n. 5.

34. For a concise account of Chrystostom's exegetical practice in his sermons on the Gospels, which highlights such issues as his preference for literal interpretation and his consequent focus on ethical exhortation, see Thomas R. McKibbens, "The Exegesis of John Chrystostom: Homilies on the Gospels," *ExpTim* 93 (1982): 264-70; cf. Amy S.

"...love your enemies, and pray for them which despitefully use you: bless them that curse you, do good to them that hate you...for [your Father] maketh his sun to rise on the evil and the good..." [18.4 {*NPNF*[1]}]), Chrysostom puts forward several reasons why Christians should literally practice this behavior. First, Chrysostom believes that only good can overcome evil: "it is said, 'ought we not to resist the evil one?' Indeed we ought...as he hath commanded, by giving one's self up to suffer wrongfully; for thus shalt thou prevail over him. For one fire is not quenched by another, but fire by water" (18.1 [*NPNF*[1]]). Second, and related, a motif running throughout his eighteenth homily is the idea that mercy and non-retaliation can actually convert one's persecutors: e.g., "it not only restrains [the wrongdoers] from rushing onward, but works upon them also to repent...even as avenging one's self does just the contrary" (18.1 [*NPNF*[1]]); "consider what a lesson [the wrongdoer] will get...to scorn vice and to seek after virtue" (18.2 [*NPNF*[1]]). Third, practicing such teachings simultaneously allows virtue to grow and vice to decrease. Thus, taking seriously Jesus' teachings allows vice to be "pull[ed] up by the roots" (e.g., "he that is persecuted and suffers insults...is practicing of course entire contempt of things present, and is clear from pride and vainglory" [18.8 {*NPNF*[1]}]). Further, virtue is enabled to grow as one progresses from non-retaliation alone to non-retaliation accompanied by prayer: "[Jesus] goes on to say, 'pray for them which despitefully use you:' leading us to the very highest summit of self control" (18.8 [*NPNF*[1]]; cf. 18.4). Fourth, to those who think that this teaching is too hard, Chrysostom notes that Jesus has done something far greater than what his disciples are called to do. Jesus, the master, was cursed by slaves, yet he not only prays, "Forgive them, for they know not what they do," but after he is crucified he sends his disciples "to bring them his ten thousand blessings"; in contrast, Christians are only enduring the slander of "fellow-slaves" (18.5 [*NPNF*[1]]). "[S]urely in no respect is the case parallel, not only because of the surpassing nature of his benefits, but also by reason of the excellence of his dignity" (18.5 [*NPNF*[1]]). Thus, the example of Jesus in Luke 23:34a confirms and illustrates Chrysostom's exhortation from Matt 5:43-45. It is also noteworthy that, while not making an explicit connection to the excuse of ignorance, Chrysostom may have this in mind when he exhorts Christians to be understanding and merciful toward their enemies who are like the insane: "the physicians, when they are kicked, and shamefully handled by the insane, then most of all pity them, and take measures for their perfect cure, knowing that the insult comes of the extremity of their disease...Yea, for if we see persons possessed by devils, we weep for them; we do not seek to be ourselves also possessed" (18.6 [*NPNF*[1]]).[35] Love of enemies and non-

---

McCormick, "John Chrysostom's Homily 50 as an Example of the Antiochene Exegetical Tradition," *PatByzRev* 12 (1993): 70-71.

35. On such use of imagery as the "hallmark" of Chrysostom's homilies, see Pamela Jackson, "John Chrysostom's Use of Scripture in Initiatory Preaching," *GOTR* 35 (1990): 359-63.

retaliation, then, become the prescription that can help bring one's diseased persecutors to health (18.1).

It would seem that Chrysostom offers here a good ecclesially located reading of Luke 23:34a (and perhaps of Matt 5:38-43, though that is beyond the scope of this work). Jesus' prayer for his persecutors primarily functions as support for another reading, which is a legitimate and necessary function for Scripture in an Augustinian-informed hermeneutic. Chrysostom's comment about bringing Jesus' ten thousand blessings to "the Jews that had slain him" is coherent with the Lukan text insofar as such Jews are not identified with all Jews, but those Jews specified as responsible for the crucifixion in Luke-Acts (specifically, the Jewish leaders and Jerusalem inhabitants [see ch. 5]).

Particularly noteworthy is the degree to which Chrysostom's exegesis is shaped by love of enemies—a chief end of an ecclesially located reading. There is little doubt when reading his eighteenth homily that loving one's enemies goes beyond not desiring bad for them, and extends to desiring good for them (e.g., hoping for their repentance). Jesus' prayer for his persecutors' forgiveness becomes an illustration of just such enemy-love. Further, by seeing Luke 23:34a in light of ecclesially informed christology that attests to Jesus' divinity, Chrysostom amplifies the shocking mercy of Christ's prayer: "Having seen *God become [hu]man, and descend so far*, and suffer so much for thy sake, dost thou still inquire and doubt, how it is possible to forgive thy fellow-servants their injuriousness?" (*Homilies on Matthew* 18.5). If anything, what is most unpalatable about this homily from Chrysostom is the extent to which it convicts the reader. It is perhaps *too* good an ecclesially located reading.

In his sixtieth *Homily on Matthew*, Chrysostom writes:

> Therefore I say, he who thus loves inquires not about race, nor country, nor wealth, nor his love to himself…but though he be hated, though he be insulted, though he be slain, continues to love, having as a sufficient ground for love, Christ…. And those even that crucified [Christ], and acted in so many instances with contumely against him, see how he continues to treat with kindness. For even to his father he speaks for them, saying, "Father, forgive them, for they know not what they do." And he sent his disciples moreover, after these things, unto them. This love then let us also imitate. (60.3 [*NPNF*[1]])

In this passage, Chrysostom is expounding on Matt 18:20 ("For where two or three are gathered in my name, there I am in the midst of them"). Specifically, he is concerned with the motives of those who gather together: "For not merely of the assembling doth [Jesus] speak…but most surely…the rest of virtue together with this" (60.3 [*NPNF*[1]]). Chrysostom explains that often a person loves another because he receives a "worldly" benefit from the relationship: "For one loves, because he is loved, another because he hath been honored…" (60.3 [*NPNF*[1]]). Yet, such love disappears because the "temporal" benefit of the relationship ceases (60.3). In contrast, "love for Christ's sake is firm, and not to be broken, and impregnable, and nothing can tear it asunder"; rather "he who thus loves inquires not about race, nor country, nor wealth, nor his love to himself...but though he be hated, though he be insulted, though he be slain, continues to love, having as a sufficient ground for love, Christ" (60.3 [*NPNF*[1]]). Exemplifying such resilient love is Christ, who not only prays for his crucifiers— "Father, forgive them, for they know not what they do"—but also sends his disciples to these very persons (60.3).

As with Chrysostom's reading of Luke 23:34a in his eighteenth homily, this too may be a good ecclesially located reading. It does not exhort readers to some generic love, but to the selfless and "impregnable" love of Christ. As mentioned in ch. 4, loving one's neighbor is a benchmark for proper interpretation, and is characterized by Augustine in a way congruent with Chrysostom's description here—namely, as loving another person "more than our own bodies," loving "the person to whom an act of compassion is due" even if he is an enemy, and having the same compassion for others as God had for oneself (*DDC* 1.27, 30). Furthermore, Chrysostom's reading coheres with the Lukan text wherein Jesus does indeed send his disciples to those who crucified him (e.g., Luke 24:47; Acts 3:12-21). In fact, had Chrysostom focused on Luke's Gospel, he would have found even more support for his claim that Christian love "inquires not about race, nor country, nor wealth." Examples abound where those who would be considered low-status in their socio-cultural milieu are dignified and loved, even though they might seem to have little to offer (e.g., the widow at Nain [7:11-17]; the sinful woman [7:36-50]; the children blessed by Jesus [18:15-17]). Rightly, therefore, Chrysostom exhorts: "This love then let us also imitate, unto this let us look" (60.3 [*NPNF*[1]]).[36] What is perhaps missing in Chrysostom's teaching on Matt 18:20 is a more explicit interaction with the *Matthean* text (e.g., how Matthew addresses the matters of gathering together and the foundation for loving others). As already mentioned, the ecclesially located reader prioritizes authorial communicative intent; at the same time, such a reader recognizes that the human author's voice may not be the most necessary voice for one's context. Consequently, it is entirely plausible that Chrysostom's reading of Matt 18:20, in which he references Jesus' enduring love in Luke 23:34a, was the best reading for Chrysostom's particular audience. In other words, it may have been the reading that would best build faith, hope, and love. As Augustine writes in his *Confessions*, "Lord, point out either [the author's] meaning or such other true meaning as pleases you. Hence, whether you uncover the same meaning to us as to your servant [the author], or some other meaning ...you will still nourish us and error will not delude us" (12.32).

---

36. For further references to Luke 23:34a by Chrysostom, see Blum, *Denn Sie Wissen Nicht*, 153-59; Eubank, "A Disconcerting Prayer," 529, 535.

Leo the Great (Pope from AD 440-461)
In *Sermon* 65, Leo addresses the ignorance of the crucifiers:[37]

> Wherefore, the merciful Lord Jesus—who wanted to save even his murderers by his death—prayed from the height of the cross for the ignorance of those raging against him, saying, "Father, forgive them, for they know not what they do." Not by the understanding of their heart, nor by the hearing of their ear, nor by the sight of their eyes did they perceive who it was they had assailed…. They do not recognize in his human body the substance of divinity. They saw him to be lowly. They did not worship him as maker of the universe. Disparaging the meekness of the one who had been judged, they did not understand the power of the one who would judge. One wickedness joined the persecution of true God and the rejection of true man. (65.3 [FC])

Leo states at the beginning of this sermon that he aims to "counteract the effrontery of wicked error," namely, the error of "[t]hose who deny that the Son of God took on the true nature of our flesh" so that "the cross of Christ was either the pretense of an imaginary being or a punishment endured by the divinity" (65.1 [FC]). According to Leo, such claims are incompatible with "Catholic integrity," which "confesses one Christ, both God and man, in such a way that it cannot say either that the man was false or that God was capable of suffering" (65.1 [FC]). Murphy writes, "On one truth Leo is absolute and unbending—that Jesus Christ was of two natures, the divine and human…. This theological insight underlies his every thought."[38] Leo goes on to argue that this dual nature of Christ is necessary for human salvation: "Certainly a mere semblance would have been worthless, and the appearance of suffering would not have benefited anyone, had true divinity not clothed itself with the true feelings of human flesh. Son of God and of a human being…he renewed our mortal essence through his immortal one" (65.2 [FC]).

Leo explains that, though the divinity cannot suffer, the human suffering of Jesus "redounded" in a sense onto the divinity; so Paul writes: "For if they had known, they would never have crucified the Lord of Majesty" (65.3 [FC], quoting 1 Cor 2:8). The reference to the crucifiers' ignorance in 1 Cor 2:8 leads to a quotation of Jesus' prayer "for the ignorance of those raging against him" (65.3). Although Leo makes a brief comment that the Jews were "blinded in their mal-

---

37. Regarding Leo's exegetical framework, Kannengiesser writes, "Leo shows little consciousness of specific hermeneutical concerns. He mentions scripture only for the purpose of quoting it" ("Leo I, The Great," in *Handbook of Patristic Exegesis: The Bible in Ancient Christianity* [2 vols.; by Charles Kannengiesser; Leiden: Brill, 2004], 2:1288); for recurring themes and theology that, nevertheless, seems to guide Leo's use of Scripture, see Francis X. Murphy, "The Sermons of Pope Leo the Great: Content and Style," in *Preaching in the Patristic Age: Studies in Honor of Walter J. Burghart, S.J.* (ed. David G. Hunter; New York: Paulist, 1989), 183-97.

38. Murphy, "The Sermons of Pope Leo," 185.

ice," his emphasis is placed on how the crucifiers' ignorance resulted from a misperception of Jesus' lowliness: "They saw him to be lowly...[and disparaged] the meekness of the one who had been judged" (65.3).[39] Apparently the crucifiers could not reconcile Jesus' lowliness with his "divinity," his meekness with his identity as "maker of the universe" and "judge" (65.3). Leo closes his sermon by restating the necessity of acknowledging the humanity and divinity of Jesus, which is essential for the hope that "what had been initiated in the head is to be completed also in the members" (65.4-5 [FC]).

Much of Leo's use of Luke 23:34a fits well in an ecclesially located hermeneutic. For instance, it is clear from this survey of *Sermon* 65 that Leo would agree with Augustine that "[Scripture] asserts nothing except the catholic faith" (*DDC* 3.10). By reading through an ecclesial lens that recognizes Jesus' divinity, Leo interprets the crucifiers' ignorance as more far-reaching than is explicit in Luke. As argued in ch. 5, the crucifiers of Luke 23:34a appear ignorant of Jesus' identity as *Messiah, king,* and *savior.* Leo, however, states that they are blind to his identity as *the divine judge and creator.* As was the case above with Gregory's reading, Leo's christologically informed reading is also legitimate, being a natural consequence of reading Scripture through the rule of faith. Nevertheless, one should not overlook the Lukan focus either. Thus, if Leo were to take seriously Jesus' identity as (*Israel's*) Messiah, it might curb some of the regrettable language and tone here and elsewhere by which the Jewish people are addressed (e.g., "Jews, blinded in their malice..." [65.3]; cf. 35.2). As for Leo's interpretation of the crucifiers' ignorance, specifically that it resulted from a misperception of Jesus' lowliness, this is in line with the authorial communicative intent (see ch. 5) and is, accordingly, a good reading. In sum, Leo's use of Luke 23:34a in *Sermon* 65 reminds the ecclesially located reader of the benefits of paying attention to both tradition and text.

Augustine, Sermon 317 (ca. AD 425)

Fittingly, our survey concludes with Augustine, who refers to Luke 23:34a four times in his *Sermon* 317. The primary focus of his sermon is to convince listeners to carry out Jesus' teaching to love one's enemies, because "among the great and salutary instructions...people think this one is very hard" (317.1 [WSA]). To persuade his audience, he offers the examples of God, Jesus, and Stephen. Thus, Augustine reminds his audience that God lets bad people experience his blessings, citing Matt 5:44-45 as evidence: "Love your enemies...that you may be children of your Father...who makes his sun rise on the good and the bad, and sends rain upon the just and the unjust" (317.1). Having shown God loving his enemies, he turns to the example of Jesus who "came into the world as a lover of his enemies" and "[w]ith his blood he wiped out his enemies'

---

39. Cf. Leo's *Sermon* 70.3: "What, then, was it that both took away the understanding of the Jews and disturbed the hearts of 'the wise of the world' [1 Cor 1:19-20]? What else beside the Cross of God's Son, which both made the prudence of philosophers vanish and caused the teaching of the Israelites to become blurred?" (FC).

sins…[and] made friends out of his enemies" (317.2 [WSA]). As a specific example of Jesus' love for his enemies, Augustine points to Luke 23:34a:

> Yet the Lord himself was the first to show on the cross what his instructions
> were. With the Jews, you see, howling at him from all sides, furious, mock-
> ing, jeering, crucifying him, he could still say, *Father , forgive them, for they
> do not know what they are doing*; after all, it's blindness that is crucifying
> me. Blindness was crucifying him; and the crucified was making an eye-salve
> for them from his blood. (317.2 [WSA])

Although Jesus' prayer is obviously an example of enemy-love, Augustine could
have additionally pointed to Lukan passages such as Luke 6:27-28 ("Love your
enemies…pray for those who abuse you") to show how the text itself prepares
the readers for such an enemy-loving response from Jesus. Further, regarding
Augustine's references here and below to the Jewish persecutors, such a reading
is textually coherent with Jesus' prayer in Luke 23:34a insofar as these Jewish
persecutors are limited to the Jewish leaders and the Jerusalem inhabitants
(see ch. 5).[40]

Having held up the example of Jesus' prayer, Augustine immediately prepares for the counterargument that humans cannot do what the divine did:

> But people who are reluctant to carry out [this] precept…don't pay attention
> to the Lord, who would have had nobody left to praise him, if he had wanted
> to avenge himself on his enemies. So when they hear this place in the gospel,
> where the Lord says on the cross, *Father, forgive them, because they do not
> know what they are doing*, they say to themselves, "He could do that, as the
> Son of God…. Yes it was flesh hanging there, but God was hidden within. As
> for us, though, what are we, to do that sort of thing." (317.3 [WSA])

In response, Augustine points to Stephen, a mere Christian human: "He was
born in the same way as you…from the same source…of the same Spirit…redeemed by the same price…capable of just as much as you" (317.3
[WSA]).[41] Augustine's linking Jesus' prayer with Stephen's is certainly a proper
reading, not least because the Lukan parallels between Jesus' and Stephen's
martyrdoms nearly necessitate such a comparison (see ch. 2 for other parallels
such as a cry with a great voice [Luke 23:46; Acts 7:60], seeing Jesus/Son of

---

40. One wishes that Augustine had said more about how Jesus' blood became the
"eye-salve" for the crucifiers' blindness. As it is, he only makes this passing comment,
then moves on.

41. To be clear, "it wasn't from himself that [Stephen] got the capacity" to love his
enemies; but neither was it from a source to which he had exclusive access: "It's a common spring; drink from where he drank. He received it as a free gift from God. The one
who gave it has plenty more" (317.4 [WSA]).

Man at the right hand [Luke 22:69; Acts 7:55], and the prayer of committing one's spirit [Luke 23:46; Acts 7:59]). Whether Augustine's linkage of these prayers results from a close reading of Luke-Acts is, however, not specified.

Although Augustine does not state it explicitly, he may be anticipating another rebuttal wherein those who do not want to love their enemies counter by citing Jesus' and Stephen's severe rebukes of their adversaries (see examples below), which might not seem enemy-loving. Such readings, however, would be misreadings, for they do not take into account other Scriptures:

> The Lord had some harsh and bitter rebukes for the Jews, but it was out of love. *Woe to you, scribes and Pharisees, hypocrites!* (Matt 23:13). When he was saying all that, wouldn't anybody say that he hated them? It came to the cross, and he said, *Father, forgive them, because they do not know what they are doing.* In the same way Stephen too first rebuked them savagely...*Stiff-necked, and uncircumcised of hearts and ears...*(Acts 7:51-52).... His tongue is shouting, his heart is loving. (317.5 [WSA])

In light of Augustine's belief that Scripture builds up one's love for enemies, it is not surprising that he directs his audience to interpret Jesus' and Stephen's stern rebukes with reference to their love for those very persons to whom they spoke harshly. Thus, *Scripture helps interpret Scripture according to a hermeneutical paradigm that prioritizes love for one's enemies!*

Lastly, Augustine notes the parallel prayers coming from the mouths of the two dying martyrs:

> [Stephen] proved to be a true imitator of the Lord's passion, and a perfect disciple of Christ, completing in his own passion what he had heard from the master. The Lord, you see, while hanging on the cross, had said, *Father, forgive them, because they do not know what they are doing.* And the blessed Stephen, when he was already almost buried under the stones, spoke like this: *Lord Jesus, do not hold this sin against them* (Acts 7:60). Oh, what an apostolic man, already from being a disciple become a master! It was necessary, after all, for the first martyr of Christ to follow the teaching of the Master. (317.6 [WSA])[42]

Once again, Augustine points to Stephen as a model for his hearers. As Stephen imitates the Lord, so they should imitate Stephen.[43] As mentioned above, the Lukan parallels between Jesus' and Stephen's death invite such a comparison.

---

42. Cf. Bovon, *Lukas*, 474.

43. Interestingly, Augustine suggests that there is proof that Stephen's prayer was answered—namely, Saul, who stood by the coats of Stephen's executioners and was soon after commissioned by the Lord (Acts 7:58; 9:4-18).

By means of this parallel between Christ and a Christ-follower, the Lukan text shows its Christian readers that they too are called to imitate Christ, which is the very point that Augustine is making throughout this sermon. Again, whether Augustine draws these parallels from a close analysis of Luke-Acts is unclear. What is clear, however, is that Augustine's *Sermon* 317 offers a valuable ecclesially located reading of Luke 23:34a, one that certainly builds up love of one's enemies.

Summary

In sum, this chapter has attempted to appreciate and evaluate the various ways that the Fathers read Luke 23:34a:

- Irenaeus reasons from Jesus' prayer that Christ did suffer as a human; otherwise the suffering one would be greater than the one who flew away. His reading, supported by other scriptural texts, the rule of faith, and textual coherency was seen as a good ecclesially located reading.
- Origen reads this text 1) as proof that an entire congregation can sin in ignorance, and 2) as pointing to the crucifiers' ignorance of spiritual readings of scriptural texts. The latter reading received the most attention, being challenged in its devaluing of literal readings, and being cautioned about its inattention to the Lukan cotext.
- Gregory puts forward Jesus' prayer as the supreme model of patience that Christians are to imitate, painting their own lives with such virtue. His harmonizing of the crucifixion was called into question, whereas his reading through ecclesial lenses (e.g., seeing Christ as divine) was seen as suitable for a Christian reading. Most importantly, however, Gregory's reading rightly built up love for one's neighbor, particularly one's enemies.
- Ambrose brings Luke 23:34a into conversation with the OT via the Joseph narrative and Job. The former results in a hyper-typological reading where Joseph's actions point to Jesus. Such a reading is acceptable insofar as it 1) is in line with our aforementioned ecclesially located delimiters, and 2) allows privileged space for attending to the authorial communicative intent. However, Ambrose's *De Interpellatione Job et David* claims that literal readings of the OT are no longer useful, which clashes with our ecclesially located exegetical paradigm. Also problematic are both Ambrose's textually incoherent limitation of the excuse of ignorance as well as his ungraceful tenor that would seem to undermine love of one's neighbor.
- By reading Luke 23:34a through an ecclesial lens that acknowledges Jesus' divinity, Chrysostom further reveals the depths of Christ's love for his enemies, which is an example of the enemy-love that Christians should practice. He also offers Jesus' prayer as an illustration of the resilient love that should characterize Christians who gather together. Given the extent to which both of Chrysostom's readings exhort love

for one's enemies, they would seem to be good ecclesially located readings. One area that might be questioned, however, was in *Homily*
60 where Chrysostom did not include the Matthean perspective on a
Matthean text.

- Leo, clearly reading within a *regula fidei*, explains that the crucifiers'
  ignorance in Luke 23:34a resulted from an inability to reconcile Jesus'
  lowliness with his divinity. Although this reading can find coherence
  with the Lukan text, it was nonetheless suggested that it could have
  benefited from paying more attention to the Lukan cotext. Specifically,
  by recognizing how the cotext also points to the crucifiers' ignorance of
  Jesus' identity as *Israel's Messiah*, it might have altered the seemingly
  harsh way that Leo addresses the Jewish people in his *Sermon 65*.

- Lastly, Augustine points to Jesus' prayer to persuade his audience to
  practice enemy-love. For those who think this too difficult, Augustine
  helpfully points to the parallel prayer of Stephen to show that humans
  can indeed love their enemies in such a way. Most notably, Augustine
  reveals how scriptural texts are mutually interpreting within an exegetical framework that prioritizes love (e.g., texts such as Matt 23:13
  ["Woe to you, scribes and Pharisees"] must be understood with reference to texts such as Luke 23:34a ["Father, forgive them, for they know
  not what they do"]).

Conclusion

The present chapter was an attempt to take seriously the polysemy of Scripture
by attending to the various patristic readings of Jesus' prayer in Luke 23:34a:
"Father, forgive them, for they know not what they do." The Augustinian-
informed, ecclesially located framework took this chapter in a different direction
than that of Blum who primarily focused on the Fathers' (alleged) misreading of
our text (that implied Jewish culpability by applying Jesus' forgiveness to them),
which he attempted to correct by appeal to the findings of historical-critical research. In contrast, this chapter has been a case study in gaining forgotten or
undervalued insight into our text, while simultaneously delimiting certain readings within an ecclesially informed interpretive paradigm. Thus, our survey revealed how the patristic authors read this text in various ways, finding in it such
things as Jesus' grace, his exemplary love for enemies, his tie with OT texts, and
his concurrent divinity and humanity. An attempt was also made to shed light on
places where the patristic readings needed to be challenged or supplemented,
such as wrongful characterizations of the Jews, devaluing literal readings of
Scripture, and neglecting the Lukan cotext of Jesus' prayer.

In the following chapter, I will conclude our study by summarizing the preceding chapters and offering Martin Luther King Jr.'s sermon on Luke 23:34a as
a helpful example of a contemporary ecclesially located reading.

7

Summary, Conclusion, and a Contemporary Exemplar

Summary

This study opened by highlighting the various ambiguities associated with Luke 23:34a. Is this text original? Does it contain an intertextual echo, and if so, with what Scripture(s): Isa 53:12, Lev 5:18, or some other text? What is the nature of the persecutors' misunderstanding: lack of knowledge or misperception? What socio-cultural presuppositions are present in this text: the clemency practices of emperors, God's working through unintentional sinners, or something else? Who is forgiven: the Romans, the Jewish leaders, the Jewish people, or some combination? What does, or what can, this text mean? How does one evaluate readings of scriptural texts?

Accordingly, in ch. 2, I argued for the originality of Luke 23:34a. I showed that the external evidence was balanced, particularly when one notes the likelihood that certain second- and third-century Fathers were quoting Luke and not a logion from the tradition. The internal evidence, however, was noticeably Lukan, thus indicating the text's originality.

In ch. 3, I challenged the notion that proper readings of scriptural texts are limited exclusively by historical-critical research and/or authorial intent and/or the interpretations of early readers: the details about the Scriptures' early audiences are too limited to know precisely how early readers would have read the texts; the gap between ancient authors and readers combined with the inherent equivocality of language means that the author's intent cannot be known with certainty; and even if one could know the author's intent or the early readers' interpretations, there are no certainly verifiable norms that prohibit (scriptural) texts from being interpreted in ways that go beyond those parameters. Because all reading strategies come with biases attached, I claimed that Christians should read scriptural texts from an ecclesial location, from the bias of Christian faith.

Hence, ch. 4 offered an example of what an ecclesially located reading might look like by starting with Augustine's *De Doctrina Christiana*. In brief, Augustine calls for interpreters to approach Scripture humbly and submissively, to attach special importance to authorial communicative intent, and to allow for polysemic readings that are bounded by the rule of faith, the twofold love commandment, and clearer canonical texts. The *a priori* theological convictions assumed in *DDC* led to an interpretive paradigm that was seen to be at odds with

113

both Räisänen's foundation of modern historical criteria and Stendahl's exclusive privileging of authorial intent.

Next, in light of the importance of authorial communicative intent in *DDC*, ch. 5 argued for the most textually coherent reading of the ambiguities of Luke 23:34a. Specifically, it was demonstrated:

1) that the cotext indicates that the persecutors' misunderstanding is best interpreted as a misperception of Jesus' paradoxical identity and ministry—exemplified by the cross;

2) that the larger story of Luke-Acts attests a) that the Jewish leaders and Jerusalem inhabitants are the primary referents of Jesus' prayer with the Roman actors being less emphasized, and b) that misperceiving the cross is linked not only with untransformed minds and untransformed exegesis but also with the fulfillment of God's purposes; and

3) that linguistic, thematic, and socio-cultural evidence suggest that the most likely intertextual echo in Luke 23:34a is to the Pentateuchal laws on unintentional sin (esp. Lev 5:18).

Finally, ch. 6 was an attempt to deal with the polysemy of our text through a case study of patristic readings. From this case study we learned not only that the Fathers may have benefited from sticking closer to the Lukan cotext, but also that this single text has a rich history, able to speak in diverse ways to diverse contexts in ways that build up faith, hope, and love. The following section brings our study closer to the present, by looking at a helpful example of how Luke 23:34a might be read from an ecclesially located perspective in a more contemporary context.

Martin Luther King Jr.'s Sermon on Luke 23:34a

In the last book of *DDC*, Augustine writes, "There are two things on which all interpretation of scripture depends: the process of discovering what we need to learn, and the process of presenting what we have learnt" (*DDC* 4.1).[1] Augustine goes on to describe a good presenter: "The aim of our orator...is to be listened to with understanding, with pleasure, and with obedience" (*DDC* 4.15). Such would seem a fitting introduction to the preaching of Martin Luther King Jr..

Few contemporary writings on Luke 23:34a seem to carry the impact and authority as those of Martin Luther King Jr.'s "Love in Action." Perhaps this is because King reads Jesus' prayer for his persecutors through the lens of one undergoing persecution. He writes, "I have known very few quiet days in the

---

1. Although beyond our scope, theological interpretation would seem incomplete if it ends at the process of discovery. As James Andrews writes, "Augustine reminds interpreters that reading is not an end in itself. Grasping the sense of the text is not enough.... It is simply the first half of it" ("Relevant Augustine: What *De Doctrina Christiana* Says Today," StPatr 50 [2011], 319).

last few years. I have been imprisoned in Alabama and Georgia jails twelve times. My home has been bombed twice. A day seldom passes that my family and I are not the recipients of threats of death. I have been the victim of a near-fatal stabbing."[2] Even the sermon we are studying, "Love in Action," was composed from jail.[3]

In what follows we will examine King's reading of Luke 23:34a. Along the way, we will note 1) where his reading strategy is in line with our ecclesially located hermeneutic, 2) where his reading could possibly be enhanced by our ecclesially located hermeneutic, and 3) where his reading is similar to certain patristic readings from the previous chapter. This survey reveals that, in this sermon, King appears on the whole to model what I have sketched as an ecclesially located hermeneut, one who reads along with the biblical author, interprets via the church's faith-informed lenses, and most importantly uses Scripture to build up love for one's neighbors, especially one's enemies.

King delivered this sermon in a context he describes as "these turbulent days of uncertainty [when] the evils of war and of economic and racial injustice threaten the very survival of the human race."[4] The sermon opens with the following statement: "Few words in the NT more clearly and solemnly express the magnanimity of Jesus' spirit than the sublime utterance from the cross, 'Father, forgive them; for they know not what they do.' This is love at its best."[5] Demonstrating how this is "love at its best," King explains:

> We shall not fully understand the great meaning of Jesus' prayer unless we first notice that the text opens with the word "then." The verse immediately preceding reads thus: "And when they were come to the place, which is called Calvary, there they crucified him with two malefactors, one on the right hand, and the other on the left." Then said Jesus, "Father, forgive them." *Then*—when he was being plunged into the abyss of nagging agony. *Then*—when man had stooped to his worst. *Then*—when he was dying, a most ignominious death. *Then*—when the wicked hands of the creature had dared to crucify the only begotten Son of the Creator. Then said Jesus, "Father, forgive them." That "then" might well have been otherwise. He could have said, "Father, get even with them," or "Father, let loose the mighty thunderbolts of righteous wrath and destroy them" or "Father, open the flood gates of justice and permit the staggering avalanche of retribution to pour upon them." But none of these was his response. Though subjected to inexpressible agony,

---

2. King, *Strength to Love*, 152.

3. Ibid., 11.

4. Ibid.

5. Ibid., 39. Cf. also his sermon, "Levels of Love," where King notes that Jesus' love of his enemies is an example of the highest form love (in *The Papers of Martin Luther King, Jr: Advocate of the Social Gospel, September 1948-March 1963* [vol. 6; ed. Clayborne Carson; Berkeley: University of California Press, 2007], 442).

suffering excruciating pain, and despised and rejected, nevertheless, he cried,
"Father, forgive them."[6]

By highlighting the simple term "then," King focuses his readers on the immediate cotext of v. 34a, specifically the preceding verse ("...they crucified him..."
[v. 33]). Rightly, then, he shows how the text itself frames the prayer to reveal
the depths of Jesus' forgiveness. King's reading also suggests an awareness of
socio-cultural matters, such as recognizing that crucifixion was not simply pain-
ful, but humiliating ("ignominious") as well.[7] King, however, likely moving
beyond the Lukan text, notes that the one being crucified was "the begotten Son
of the Creator."[8] As with Gregory and Chrysostom who read Luke 23:34a in
light of ecclesial convictions about Jesus' identity, so too King would seem to
read the prayer appropriately in light of the church's witness to Jesus' identity as
the begotten Son of the Father. By doing so, he underscores the magnitude of
Jesus' compassion, for the creator's son forgives the created.

Having introduced this text, King hopes to make two points. First, Jesus'
prayer is "a marvelous expression of Jesus' ability to match words with actions."
King notes how Jesus has already taught "that there is no limit to forgiveness"
by telling Peter to forgive the one who sins against him "seventy times seven"
times (Matt 18:21-22 [KJV]).[9] Further, "Jesus also admonished his followers to
love their enemies and to pray for them that despitefully used them" (Luke 6:27-
28; Matt 5:44 [KJV]).[10] If King were quoting Luke 6:27-28 here instead of likely quoting Matt 5:44,[11] he would rightly note how the *Lukan* text prepares its
readers for Jesus' response from the cross, thereby avoiding any problems that
might come with conflating the Matthean and Lukan narratives.[12] With his characteristic talent for words, King captures the drama of Luke 23:34a:

> The moment of testing emerges. Christ, the innocent Son of God, is stretched
> in painful agony on an uplifted cross. What place is there for love and for-
> giveness now? How will Jesus react? What will he say? The answer to these
> questions bursts forth in majestic splendor. Jesus lifts his thorn-crowned head

---

6. King, *Strength to Love*, 39 (italics original).

7. Cf. Augustine, who claims, "we must pay careful attention to the conduct appropriate to different, places, times, and persons..." (*DDC* 3.12-15). Although Augustine's
teaching on socio-cultural awareness is intended to prevent misinterpretation, it would
nonetheless seem to apply to proper interpretation of the authorial communicative intent.

8. The language of "begotten" is possibly Lukan (Acts 13:33), though it is more
characteristically Johannine (John 1:14, 18; 3:16, 18).

9. King, *Strength to Love*, 40.

10. Ibid., 41.

11. King does not specify whether he is referencing Matthew or Luke; the former is
suggested by King's citing this text as Matthean in a later sermon (ibid., 49).

12. For problems related to conflating gospel narratives, see the commentary on
Gregory of Nyssa in ch. 6.

and cries in words of cosmic proportions: "Father, forgive them, for they know not what they do." This was Jesus' finest hour; this was his heavenly response to his earthly rendezvous with destiny.[13]

Recalling our survey in ch. 6, one sees parallels between King's reading and the Fathers. Like Irenaeus, King recognizes that Luke 23:34a illustrates Jesus practicing his own teachings. Like Chrysostom, King expects his readers to practice what Jesus teaches and models, as it is the only hope of overcoming evil: "[Jesus] did not seek to overcome evil with evil. He overcame evil with good. Although crucified by hate, he responded with aggressive love.... [E]ver and again this noble lesson of Calvary will be a nagging reminder that only goodness can drive out evil and only love can conquer hate."[14] And like Augustine, King avers throughout *Strength to Love* that such teachings are not overly idealistic, but must be imitated. Clearly, King's reading builds up love of one's enemies.[15]

The second point King hopes to draw from Luke 23:34a regards "Jesus' awareness of man's intellectual and spiritual blindness."[16] King focuses on how those "who cried 'Crucify him' were not bad men but rather blind men."[17] This leads him to give example after example throughout history of how "sincere" people committed evil even while assuming they were doing good (e.g., Saul's persecuting Christians; the church's persecuting Copernicus).[18] In his own context, King notes how supporters of segregation can be "sincere in their beliefs and earnest in their motives" with the result that they ignorantly perpetuate evil while thinking they are doing good. Recognizing their ignorance, one forgives them:

---

13. Ibid., 41.

14. Ibid., 42; Chrysostom writes, "it is said, 'ought we not to resist the evil one?' Indeed we ought...as he hath commanded, by giving one's self up to suffer wrongfully; for thus shalt thou prevail over him. For one fire is not quenched by another, but fire by water" (*Homilies on Matthew* 18.1 [*NPNF*[1]]).

15. A stirring example of King's call to enemy-love is found later in *Strength to Love*: "To our most bitter opponents we say: We shall match your capacity to inflict suffering by our capacity to endure suffering. We shall meet your physical force with soul force. Do to us what you will, and we shall continue to love you.... Throw us in jail, and we shall still love you. Send your hooded perpetrators of violence into our community at the midnight hour and beat us and leave us half dead, and we shall still love you. But be ye assured that we will wear you down by our capacity to suffer. One day we shall win freedom, but not only for ourselves. We shall so appeal to your heart and conscience that we shall win *you* in the process, and our victory will be a double victory" (56).

16. Ibid., 42-43.

17. Ibid., 43.

18. Ibid., 43-46.

What a tragedy! Millions of Negroes have been crucified by conscientious blindness. With Jesus on the cross, we must look lovingly at our oppressors and say, "Father, forgive them, for they know not what they do."[19]

In ch. 5, it was argued that, in Luke 23:34a, ignorance is particularly tied to unillumined minds and unillumined readings of Scripture, and that such ignorance is corrected when Scripture is interpreted according to the reading opened by the Resurrected One. King, however, preaches from this text about the need to overcome ignorance through intelligence. Specifically, "the call for intelligence is a call for openmindedness, sound judgment, and love for truth."[20] In the case of segregationists, this might mean, for example, opening one's eyes to the evidence that "the idea of an inferior or superior race has been refuted by the best evidence of the science of anthropology."[21]

Although King's reading of "ignorance" is not identical to the authorial communicative intent, he nonetheless brings the text into his contemporary situation in a way that promotes love for one's neighbor and compassion for one's enemy. Nevertheless, King's exhortation for "openmindedness, sound judgment, and love for truth" might have been enhanced by the authorial communicative intent. For example, I claimed in ch. 5 that overcoming ignorance required not only information (the disciples had been given information that the Messiah must suffer, yet they could not comprehend it), but also the illumined minds to *process* the information (Jesus' opening their minds to understand the Scriptures). Though not an identical parallel, one can see, for example, how segregationists might not simply lack information (e.g., anthropological evidence), but the ability to process the information (i.e., they might require a far-reaching worldview shift away from the belief "in the eternal validity" and "timeless truth" of the superiority of the white race). In fact, it would seem that King is already working to enable this paradigm shift by leading a people to respond to ignorance and evil with resilient love. It would seem that such non-retaliating love helped make it possible for others to reconsider and internalize the evidence of racial equality with openmindedness and sound judgment.

In ch. 4, an ecclesially located exegetical framework was offered that upheld love of God and neighbor as its chief aim, prioritized authorial communicative intent, allowed for a theologically delimited polysemy, and recognized the need for virtuous interpreters. According to this framework, King's "Love in Action" should be regarded as a particularly good reading of Luke 23:34a. Certainly, there were places where more attention might have been paid to authorial communicative intent (e.g., by explicitly tying Luke 23:34a to Jesus' earlier teaching in Luke 6:27-28). Even so, King's sermon opens with a close reading of the text, specifically noting how "then" is connected to the preceding verse.

---

19. Ibid., 46.
20. Ibid., 47.
21. Ibid., 45.

And, most importantly, if "the chief purpose" and "fulfillment and end of the law and all the divine Scriptures" is love of God and neighbor (*DDC* 1.35), and if love of one's neighbor includes loving "the person to whom an act of compassion is due" even if that person is an enemy (*DDC* 1.30), then King's reading is especially good—indeed, better than those readings that stick closer to the authorial communicative intent but fail to build up love. Recall Augustine's maxim: "anyone who thinks that he has understood the divine Scriptures or any part of them, but cannot by his understanding build up this double love of God and neighbor, has not yet succeeded in understanding them" (*DDC* 1.36). Perhaps King's ability to read well, even when going beyond authorial communicative intent, is tied to his being a person of virtue. As Fowl observes, "It is not surprising that those who have grown and advanced in virtue will tend to be masterful interpreters of Scripture.... [I]t simply stands to reason that those who have advanced in the Christian life will tend to offer the best interpretations for those whose primary aim is to advance in the Christian life."[22]

Conclusion

The focus of this book has been on the various ambiguities associated with Luke 23:34a, with particular attention paid to how one evaluates interpretations of an ambiguous scriptural text. Through this study, I hope to have demonstrated the likeliness of the text's originality, to have made a convincing case for the most textually coherent reading of this verse, and to have called into question prominent methods for evaluating interpretations. I also hope to have advanced the field of theological interpretation by bringing Augustine's *De Doctrina Christiana* into conversation with contemporary theological interpreters. Although I do not think that *DDC* holds the answers to all the questions that theological interpreters wrestle with, I do think that *DDC* proves itself to have insight that is especially valuable to those who "seek to read biblical texts as the church's Scripture."[23]

---

22. Fowl, "Virtue," 838.
23. Wall, review of *World Upside Down*, 4.

Bibliography

Adam, A.K.M. *Faithful Interpretation: Reading the Bible in a Postmodern World*. Minneapolis: Fortress, 2006.

Aland, Kurt, and Barbara Aland. *The Text of the New Testament: An Introduction to the Critical Editions and to the Theory and Practice of Modern Textual Criticism*. Rev. ed. Grand Rapids: Eerdmans, 1989.

Anderson, Gary A. "Intentional and Unintentional Sin in the Dead Sea Scrolls." Pages 49-64 in *Pomegranates and Golden Bells: Studies in Biblical, Jewish, and Near Eastern Ritual, Law, and Literature in Honor of Jacob Milgrom*. Edited by David P. Wright, David Noel Freedman, and Avi Hurvitz. Winona Lake, IN: Eisenbrauns, 1995.

Andrews, James. "Relevant Augustine: What *De Doctrina Christiana* Says Today." StPatr 50 (2011): 309-20.

_____. "Why Theological Hermeneutics Needs Rhetoric: Augustine's *De Doctrina Christiana*." *IJST* 12 (2010): 184-200.

Augustine. *De Doctrina Christiana*. Edited by R.P.H. Green. OECT. Oxford: Clarendon Press, 1995.

_____. *The Confessions of Saint Augustine*. Translated by John K. Ryan. New York: Doubleday, 1960.

Baehr, Jason. "Four Varieties of Character-Based Virtue Epistemology." *SJP* 46 (2008): 469-502.

Barrett, C.K. "Is There a Theological Tendency in Codex Bezae?" Pages 15-27 in *Text and Interpretation: Studies in the New Testament Presented to Matthew Black*. Edited by Ernest Best and R. McL. Wilson. Cambridge: Cambridge University Press, 1979.

Barton, Stephen C. "Can We Identify the Gospel Audiences?" Pages 173-94 in *The Gospels for All Christians: Rethinking the Gospel Audiences*. Edited by Richard Bauckham. Grand Rapids: Eerdmans, 1998.

Blum, Matthias. *"... denn sie wissen nicht, was sie tun": Zur Rezeption der Fürbitte Jesu am Kreuz (Lk 23, 34a) in der antiken jüdisch-christlichen Kontroverse*. NTAbh N.F. 46. Münster: Aschendorff, 2004.

Bock, Darrell L. *Luke 9:51-24:53*. BECNT 2. Grand Rapids: Baker Academic, 1994.

_____. *Proclamation from Prophecy and Pattern: Lucan Old Testament Christology*. JSNTSS 12. Sheffield: Sheffield Academic Press, 1987.

Bolin, Thomas. "A Reassessment of the Textual Problem of Luke 23:34a." *PEGLMWBS* 12 (1992): 131-44.

Bonner, Gerald. "Augustine as Biblical Scholar." Pages 541-63 in *The Cambridge History of the Bible*. Vol. 1: *From the Beginnings to Jerome*. Cambridge: Cambridge University Press, 1970.

Bovon, François. *Das Evangelium nach Lukas*. EKKNT 3/4. Zürich: Benziger Verlag, 2010.

_____. "Issues in Reception History and Reception Theory: The Reception and Use of the Gospel of Luke in the Second Century." Pages 379-400 in *Reading Luke: Interpretation, Reflection, Formation*. Edited by Craig G. Bartholemew et al. Grand Rapids: Zondervan, 2005.

_____. *Luke the Theologian: Fifty-five Years of Research (1950-2005)*. 2d ed. Waco, TX: Baylor University Press, 2005.

Briggs, Richard S. *The Virtuous Reader: Old Testament Narrative and Interpretive Virtue*. Grand Rapids: Baker Academic, 2010.

Bright, Pamela. "Augustine: The Hermeneutics of Conversion." Pages 1219-33 in *Handbook of Patristic Exegesis: The Bible in Ancient Christianity*. 2 vols. By Charles Kannengiesser. Leiden: Brill, 2004.

Brown, Raymond E. *The Death of the Messiah—From Gethsemane to the Grave: A Commentary on the Passion Narratives in the Four Gospels*. 2 vols. ABRL. New York: Doubleday, 1994.

Burnett, Richard E. *Karl Barth's Theological Exegesis: The Hermeneutical Principles of the Römerbrief Period*. WUNT 2/145. Tübingen: Mohr Siebeck, 2001.

Cadbury, Henry J. "Four Features of Lucan Style." Pages 87-102 in *Studies in Luke-Acts*. Edited by Leander E. Keck and J. Louis Martyn. Nashville: Abingdon, 1966.

_____. *The Style and Literary Method of Luke*. HTS 6. Cambridge, MA: Harvard University Press, 1920. Repr., New York: Kraus, 1969.

Carlson, Richard P. "The Role of the Jewish People in Luke's Passion Theology." Pages 82-102 in *SBL Seminar Papers, 1991*. SBLSP 30. Atlanta: Scholars Press, 1991.

Carras, G.P. "A Pentateuchal Echo in Jesus' Prayer on the Cross: Intertextuality between Numbers 15:22-31 and Luke 23:34a." Pages 605-16 in *The Scriptures in the Gospels*. Edited by C.M. Tucket. Leuven: Leuven University Press, 1997.

Carroll, John T. "Luke's Crucifixion Scene." Pages 108-24 in *Reimagining the Death of the Lucan Jesus*. Edited by Dennis D. Sylva. Frankfurt am Main: Hain, 1990.

Carroll, John T. and Joel B. Green. *The Death of Jesus in Early Christianity*. Peabody, MA: Hendrickson, 1995.

Catchpole, David R. "The Problem of the Historicity of the Sanhedrin Trial." Pages 47-65 in *The Trial of Jesus: Cambridge Studies in Honour of C.F.D. Moule*. Edited by Ernst Bammel. Naperville, IL: SCM, 1970.

Chance, J. Bradley. "The Jewish People and the Death of Jesus in Luke-Acts: Some Implications of an Inconsistent Narrative Role." Pages 50-81 in *SBL Seminar Papers, 1991*. SBLSP 30. Atlanta: Scholars Press, 1991.

Childs, Brevard S. *The New Testament as Canon: An Introduction*. Philadelphia: Fortress, 1984.

Chilton, Bruce D. *The Isaiah Targum: Introduction, Translation, Apparatus and Notes*. The Aramaic Bible 11. Wilmington, DE: Michael Glazier, 1987.

Clancy, Finbarr G. "*Fide et Symbolo, De*." Pages 360-61 in *Augustine through the Ages: An Encyclopedia*. Edited by Allan D. Fitzgerald. Grand Rapids: Eerdmans, 1999.

_____. "St Augustine's Commentary on the Emmaus Scene in Luke's Gospel." StPatr 43 (2006): 51-58.

Clark, Elizabeth A. *History, Theory, Text: Historians and the Linguistic Turn.* Cambridge, MA: Harvard University Press, 2004.

Colson, F.H. and G.H. Whitaker. Introduction and Notes to *Philo*. 10 vols. LCL. Cambridge, MA: Harvard University Press, 1929-62.

Comfort, Philip Wesley. *Early Manuscripts and Modern Translations of the New Testament*. Grand Rapids: Baker, 1990.

Cook, Albert S. *History/Writing: The Theory and Practice of History in Antiquity and in Modern Times.* Cambridge: Cambridge University Press, 1988.

Creed, John Martin. *The Gospel According to St. Luke: The Greek Text with Introduction, Notes, and Indices.* London: Macmillan, 1950.

Crossan, John Dominic. *The Cross That Spoke: The Origins of the Passion Narrative.* San Francisco: Harper & Row: 1988.

Crump, David Michael. *Jesus the Intercessor: Prayer and Christology in Luke-Acts.* WUNT 2/49. Tübingen: Mohr Siebeck, 1992.

Daly, Robert J. Introduction to *Origen: Treatise on the Passover and Dialogue of Origen with Heraclides and His Fellow Bishops on the Father, the Son, and the Soul.* ACW 54. New York: Paulist, 1992.

Daube, D. "'For They Know Not What They Do': Luke 23:34." StPatr 4 (1961): 58-70.

Dearman, J. Andrew. *Hosea.* NICOT 28. Grand Rapids: Eerdmans, 2010.

Delobel, Joël. "Luke 23:34a: A Perpetual Text-Critical Crux?" Pages 25-36 in *Sayings of Jesus: Canonical and Non-canonical: Essays in Honour of Tjitze Baarda.* Edited by William L. Peterson et al. Leiden: Brill, 1997.

Du Plessus, I.J. "The Saving Significance of Jesus and His Death on the Cross in Luke's Gospel—Focusing on Luke 22:19b-20." *Neot* 28 (1994): 523-40.

Eco, Umberto. *The Limits of Interpretation.* Indianapolis: Indiana University Press, 1990.

_____. *The Role of the Reader: Explorations in the Semiotics of Texts.* London: Hutchinson, 1981.

Ehrman, Bart D. "The Cup, the Bread, and the Salvific Effect of Jesus' Death in Luke-Acts." Pages 576-91 in *SBL Seminar Papers, 1991.* SBLSP 30. Atlanta: Scholars Press, 1991.

Ernst, Josef. *Das Evangelium nach Lukas.* RNT 3. Regensburg: Friedrich Pustet, 1993.

Epp, Elton J. "The 'Ignorance Motif' in Acts and the Antijudaic Tendencies in Codex Bezae." *HTR* 55 (1962): 51-62.

_____. "The Multivalence of the Term 'Original Text' in New Testament Textual Criticism." *HTR* 92 (1999): 245-81.

Eubank, Nathan. "A Disconcerting Prayer: On the Originality of Luke 23:34a." *JBL* 129 (2010): 521-36.

Evans, C.F. *Saint Luke.* TPINTC. London: SCM, 1990.

Ferguson, Everett. "Some Aspects of Gregory of Nyssa's Interpretation of Scripture Exemplified in His *Homilies on Ecclesiastes.*" StPatr 27 (1993): 29-33.

Fitzmyer, Joseph A. *The Gospel According to Luke.* AB 28a. New York: Doubleday, 1985.

_____. *To Advance the Gospel: New Testament Studies.* 2d ed. Grand Rapids: Eerdmans, 1998.

Flusser, David. "'Sie Wissen Nicht, Was Sie Tun': Geschichte eines Herrnwortes." Pages 393-410 in *Kontinuitaet und Einheit: Für Franz Mussner.* Edited by Paul-Gerhard Müller and Werner Stenger. Freiburg: Herder, 1981.

Fowl, Stephen E. *Engaging Scripture: A Model for Theological Interpretation.* Oxford: Blackwell, 1999.

_____. *Philippians.* THNTC 11. Grand Rapids: Eerdmans, 2005.

_____. "The Role of Authorial Intention in the Theological Interpretation of Scripture." Pages 71-87 in *Between Two Horizons: Spanning New Testament Studies and Systematic Theology.* Edited by Joel B. Green and Max Turner. Grand Rapids: Eerdmans, 2000.

_____. *Theological Interpretation of Scripture.* Eugene, OR: Cascade, 2009.

_____. "Virtue." Pages 837-39 in *Dictionary for Theological Interpretation of the Bible.* Edited by Kevin J. Vanhoozer. Grand Rapids: Baker Academic, 2005.

González, Justo L. *The Changing Shape of Church History.* St. Louis, MO: Chalice, 2002.

Green, Joel B. "Afterword: Rethinking History (and Theology)." Pages 237-42 in *Between Two Horizons: Spanning New Testament Studies and Systematic Theology.* Edited by Joel B. Green and Max Turner. Grand Rapids: Eerdmans, 2000.

_____. "Learning Theological Interpretation from Luke." Pages 55-78 in *Reading Luke: Interpretation, Reflection, Formation.* Edited by Craig G. Bartholemew et al. Grand Rapids: Zondervan, 2005.

_____. "Reading Luke" Pages 1-8 in *Methods for Luke. Edited by* Joel B. Green. New York: Cambridge University Press, 2010.

_____. "Scripture and Theology: Uniting the Two So Long Divided." Pages 23-43 in *Between Two Horizons: Spanning New Testament Studies and Systematic Theology.* Edited by Joel B. Green and Max Turner. Grand Rapids: Eerdmans, 2000.

_____. *The Gospel of Luke.* NICNT 42. Grand Rapids: Eerdmans, 1997.

Gregory, Andrew. "Looking for Luke in the Second Century: A Dialogue with François Bovon." Pages 401-15 in *Reading Luke: Interpretation, Reflection, Formation.* Edited by Craig G. Bartholemew et al. Grand Rapids: Zondervan, 2005.

_____. *The Reception of Luke and Acts in the Period before Irenaeus: Looking for Luke in the Second Century.* WUNT 2/169. Tübingen: Mohr Siebeck, 2003.

Gregory of Nyssa. *Gregorii Nysseni: Opera Ascetica.* Edited by Wernerus Jaeger, Johannes P. Cavarnos, and Virginia Woods Callahan. Leiden: Brill, 1986.

_____. *Saint Gregory of Nyssa: Ascetical Works*. Translated by Virginia Woods Callahan. FC 58. Washington, D.C.: Catholic University of America Press, 1966.

Haines-Eitzen, Kim. *Guardians of Letters: Literacy, Power, and the Transmitters of Early Christian Literature*. New York: Oxford University Press, 2000.

Hamilton, Gordon J. "Augustine's Methods of Biblical Interpretation." Pages 103-19 in *Grace, Politics and Desire: Essays on Augustine*. Edited by Hugo A. Meynell. Calgary, Alberta: University of Calgary Press, 1990.

Harnack, A. von. "Probleme im Texte der Leidensgeschichte Jesu." Pages 470-85 in *Kleine Schriften zur alten Kirche: Berliner Akademieschriften, 1890-1920*. Edited by A. von Harnack and Jürgen Dummer. 2 vols. Leipzig: Zentralantiquariat der Deutschen Demokratischen Republik, 1980.

Harrison, Carol. *Beauty and Revelation in the Thought of Saint Augustine*. Oxford: Clarendon Press, 1992.

Hart, Trevor. "Tradition, Authority, and a Christian Approach to the Bible as Scripture." Pages 183-204 in *Between Two Horizons: Spanning New Testament Studies and Systematic Theology*. Edited by Joel B. Green and Max Turner. Grand Rapids: Eerdmans, 2000.

Hays, Richard B. *Echoes of Scripture in the Letters of Paul*. New Haven, CT: Yale University Press, 1989.

_____. "Reading the Bible with Eyes of Faith: The Practice of Theological Exegesis." *JTI* 1 (2007): 5-21.

_____. "Reading Scripture in Light of the Resurrection." Pages 216-38 in *The Art of Reading Scripture*. Edited by Ellen F. Davis and Richard B. Hays. Grand Rapids: Eerdmans, 2003.

_____. *The Moral Vision of the New Testament: Community, Cross, New Creation: A Contemporary Introduction to New Testament Ethics*. New York: HarperOne, 1996.

Heine, Ronald. "Reading the Bible with Origen." Pages 131-48 in *The Bible in Greek Christian Antiquity*. Edited and translated by Paul M. Blowers. Notre Dame, IN: University of Notre Dame Press, 1997.

Hengel, Martin. *Crucifixion in the Ancient World and the Folly of the Message of the Cross*. Philadelphia: Fortress, 1977.

Holmes, Michael W. "Reconstructing the Text of the New Testament." Pages 77-89 in *The Blackwell Companion to the New Testament*. Edited by David Aune. Oxford: Wiley-Blackwell, 2010.

Holtz, Traugott. *Untersuchungen über die Alttestamentlichen Zitate bei Lukas*. TUGAL 104. Berlin: Akademie-Verlag, 1968.

Jackson, Pamela. "John Chrysostom's Use of Scripture in Initiatory Preaching." *GOTR* 35 (1990): 345-66.

Johnson, Luke Timothy. "A Historiographical Response to Wright's Jesus." Pages 206-24 in *Jesus and the Restoration of Israel: A Critical Assessment of N.T. Wright's Jesus and the Victory of God.* Edited by Carey C. Newman. Downers Grove, IL: InterVarsity, 1999.

_____. "Luke 24:1-11." *Int* 46 (1992): 57-61.

_____. *The Acts of the Apostles.* SP 5. Collegeville, MN: Liturgical, 1992.

_____. *The Gospel of Luke.* SP 3. Collegeville, MN: Liturgical, 1991.

_____. *The Real Jesus: The Misguided Quest for the Historical Jesus and the Truth of the Traditional Gospels.* San Francisco: HarperSanFrancisco, 1996.

Jourjon, Maurice. "Irenaeus's Reading of the Bible." Pages 105-11 in *The Bible in Greek Christian Antiquity.* Edited and translated by Paul M. Blowers. Notre Dame, IN: University of Notre Dame Press, 1997.

Kannengiesser, Charles. "Ambrose of Milan." Pages 1045-80 in *Handbook of Patristic Exegesis: The Bible in Ancient Christianity.* 2 vols. By Charles Kannengiesser. Leiden: Brill, 2004.

_____. "Leo I, The Great." Pages 1287-89 in *Handbook of Patristic Exegesis: The Bible in Ancient Christianity.* 2 vols. By Charles Kannengiesser. Leiden: Brill, 2004.

Karris, Robert J. "Luke 24:13-35." *Int* 41 (1987): 57-61.

_____. *Luke: Artist and Theologian: Luke's Passion Account as Literature.* New York: Paulist, 1985.

Kilpatrick, G.D. *The Eucharist in Bible and Liturgy.* New York: Cambridge University Press, 1983.

King, Martin Luther, Jr. *Strength to Love.* Philadelphia: Fortress, 1963.

_____. "Levels of Love: Sermon Delivered at Ebenezer Baptist Church." Pages 437-45 in *Papers of Martin Luther King, Jr: Advocate of the Social Gospel, September 1948-March 1963.* Vol. 6. Edited by Clayborne Carson. Berkeley: University of California Press, 2007.

Kingsbury, Jack Dean. *Conflict in Luke: Jesus, Authorities, Disciples.* Minneapolis: Fortress, 1991.

_____. "Luke 24:44-49." *Int* 35 (1981): 170-74.

Klink III, Edward W. "Gospel Audience and Origin: The Current Debate." Pages 1-26 in *The Audience of the Gospels: The Origin and Function of the Gospels in Early Christianity.* Edited by Edward Klink III. New York: T&T Clark, 2010.

Laytham D. Brent. "Interpretation on the Way to Emmaus: Jesus Performs His Story." *JTI* 1 (2007): 101-15.

Lemcio, Eugene E. "The Gospels and Canonical Criticism." Pages 28-47 in *The New Testament as Canon: A Reader in Canonical Criticism.* By Robert W. Wall and Eugene E. Lemcio. JSNTSS 76. Sheffield: JSOT Press, 1992.

Loewen, Howard J. "The Use of Scripture in Augustine's Theology." *SJT* 34 (1981): 201-24.

Levering, Matthew. *Participatory Biblical Exegesis: A Theology of Biblical Interpretation.* Notre Dame, IN: University of Notre Dame Press, 2008.

Lewis, C.S. Introduction to Athanasius, *Incarnation of the Word of God.* New York: MacMillan, 1996.

Lienhard, Joseph T. Forward to *Origen: Homilies on Luke, Fragments on Luke.* FC 94. Washington, D.C.: Catholic University of America Press, 1996.

Macintosh, A.A. *Hosea.* ICC 28. Edinburgh: T&T Clark, 1997.

Marshall, I. Howard. *Luke: Historian and Theologian.* Downers Grove, IL: InterVarsity, 1998.

_____. *The Gospel of Luke: A Commentary on the Greek Text.* NIGTC 3. Grand Rapids: Eerdmans, 1978.

Matera, Frank. "Responsibility for the Death of Jesus according to the Acts of the Apostles." *JSNT* 39 (1990): 77-93.

Matthews, Shelly. "Clemency as Cruelty: Forgiveness and Force in the Dying Prayers of Jesus and Stephen." *BibInt* 17 (2009): 118-46.

McCormick, Amy S. "John Chysostom's Homily 50 as an Example of the Antiochene Exegetical Tradition." *PatByzRev* 12 (1993): 65-82.

McHugh, Michael P. Introduction to *Joseph.* FC 65. Washington, D.C.: Catholic University of America Press, 1972.

McKibbens, Thomas R. "The Exegesis of John Chrystostom: Homilies on the Gospels." *ExpTim* 93 (1982): 264-70.

Metzger, Bruce M. *The Canon of the New Testament: Its Origin, Development, and Significance.* Oxford: Clarendon Press, 1987.

_____. *Textual Commentary on the Greek New Testament: A Companion Volume to the United Bible Societies' Greek New Testament (Fourth Revised Edition).* 2d ed. Stuttgart: United Bible Societies, 1994.

Mowery, Robert L. "The Divine Hand and the Divine Plan in the Lukan Passion Narrative." Pages 558-75 in *SBL Seminar Papers, 1991.* SBLSP 30. Atlanta: Scholars Press, 1991.

Murphy, Francis X. "The Sermons of Pope Leo the Great: Content and Style." Pages 183-97 in *Preaching in the Patristic Age: Studies in Honor of Walter J. Burghart, S.J..* Edited by David G. Hunter. New York: Paulist, 1989.

Nolland, John. *Luke 18:35-24:53.* WBC 35c. Dallas: Word, 1993.

O'Donnell, James J. *Augustine Confessions III: Commentary on Books 8-13.* Oxford: Oxford University Press, 1992.

O'Toole, Robert F. "Luke's Message in Luke 9:1-50." *CBQ* 49 (1987): 74-89.

Origen. *Origène: Sur la Pâque.* Edited by O. Guérand and P. Nautin. ChristAnt 2. Paris: Beauchesne, 1979.

Parsons, Mikeal C. "A Christological Tendency in P^{75}." *JBL* 105 (1986): 463-79.

Penner, Todd. "The Challenge from Within: Reading Räisänen against Dominant Methodological Discourse." Pages 1-31 in *Moving Beyond New Testament Theology: Essays in Conversation with Heikki Räisänen*. Edited by Todd Penner and Caroline Vander Stichele. Göttingen: Vandenhoeck & Ruprecht, 2005.

Petzer, Jacobus H. "Anti-Judaism and the Textual Problem of Luke 23:34." *FN* 5 (1992): 199-203.

Philo. LCL. 10 vols. Translated by F.H. Colson and G.H. Whitaker. Cambridge, MA: Harvard University Press, 1929-62.

Plevnik, Joseph. "The Eyewitnesses of the Risen Jesus in Luke 24." *CBQ* 49 (1987): 90-103.

Porter, Calvin L. "Papyrus Bodmer XV (P75) and the Text of Codex Vaticanus." *JBL* 81 (1962): 363-76.

Powell, Mark Allan. "Narrative Criticism." Pages 240-58 in *Hearing the New Testament: Strategies for Interpretation*. Edited by Joel B. Green. 2d ed. Grand Rapids: Eerdmans, 2010.

Quimron, E. "Al Shegagot u-Zdnonot bi-Mgillot Midbar Yehuda: Iyyun ba-Munahim ha-Meshamshim le-Tsiyyunam." Pages 103-10 in *Proceedings of the Tenth World Congress of Jewish Studies*. Jerusalem: World Union of Jewish Studies, 1990.

Rae, Murray. "Texts in Context: Scripture and the Divine Economy." *JTI* 1 (2007): 23-45.

Räisänen, Heikki. *Beyond New Testament Theology: A Story and a Programme*. 2d ed. London: SCM, 2000.

_____. "What I Meant and What It Might Mean…An Attempt at Responding." Pages 400-43 in *Moving Beyond New Testament Theology: Essays in Conversation with Heikki Räisänen*. Edited by Todd Penner and Caroline Vander Stichele. Göttingen: Vandenhoeck & Ruprecht, 2005.

Ramm, Bernard L. *Protestant Biblical Interpretation: A Textbook of Hermeneutics*. 3d ed. Grand Rapids: Baker Book House, 1970.

Rice, George F. "The Anti-Judaic Bias of the Western Text in the Gospel of Luke." *AUSS* 18 (1980): 51-57.

_____. "Some Further Examples of the Anti-Judaic Bias in the Western Text of the Gospel of Luke." *AUSS* 18 (1980): 149-56.

Royce, James R. *Scribal Habits in Early Greek New Testament Papyri*. NTTSD 36. Leiden: Brill, 2008.

Sanders, J.T. *The Jews in Luke-Acts*. Philadelphia: Fortress, 1987.

Schaff, Philip. *The Creeds of Christendom: With a History and Critical Notes*. 3 vols. 6th ed. Grand Rapids: Baker, 1985.

Schille, Gottfried. *Die Apostelgeschichte des Lukas*. THKNT 5. Berlin: Evangelische Verlagsanstalt, 1983.

Schmithals, Walter. *Das Evangelium nach Lukas*. ZBK 3. Zurich: Theologischer, 1980.

Schneider, Gerhard. *Das Evangelium nach Lukas: Kapitel 11-24*. ÖTK 3. Gütersloh: Gütersloher Verlagshaus Mohn, 1977.

_____. *Die Apostelgeschichte I. Teil: Einleitung. Kommentar zu Kap 1:1-8:40.* HTKNT 5. Freiburg: Herder, 1980.

Schweizer, Eduard. *The Good News According to Luke.* Atlanta: John Knox, 1984.

Seitz, Christopher R. *Word without End: The Old Testament as Abiding Theological Witness.* Grand Rapids: Eerdmans, 1998.

Spencer, F. Scott. "Preparing the Way of the Lord: Introducing and Interpreting Luke's Narrative: A Response to David Wenham." Pages 104-24 in *Reading Luke: Interpretation, Reflection, Formation.* Edited by Craig G. Bartholemew et al. Grand Rapids: Zondervan, 2005.

Stendahl, Krister. "Biblical Theology, Contemporary," Pages 418-32 in vol. 1 of *The Interpreter's Dictionary of the Bible.* Edited by G.A. Buttrick. 4 vols. Nashville: Abingdon, 1962.

Stuart, Douglas. *Hosea-Jonah.* WBC 31. Waco, TX: Word, 1987.

Taeger, Jens-W. *Der Mensch und sein Heil: Studien zum Bild des Menschen und zur Sicht der Bekehrung bei Lukas.* SNT 14. Gütersloh: Gütersloher Verlagshaus Gerd Mohn, 1982.

Tannehill. Robert C. *The Narrative Unity of Luke-Acts: A Literary Interpretation.* Vol. 1: *The Gospel according to Luke.* Philadelphia: Fortress, 1986.

Thomas Aquinas. *Summa Theologiae.* Edited by Brian Davies and Brian Leftow. Cambridge: Cambridge University Press, 2006.

Tilley, Terrence W. *History, Theology and Faith: Dissolving the Modern Problematic.* Maryknoll, NY: Orbis, 2004.

Tortorelli, Kevin M. "Some Methods of Interpretation in St. Irenaeus." *VetChr* 30 (1993): 123-32.

Turner, Max. "Historical Criticism and Theological Hermeneutics of the New Testament." Pages 44-70 in *Between Two Horizons: Spanning New Testament Studies and Systematic Theology.* Edited by Joel B. Green and Max Turner. Grand Rapids: Eerdmans, 2000.

Van Zyl, H.C. "The Soteriological Meaning of Jesus' Death in Luke-Acts: A Survey of Possibilities." *Verbum et Ecclesia* 23 (2002): 533-57.

Vanhoozer, Kevin J. "The Apostolic Discourse and Its Developments." Pages 191-207 in *Scripture's Doctrine and Theology's Bible: How the New Testament Shapes Christian Dogmatics.* Edited by Markus Bockmuehl and Alan J. Torrance. Grand Rapids: Baker Academic, 2008.

_____. "Four Theological Faces of Biblical Interpretation." Pages 131-42 in *Reading Scripture with the Church: Toward a Hermeneutic for Theological Interpretation.* By A.K.M. Adam et al. Grand Rapids: Baker, 2006.

_____. "Imprisoned or Free? Text, Status, and Theological Interpretation in the Master/Slave Discourse of Philemon." Pages 51-93 in *Reading Scripture with the Church: Toward a Hermeneutic for Theological Interpretation.* By A.K.M. Adam et al. Grand Rapids: Baker, 2006.

Vogt, Hermann J. "Origen of Alexandria." Pages 536-74 in *Handbook of Patristic Exegesis: The Bible in Ancient Christianity*. 2 vols. By Charles Kannengiesser. Leiden: Brill, 2004.

Walaskay, Paul W. "Trial and Death of Jesus in the Gospel of Luke." *JBL* 94 (1975): 81-93.

Wall, Robert W. "Canonical Context and Canonical Converstations." Pages 165-82 in *Between Two Horizons: Spanning New Testament Studies and Systematic Theology*. Edited by Joel B. Green and Max Turner. Grand Rapids: Eerdmans, 2000.

_____. Review of C. Kavin Rowe, *World Upside Down: Reading Acts in the Graeco-Roman Age*. Paper presented at the Annual Meeting of the Society of Biblical Literature. Atlanta, Nov 21, 2010.

Wallis, Richard T. *The Idea of Conscience in Philo of Alexandria: Protocol of the Thirteenth Colloquy 12 January 1975*. Berkeley, CA: The Center for Hermeneutical Studies in Hellenistic and Modern Culture, 1975.

Watson, Francis. *Text, Church and World: Biblical Interpretation in Theological Perspective*. Grand Rapids: Eerdmans, 1994.

Webster, John. *Holy Scripture: A Dogmatic Sketch*. Cambridge: Cambridge University Press, 2003.

Whitlark, Jason A. and Mikeal C. Parsons. "The 'Seven' Last Words: A Numerical Motivation for the Insertion of Luke 23:34a." *NTS* 52 (2006): 188-204.

Wilcox, Max. "Text Form." Pages 193-204 in *It Is Written: Scripture Citing Scripture: Essays in Honour of Barnabas Lindars*. Edited by D.A. Carson and H.G.M. Williamson. Cambridge: Cambridge University Press, 1988.

Williams, Thomas. "Biblical Interpretation." Pages 59-70 in *The Cambridge Companion to Augustine*. Edited by Eleonore Stump and Norman Kretzmann. Cambridge: Cambridge University Press, 2001.

Winter, Paul. *On the Trial of Jesus*. 2d. ed. Berlin: Walter de Gruyter, 1974.

Wolter, Michael. *Das Lukasevangelium*. HNT 5. Tübingen: Mohr Siebeck, 2008.

Wright, N.T. *The New Testament and the People of God*. Minneapolis: Fortress, 1992.

_____. Review of Heiki Räisänen, *Beyond New Testament Theology: A Story and a Programme*. *JTS* 43 (1992): 626-30.

Index: Biblical Citations

Author and Subject